*Greece & Rome*

NEW SURVEYS IN THE CLASSICS No. 43

# EARLY GREEK HEXAMETER POETRY

BY
PETER GAINSFORD

*Published for the Classical Association*
CAMBRIDGE UNIVERSITY PRESS
2015

CAMBRIDGE UNIVERSITY PRESS
The Edinburgh Building, Cambridge CB2 8BS, United Kingdom
32 Avenue of the Americas, New York, NY 10013-2473, USA
477 Williamstown Road, Port Melbourne, VIC 3207, Australia
Ruiz de Alarcón 13, 28014 Madrid, Spain
Dock house, The Waterfront, Cape Town 8001, South Africa

www.cambridge.org
Information on this title: www.cambridge.org/9781316608883

Printed in the United Kingdom by Bell and Bain, Glasgow, UK

*A catalogue record for this publication is available from the British Library*

ISBN 9781316608883

# CONTENTS

# ACKNOWLEDGEMENTS

All students of early hexameter are very deeply indebted to Alberto Bernabé, Malcolm Davies, and the late M. L. West; their editions of early hexameter poetry have made the material far more accessible than it has ever been before. I am very happy to acknowledge more personal debts to Jonathan Burgess, Pat Easterling, Adrian Kelly, Simon Perris, Art Pomeroy, Christian Schäfer, Tatjana Schaefer, Michael Sharp, John Taylor, Stefano Vecchiato, and Alex Wilson, for a variety of help, pointers, and kind words of encouragement. Unfortunately, I was unable to make full use of Fantuzzi and Tsagalis' superb companion to *The Greek Epic Cycle and Its Ancient Reception* (2015) before finalizing the manuscript of the present book; I am grateful to Professor Tsagalis for kindly allowing me to read part of the introduction in advance of publication.

I also thank the endlessly helpful staff of the Interloans Department at Victoria University of Wellington library: without their professionalism and assistance I should never have been able to dream of obtaining all the material I have used.

Greek texts and translations of the Hesiodic corpus, Homeric *Hymns* and *Lives*, and most fragments of heroic and genealogical poems follow those in the Loeb editions of M. L. West (2003a, 2003b) and Most (2006, 2007) unless otherwise stated. Other translations are my own.

Peter Gainsford
Wellington, August 2015

# INTRODUCTION

Some epics need no introduction. The *Odyssey* is a ripping yarn for any reader. The *Iliad*'s insight into the human condition offsets much of its violence and slow plot-pacing. There is much more to Homer than that, of course: these epics have nearly limitless depths of poetic richness and historical significance, and that is where the scholarship comes into its own – the philology, the literary criticism, the linguistics, the archaeology.

But not all early Greek hexameter poetry is so accessible. Many people can read and enjoy the Hesiodic *Theogony* without preface; some of the major Homeric *Hymns* too. But the *Works and Days* is tough going for general readers, and stepping into the world of fragments can be like trying to find your way in a hospital where there are no signs, no coloured lines to follow, and all the doors are shut. These things need guidance.

Things have become much easier in the last fifteen years thanks to new Loeb editions, edited by M. L. West (2003a, 2003b) and Glenn Most (2006, 2007), of Hesiodic, hymnic, heroic, and antiquarian poetry. Previously, Anglophone readers had to rely on Evelyn-White's (1914) edition, which had been obsolete for a long time. The present volume takes advantage of Most's and West's texts and translations. For specialists, the biggest consequence of this is the use of Most's numbering of the Hesiodic fragments, rather than the more widely cited Merkelbach–West numbering. For non-specialists, a more pressing consequence is that this book gives Greek names in Latin translation, following the practice of the Loeb editions. For poems not included in the Loeb editions – oracles, Orphic poems, inscriptions, and so on – I supply my own translations.

This survey's main aim is to make the esoteric not easy, perhaps, but at least accessible. Its secondary aim is to emphasize that there was a tremendous amount of poetic material that we *do not* have, and that what remains to us is only a very partial reflection of a much larger reality. All Greek is translated. The gentlest part of the book is Chapter V, which gives an introduction to fragments targeted at the lay reader or apprentice classicist.

In a few places, these two aims mean abandoning the format of discursive prose. Like a reader embarking on the *Iliad* for the first time, you should be warned: there are catalogues ahead – of Archaic hexameter inscriptions (pp. 31–2); of evidence for the existence of ancient editions in which poems were excerpted or spliced together (pp. 112–26); and of modern editions of fragmentary poems (Appendix, pp. 127–33). These are not intended as exercises in boring the reader, but as cheat-sheets. Some other topics demand technical details: so also lying in wait for you are some sample formal analyses of genre conventions (Chapter II); linguistic details about early Greek dialects and their impact on the epic tradition (Chapter III); tuning in ancient Greek music (Chapter IV); and the mysteries of Hellenistic mythography (Chapter V). These sections are more selective.

Homer is already covered in the 'New Surveys' series by Richard Rutherford's sublime book of the same name (1996), recently republished in an expanded edition (2013). The present book tries to avoid overlapping with Rutherford, but there are places where it would make no sense to skirt around the *Iliad* and *Odyssey*: for example, when discussing the prehistory of the epic tradition (Chapter III) or relationships between poems (Chapter VI). In those contexts Homer is usually the starting point for modern scholarship, and it would be silly to pretend otherwise.

Another matter that needs to be highlighted before we begin is the odd nature of the authorial persona in early Greek literature. Someone who has started to read this book is probably already aware that there are many poems that we call 'Hesiodic' but that cannot possibly be assigned to a historical individual of that name, either because the poems are too late, or because ancient sources were already sceptical of Hesiod's authorship, or for some other reason: they include the *Shield*, the *Catalogue of Women*, the *Astronomy*, the *Melampodia*, and half a dozen more. This is not just a Hesiodic problem: he is only the most visible example.

Once upon a time, the way of dealing with this was to divide the world of hexameter poetry into 'Ionian' and 'Boeotian' schools, with Homer and Hesiod as their respective models.[1] So the *Shield* was not by Hesiod himself, but was composed by one of his intellectual heirs; the *Hymn to Apollo* was not by Homer but one of the 'Homeridae', a group of poets based on Chios. The binary division was especially tidy thanks to a text called the *Contest of Homer and Hesiod*, an account

---

[1] Evelyn-White 1914: xi–xxxiii.

of a poetic duel, which helpfully frames Homer and Hesiod as two poles
of a universe of poetry. In its surviving form the *Contest* dates to the second century CE, but it is based on material by the fourth-century-BCE
writer Alcidamas, who in turn drew on older traditions; the poetic
duel in Aristophanes' *Frogs* between Aeschylus and Euripides played
on the same material.[2]

The trouble is that there is no hard and fast distinction to be drawn
between the 'Homeric' and 'Hesiodic' corpuses. If we were to plot the
two corpuses on a spectrum ranging from 'heroic' to 'didactic', or 'narrative' to 'non-narrative' or what have you, we would inevitably end up
with miscategorizations. The 'Hesiodic' *Shield* and *Catalogue of Women*
have much more in common with the *Iliad* than the *Works and Days*;
the Homeric *Hymns* are much more like cosmogonic poetry than heroic
legend. 'Hesiod' was supposedly Aeolian, yet 'Homer' and 'Hesiod'
both represent a tradition of Ionic poetry.

The modern solution is subtly different. Homer and Hesiod were not
models for well-defined poetic genres: they were more like *appellations
d'origine*. Poets could adopt a persona and 'be' Homer or Hesiod. The
classic case is in the *Hymn to Apollo* (166–73):

> χαίρετε δ' ὑμεῖς πᾶσαι· ἐμεῖο δὲ καὶ μετόπισθε
> μνήσασθ', ὁππότε κέν τις ἐπιχθονίων ἀνθρώπων
> ἐνθάδ' ἀνείρηται ξεῖνος ταλαπείριος ἐλθών·
> 'ὦ κοῦραι, τίς δ' ὕμμιν ἀνὴρ ἥδιστος ἀοιδῶν
> ἐνθάδε πωλεῖται, καὶ τέωι τέρπεσθε μάλιστα;'
> ὑμεῖς δ' εὖ μάλα πᾶσαι ὑποκρίνασθαι ἀφήμως·
> 'τυφλὸς ἀνήρ, οἰκεῖ δὲ Χίωι ἔνι παιπαλοέσσηι·
> τοῦ πᾶσαι μετόπισθεν ἀριστεύσουσιν ἀοιδαί.'

Think of me in future, if ever some long-suffering stranger comes here and asks, 'O
Maidens, which is your favorite singer who visits here, and who do you enjoy most?'
Then you must all answer with one voice(?), 'It is a blind man, and he lives in rocky
Chios; all of his songs remain supreme afterwards.'

If there is one thing everyone knows about Homer, it is that he was
blind.[3] Simonides (late sixth to early fifth century BCE) identifies the
'Chian man' with Homer more explicitly.[4] The *Hymn to Apollo* is a
sixth-century poem attributed to Cynaethus, so there is no question

---

[2] On the *Contest* and the Homer–Hesiod dichotomy see especially Graziosi 2002: 164–200;
Debiasi 2012: 478–93. On early material in the *Contest* see N. Richardson 1981; Rosen 2004.

[3] See further Graziosi 2002: 125–63.

[4] Simon. frs. eleg. 19–20 West[2] (see Sider 2001 on the link between the fragments).

of the poem being by a historical Homer: instead Cynaethus adopts the persona of Homer to subscribe to a particular heritage. And that can just as easily be a *cultural* as a *poetic* heritage.

Another case that is hard to miss is in Homer himself, *Odyssey* 8, when the blind poet Demodocus is treated with great honour in the court of Alcinous, and is called 'divine', 'trusty', and 'very famous'.[5] If 'Homer' is more persona than person, this is not authorial self-injection but it is at least narratorial self-injection.

If 'Homer' can be played on as a persona *even within Homer*, Homer the real person barely matters. The mythologized biographical tradition, embodied in the *Contest* and in the *Lives* of Homer, was always more important than any historical individual of that name.[6] So it becomes much harder to take the Hesiodic speaker at face value when he tells a story about how 'Hesiod' was visited by the Muses and given the gift of poetry (*Theog.* 22–34); or when he says that he once went to Euboea to win a poetry competition (*WD* 650–9), the same setting we see again in the mythologized *Contest*. The origins of the names illustrate their nature as personas too: Hesiod is 'he who sets out on a journey' or 'he who enjoys the journey', *hēsi-* (from ἵημι or ἥδομαι) + *hod-*; Homer is 'he who fits (songs) together', *hom-* + *ār-* – or, in one recent argument, a title meaning 'agonistic, competitor'.[7]

A novice's perspective finds this hard to swallow. Surely biographical traditions can only weigh in *favour* of a historical individual's existence, not *against* it? It gets easier if we compare other poets who are much more obviously inventions. For there are many. No-one would dream of taking Orpheus and Musaeus as historical figures, yet there were unquestionably real poems dating to the Archaic period that were attributed to them. One of them, we know, was written by Onomacritus, adopting the persona of Musaeus.[8] Linus and Epimenides are at least semi-mythical – Linus was a son of Apollo or took part in a musical contest with Apollo; Epimenides reportedly went to sleep for half a century – yet we have fragments of their poetry. Heracleides of Pontus treated three mythical poets in Homer – Thamyris, Demodocus, and Phemius – as

---

[5] Graziosi 2002: 138–42.

[6] For major studies on Homer and Hesiod as poetic personas see Graziosi 2002, 2013 (Homer); Koning 2010: 129–59 (Hesiod).

[7] Nagy 1979: 296–300 (ἥδομαι: Most 2006: xiv). Debiasi 2012 links Ὅμηρος to Ὁμάριος, a cult-title of Zeus ('god of the assembly') and a fifth-century Euboean personal name (*IG* XII.9 56.135 Ὁμέριος).

[8] Hdt. 7.6 (=Orphica fr. 1109 Bernabé).

historical figures, and it is possible that he knew poems attributed to them.[9] An extreme case is Abaris of Hyperborea. There were several poems attributed to him; and at least one, which pre-dated Herodotus' time (probably the one called *Apollo's Arrival among the Hyperboreans*), gave him a backstory as a Hyperborean priest of Apollo who travelled around Greece flying across rivers and mountains on the giant arrow with which Apollo had killed the Cyclopes.[10]

In other genres, too, there are poets who may possibly have been real historical individuals, but whose biographical tradition is so mythologized, so contaminated by fictional material, that the persona takes precedence over any reality. Among melic poets, Terpander was a hook on which all manner of musical firsts were hung, not least the invention of the *barbitos*, the most popular type of lyre for amateurs in the Classical period; Olympus, who invented the *aulos*, supposedly lived before the Trojan War.

In recent years scholars have been edging towards a recognition that some major lyric poets fall into this category too. Sappho and Solon are also both more persona than person.[11] The wildly romanticized biographical tradition of Sappho, leaping to her death over her unrequited love for Phaon, is obviously invented rather than historical; yet we are told that the love affair was there in 'Sappho's' own poems.[12] The oxymoron – that a rich biographical tradition only reinforces the impression of poet-as-persona – is well exemplified by a major new Sappho fragment discovered in 2014. There 'Sappho' talks to a family member about the doings of Charaxus and Larichus, her brothers; in the biographical tradition they are regularly grouped with a third brother, Erigyius, so Erigyius is presumably the purported addressee of the poem.[13] But this ostentatious dwelling on Sappho's family life is not incidental, not just a lucky corroboration of the biographical tradition: it is inescapably a *purposeful demand* to be interpreted as 'Sappho'. Similarly, when 'Solon' repeatedly stresses his identity as Solon, saying such things as 'I have come here in person as a herald',[14] it is only

---

[9] Heracleid. fr. 157 Wehrli.

[10] Hdt. 4.36; Lycurg. fr. 14.5a Conomis; Eratosth. *Cat.* 29; *Suda* α.18 (=*New Jacoby* 34 T 1).

[11] Lardinois 1994; Irwin 2005b, esp. 132–55 and 263–88. See also Irwin 1998 on Archilochus.

[12] Sappho frs. 211(a), (b.i), (b.iii) Campbell/LP.

[13] New fragment: Obbink 2014. Sappho's brothers: test. 1, 2, 14 Campbell. The vocatives Ἐρίγυιε, ὠρίγυιε fit comfortably in the Sapphic stanza.

[14] Solon fr. 1; similar emphasis on the speaker's identity as 'Solon' in frs. 2, 5; Plut. *Vit. Sol.* 14.2.

sensible to recognize that the speaker is not simply mentioning his identity in passing but ostentatiously laying claim to that identity: in Solon's case, adopting the persona of a revered sage so as to frame a political message. Whether these poets really were Sappho and Solon is scarcely relevant.

We cannot have a purely fictional Musaeus and a purely historical Hesiod. If poets could play-act one, they could play-act the other. The upshot is that we can infer essentially nothing about the real authors of these poems from the poems themselves. If later biographical traditions are already there within the poems – as in *Odyssey* 8, the *Theogony*, and Sappho – then it makes sense to speak of the narratorial voice as a 're-enacting I', as Nagy puts it.[15]

This poses historical problems. If we have two poems claiming the same *appellation d'origine* – say, the *Theogony* and *Works and Days* claiming to be spoken by 'Hesiod' – then not only must we hesitate over assigning them to a single poet but we cannot even make any assumptions about their relative dates. In the opening chapter, which surveys the major poems, we shall have to be especially cautious.

---

[15] Nagy 1994: 20.

# I THE POEMS

The early Greek hexameter poems that survive intact are the two Homeric epics; the Hesiodic *Theogony*, *Works and Days*, and *Shield*; thirty-one Homeric *Hymns*; and about two hundred short inscriptions. Homer comprises 27,803 lines of verse; the other poems comprise another 5,000 lines or so. But we can safely infer that there was once much more. For one thing, we are lucky to have what we do: as a general principle, the texts we have inherited through mediaeval manuscripts represent only a sample of what was available in ancient libraries. For another, in ancient authors who *do* survive we find references to over a hundred other poems or poets that were available to them but are now lost. In several cases we have indications of considerable length.

Here we shall look at each of the intact poems (other than the *Iliad* and *Odyssey*) and some of the most important fragmentary poems. There are too many fragmentary poems to discuss every one in detail. The Appendix gives a list of editions where all the fragments may be found. On fragmentary heroic epics not discussed in detail here, see Huxley 1969; specifically on the Theban epics, Davies 2014 and the relevant chapters in Fantuzzi and Tsagalis (eds.) 2015; on the Orphic fragments, Edmonds 2011; on the Derveni *Theogony*, Bernabé 2007; and for literary criticism of Xenophanes and Parmenides, Fränkel 1975: 325–37, 349–70.

In dating the poems it is best to err on the side of caution. Frankly we are lucky if we can pin a poem down to the correct century, let alone the correct part of a century. Ancient testimony on early poets' dates is usually untrustworthy. Averaging out the dates suggested by experts is no solution; nor is repeating a traditionally accepted date, as though consensus constituted proof. We have three types of evidence, and there are serious problems with all of them.

**1. Intertextual references.** When two poems display a shared motif, a common procedure is to treat one poem as the original source of the motif. This sets a bound on the date of both poems. For example: a reference to different kinds of Strife in *Works and Days* 11–12 might be a retraction of the genealogy given for Strife in *Theogony* 225; a distinctive choice of words in *Hymn to Demeter* 268 (τιμάοχος...τέτυκται, 'the honoured one...is') might be an echo of the same phrasing in

*Hymn to Aphrodite* 31–2.[1] But it is nearly always more parsimonious to interpret similarities like these as motifs belonging to a shared tradition, not allusions to a specific text.[2] Motifs require only that a tradition of stock elements and characters existed – something we know to be true. Strife is a traditional character; 'the honoured one' may be a traditional trope. By contrast, specific allusions involve a strong assertion that no earlier poem, legend, or story ever used the motif; or, even more strongly, that *only* the two texts in question ever used the motif. Since we have lost vastly more hexameter poetry than we possess, and since there is no guarantee that a given motif even has its origin in hexameter, this type of evidence always involves an argument from silence.

2. **Stylometry.** There is only one stylometric study of Archaic hexameter poetry that is both broad-reaching and statistically competent. Janko's *Homer, Hesiod and the Hymns* (1982) reconstructs a chronology of early hexameter poems based on the relative density of ten medium-to-low-frequency, context-sensitive, linguistic features. His research suggests some striking trends, vividly depicted by two graphs in a 2011 essay, but has also been criticized from a variety of angles.[3] Modern automated stylometric analysis looks a bit different: best practice is to treat the results as compelling only if multiple kinds of analysis point the same way, and some standard tests use forty high-frequency, context-insensitive words in a single analysis.[4] This category of evidence is certainly suggestive, but so far only the surface has been scratched.

3. **References to dateable events and material culture.** If a passage within a poem presupposes a specific and dateable historical event, or refers to a custom or aspect of material culture where external evidence shows a clear transition at a well-defined date, then that external evidence puts a constraint on the date of the poetic passage. This tactic has been especially heavily applied to the *Iliad*, where many different references of this kind consistently point to a date of about 670–650 BCE: the use of single-grip round shields; bronze greaves; soldiers

---

[1] On *WD* 11–12 see Zarecki 2007; on *Hymn. Hom. Aphr.* 31–2 see Olson 2012: 23.

[2] See pp. 57–63 on 'unrecorded traditions'; pp. 104–12 on the pitfalls involved in identifying Homeric echoes of earlier poems.

[3] Janko 1982; 2011: 26, 28. For criticism see Jones 2011; Olson 2012: 10–15; Vergados 2012: 142–5.

[4] Grieve 2007, esp. 266–7; Juola 2006 provides a useful survey (Grieve and Juola both focus on authorship attribution, not relative chronology).

armed with a single spear; the overwhelming dominance of spears as
the instrument of death in battle scenes; the Gorgoneion as a shield
device.[5] In a similar vein, the *Theogony*'s description of Pandora's head-
band (*Theog.* 578–84) may suggest a date after animal decorations
began to appear in the Late Geometric style of Greek art.[6] This form
of dating is compelling when it is practical, but that is rarely the case.
Textual critics are familiar with the problem of interpolations in ancient
texts; with literature earlier than 500 BCE, we must also worry about
adaptations in the course of oral transmission and transcription. Any
constraint based on a single passage is severely weakened by the significant, and unquantifiable, likelihood of late alterations. This method
carries little weight unless it is based on aggregate data, as is the case
with the military equipment in the *Iliad*.

## 1. The Hesiodic *Works and Days*

The most popular Hesiodic poem nowadays is the *Theogony*, thanks to
its prestige as a source text on Greek mythology. But in antiquity the
*Works and Days* was the centrepiece of the Hesiodic corpus.
According to Pausanias, there was a tradition at Mount Helicon in
Boeotia that it was the *only* authentically Hesiodic poem. He reports
that the locals even rejected the opening hymn to Zeus (lines 1–10)
as an interpolation.[7] The poem's popularity is easy to see from a set
of 'commemograms' drawn up by Koning, which tabulate references
to Hesiodic passages in later Greco-Roman authors.[8] Koning's results
are telling: ancient writers quoted the *Works and Days* more than twice
as often as the *Theogony*, and the least-quoted sections of the poem
were quoted as much as the most-quoted parts of the *Theogony*.

The speaker assumes the persona of Hesiod and addresses the poem
to his brother Perses. After their father's death, the backstory goes,
Perses brought a case before the leading figures of the community,
the big men or *basilēes* (usually translated as 'kings');[9] Perses bribed

---

[5] Van Wees 1994: 138–46 (round shields, greaves, spears); M. L. West 2011a: 15–19
(Gorgoneion).

[6] M. L. West 1966: 328, commenting on *Th.* 584 ζωοῖσιν ἐοικότα.

[7] Paus. 9.31.4 (=Hesiod test. 42).

[8] Koning 2010: 18–22.

[9] See Hall 2014: 127–34 on the meaning of βασιλεύς in Iron Age Greece. In classical Greek the
word means 'king'; in Homer its meaning is closer to the term 'big man' popularized by the

them in an effort to get more than his fair share of the patrimony. Perses himself slips out of view after the first 300 lines or so. The poem as a whole is an ethical discourse on virtue and the relationship between virtue and work, interspersed with mythological narratives and aphorisms about managing an estate. It fits into a long-standing tradition of wisdom literature, with many parallels in ancient Near Eastern and Greek literature.[10]

The present book follows Most's (2006) text and translation; for commentaries, see M. L. West (1978) and Ercolani (2010). The poem's structure is as follows:

| | |
|---|---|
| 1–10 | Hymnic prelude to Zeus |
| 11–46 | Introductory ethical discourse addressed to Perses |
| 47–212 | Mythical interlude (Prometheus and Pandora; Myth of the Races; fable of the hawk and nightingale) |
| 213–380 | Aphorisms on political (213–85) and personal (286–380) ethics |
| 381–764 | The 'works': advice on |
| | 383–492 Ploughing and sowing |
| | 493–617 The nature of the seasons |
| | 618–93 Sailing |
| | 694–764 Household management and ethics |
| 765–828 | The 'days': advice for specific days of the month |

*Works and Days* 654–7 often plays a key role in scholarship on the dating of early hexameter poetry:

ἔνθα δ' ἐγὼν ἐπ' ἄεθλα δαΐφρονος Ἀμφιδάμαντος
Χαλκίδα τ' εἰς ἐπέρησα· τὰ δὲ προπεφραδμένα πολλὰ
ἆθλ' ἔθεσαν παῖδες μεγαλήτορες· ἔνθα μέ φημι
ὕμνῳ νικήσαντα φέρειν τρίποδ' ὠτώεντα.

There I myself crossed over into Chalcis for the games of valorous Amphidamas – that great-hearted man's sons had announced and established many prizes – and there, I declare, I gained victory with a hymn, and carried off a tripod with handles.

Plutarch and the *Contest of Homer and Hesiod* tell us that this event at Chalcis was considered to be *the* Contest of Homer and Hesiod, and

anthropologist Marshall Sahlins. Homeric βασιλεύς-ship is not an inherited constitutional position but a prestigious social role linked to personal qualities and wealth. The word's meaning in Hesiod is a moot question.

[10] See pp. 37–8.

that Amphidamas was a hero of the Lelantine War.[11] The story is very doubtful, but a very old one nonetheless. The tradition of the *Contest* goes back to Alcidamas in the fourth century BCE, and before that was probably known to Aristophanes;[12] the Lelantine War is attested in Herodotus and Thucydides.[13] But the events themselves are so early that it is impossible to tell where tradition ends and history begins.[14] The reports we have of both contest and war are shaped more by tradition and legend than by accurate reporting. If the Lelantine War was a real historical event, one candidate for its date is *c.*700 BCE, based on archaeological indications that the site of Lefkandi was abandoned or destroyed near that date. Now, it would be too credulous to suppose that the composer of the *Works and Days* genuinely participated in a real-life Contest of Homer and Hesiod. But it may well be that the above passage was designed to evoke the Lelantine War in the minds of its initial audience. If so, the war would probably have been within living memory: this extremely conjectural argument would put the *Works and Days* in the first half of the seventh century. It is unlikely that we can get any closer to a secure dating.[15]

The poem's image of domestic economics, and intimations of a class struggle between working landowners and *basilēes*, cannot be taken as a faithful, impartial account of a real society. But it can be expected to possess verisimilitude. For this reason, ancient historians sometimes give it a prominent role in the study of Iron Age Greek society. That position is not really secure: the picture that the poem paints has various inconsistencies. For example, we can easily imagine the *Works and Days* being performed in the sympotic context that we routinely suppose to be a normal forum for Archaic poetry, but it is harder to imagine the severe narrator himself tolerating such a leisured environment. He has no time for handouts, yet he is happy to accept a valuable tripod as a prize for his poetry (654–7, quoted above) – even though

---

[11] Plut. *Conv. sept. sap.* 153f–54a; *Contest* 6.

[12] See Introduction, pp. vi–vii with n. 2.

[13] Hdt. 5.99; Thuc. 1.15. Archil. fr. 3 distances 'the masters of Euboea, spear-famed' from the use of bows and slings, and this is sometimes linked to the Lelantine War by a legend that a treaty forbade the war from being fought with missile weapons (Strabo 10.1.12); but that legend cannot realistically be dated earlier than Ephorus, in the fourth century (see E. Wheeler 1987).

[14] For a sceptical view see Hall 2014: 1–8; more sympathetically, Janko 1982: 94–8, with further bibliography.

[15] Cf. Janko 1982: 228–31, dating *WD* to 690–650; Kõiv 2011 makes 'Hesiod' contemporary with Archilochus (both give extensive bibliographies).

poetry is not a type of economic activity that fits easily into the conception of 'work' presented elsewhere in the poem.[16]

As a literary work, the *Works and Days* is far more than just a string of aphorisms.[17] It depicts an intimate interdependence between ethics and work. The narrator weaves back and forth between advice on household and farm management, on the one hand, and politics, justice, and obligations, on the other. As Stephanie Nelson has suggested, the poem is not a technical manual about *how to do* farming but more a self-help manual on how to *experience* farming.[18] The work ethic that emerges is not a rule imposed by an external authority but an integral part of the human experience: only a working person is a fully realized person.

Work is central to the relationship between gods and mortals. It is the gods who provide mortals with this opportunity to become fully human: the gods conceal livelihood from mortals so that they must work (*WD* 42–6), and they share out work to mortals (397–8). Work is tough and requires sweat, but it is also the only way to avoid misery (287–92):

> τὴν μέν τοι Κακότητα καὶ ἰλαδὸν ἔστιν ἑλέσθαι
> ῥηιδίως· λείη μὲν ὁδός, μάλα δ' ἐγγύθι ναίει·
> τῆς δ' Ἀρετῆς ἱδρῶτα θεοὶ προπάροιθεν ἔθηκαν
> ἀθάνατοι· μακρὸς δὲ καὶ ὄρθιος οἶμος ἐς αὐτὴν
> καὶ τρηχὺς τὸ πρῶτον· ἐπὴν δ' εἰς ἄκρον ἵκηται,
> ῥηιδίη δὴπειτα πέλει, χαλεπή περ ἐοῦσα.

Misery is there to be grabbed in abundance, easily, for smooth is the road, and she lives very nearby; but in front of Excellence the immortal gods have set sweat, and the path to her is long and steep, and rough at first – yet when one arrives at the top, then it becomes easy, difficult though it still is.

The sweat of the brow is everything. This Hesiod looks a bit like a proto-libertarian. But he is no amoral egoist: he is also adamant

---

[16] See also Hall 2014: 25–6 on mismatches between the narrator's stated philosophy on work and his vocation as a poet.

[17] A sample of recent literary approaches to *Works and Days*: Clay 2003: 31–48; 2009 (the *Works* represents a mortal outlook on the cosmos, complementing the *Theogony*); Lardinois 2003 (the *Works* is structurally similar to a Homeric angry speech); Beall 2004 (the *Works* is closer to Greek epic than to Near Eastern wisdom poetry); Canevaro 2013 (misogyny in the *Works* is an expression of anxiety about the efficacy of work); Hunter 2014 (ancient reception of the *Works*); Canevaro 2015 (self-sufficiency as an interpretive strategy for approaching the poem).

[18] Nelson 1998: 57.

about the importance of honesty, loyalty, and fair dealings with neighbours and outsiders (346–50, 707–23); this way, neighbours can be relied on for aid in the event of future disaster (351, 397–403).

And his philosophy is not blindly laissez-faire either. As mentioned above, he has no problem with handouts when it comes to poetry prizes. Even aside from that, he recognizes that ethical people need an ethical society to live in. It is the responsibility of the *basilēes* to prevent envious men from taking advantage of the labour of others (248–85), and to ensure that each man has the autonomy to work. The worst dregs of humanity are 'gift-eaters' (38–41, 220–1, 263–4), people who live off the labour of others. 'Gift-eating' in a *basileus* is worse still, and stands for corruption. A thing is noble if it encourages labour and enables self-sufficiency. If envy of another man's wealth provokes a lazy man to work and gain wealth for himself (20–6), that is competition, a form of Strife that is good for mortals. It is quite different from the resentment that just men feel against a lazy man who lives without working (303–6).

Within this broad ethical framework – the divine nature of work and the imperative of justice – the poem is full of grey areas, and various interpretations compete with each other with no clear winners. This is especially true for the mythical interludes, the Myth of the Races and the story of Prometheus and Pandora. When Prometheus gives fire to mortals, is that an endorsement of fire as a moral good, on the basis that it enables people to work? Or is it an evil, since it turns mortals into a race of gift-eaters? Pandora is another paradox.[19] On the one hand she is *all gift*, the literal meaning of her name, 'since all those who live on Olympus had given her a gift' (80–2); on the other, she counterbalances the gift of fire, since her presence increases the resources and work that a man needs to sustain life. For the narrator, all women are lazy consumers (373–5):

> μηδὲ γυνή σε νόον πυγοστόλος ἐξαπατάτω
> αἱμύλα κωτίλλουσα, τεὴν διφῶσα καλιήν·
> ὃς δὲ γυναικὶ πέποιθε, πέποιθ' ὅ γε φιλήτῃσιν.

Do not let an an arse-fancy woman deceive your mind by guilefully cajoling you while she pokes into your granary: whoever trusts a woman, trusts swindlers.

---

[19] Fraser 2011 gives a recent survey and discussion of questions surrounding Pandora.

The narrator is deeply and viciously misogynistic. But he is not entirely irrational: he never resorts to fantasizing that women had never been created, and he readily acknowledges the importance of the wife in a working household. The ambiguity extends to Pandora's jar, which infamously retains Anticipation after all its evil contents have escaped (94–104): Anticipation is Most's translation of *elpis*, more traditionally rendered as 'Hope', but the word also means 'expectation'. Is Pandora's Anticipation a gift or a curse? And does it stay in the jar for mortals to keep and treasure, or to keep it hidden and inaccessible? These questions are left open.

## 2. The Hesiodic *Theogony*

The *Theogony* is an account of the establishment of the divine world. It begins with the primordial entities Chasm (or 'Chaos'), Earth, and Eros ('desire' or 'love'); moves on to the succession of Cronus at the head of the Titans, born from Earth and Sky; then considers Zeus and the Olympians; and finally arrives at the organization of the divine world in the 'now'. Many other miscellaneous divinities, monsters, and other figures appear along the way.

Again, the text and translation used here follows Most (2006); for a critical edition and commentary, see M. L. West (1966). The poem's structure is as follows:

| | |
|---|---|
| 1–103 | Hymnic prelude to Muses |
| 104–15 | Proem (introductory paragraph)[20] |
| 116–53 | The earliest divinities: Chasm to Earth, Sky, and the Titans; various monsters born from Earth |
| 154–210 | The Titans; succession of Cronus and castration of Sky; Aphrodite born from Sky's severed genitals |
| 211–452 | Various other monsters and divinities born |
| 453–506 | The Olympians; succession of Zeus |
| 507–900 | Challenges to Zeus: |

|  | | |
|---|---|---|
| | 521–616 | Prometheus; separation at Mecone; Pandora |
| | 617–819 | Titanomachy; description of Tartarus |
| | 820–80 | Battle with Typhoeus |
| | 881–900 | Zeus devours Metis; birth of Athena |

---

[20] 'Proem' is used here to refer to the brief, semi-formulaic preface that follows a hymnic prelude and precedes the main body of a poem. See pp. 45–8.

The poet explicitly assumes the persona of Hesiod (*Theog.* 22–34), so readers who take Hesiodic authorship literally will date the poem close to the *Works and Days*. And, in fact, stylometric evidence does put the poems close together, so far as that kind of evidence can be trusted.[21] On this literalist interpretation, the conventional date is *c.*700, around the time of the Lelantine War (see under *Works and Days*, above), with the *Theogony* normally supposed to be the earlier of the two poems.[22] If a later date is accepted for *Works and Days*, the *Theogony*'s date will also change. But the nature of that change will depend on other assumptions: about the validity of linguistic evidence, and whether the two poems are to be assigned to the same 'author' or not.[23]

More than any other poem discussed in this book, the Hesiodic *Theogony* needs to be understood in the context of other cosmogonic texts. Current treatments rightly emphasize the importance of older Near Eastern parallels for the succession myth.[24] But we should also think of later fragmentary Greek theogonies. We have fragments of theogonies attributed to Epimenides and Musaeus; the Derveni *Theogony*, probably dating to the sixth century; the 'Eudemian' *Theogony*, perhaps *c.*400 BCE; maybe further Orphic and/or Cyclic theogonies; and Titanomachies by Eumelus and Musaeus. And there are other, later, theogonic poems with links to the earlier ones, especially the Hieronyman *Theogony* and Orphic *Rhapsodies*, written in the Hellenistic era.[25] No reliable comprehensive translation of all these fragments is available.

---

[21] Janko 1982: 220–1.

[22] This supposition is based on treating *WD* 11–12 as a retraction of *Theog.* 225. Identifying cross-references between early Greek poems is hazardous to say the least: see pp. 1–2 above, also pp. 57–63 and 104–12 below.

[23] Janko 1982: 228–31 dates the *Theogony* to 700–665 BCE based on stylometric evidence; Kõiv 2011 makes both the *Theogony* and *Works and Days* contemporary with Archilochus (i.e. *c.*650), based on a survey of the biographical tradition and ancient chronographies; M. L. West 2011b: 236–7 assigns the poems to 680–660 based partly on the biographical tradition, partly on the catalogue of rivers in *Theog.* 337–45. See also pp. 4–5 above.

[24] See below, pp. 38–40.

[25] All of these poems appear in Bernabé 2004–7. For the Derveni *Theogony*, see also Bernabé 2007; and (full Derveni papyrus) Kouremenos et al. 2006.

The age and intact state of the Hesiodic *Theogony* have made its version of the Greek succession myth the most prestigious one for modern readers. The cosmos begins with the primal powers Chasm and Earth, followed by Eros, Erebos, Night, and others; Cronus castrates and overthrows his father Sky; in turn his son, Zeus, overthrows Cronus in the Titanomachy. In many ways the Orphic theogonies follow the same pattern. The Derveni and Eudemian theogonies begin with symbolic entities too (though they place Night first), and proceed through the succession of Cronus and then Zeus. Aristotle, who knew the Eudemian *Theogony* well, lumps it together with Hesiod in places, on the basis that the two poems' cosmogonies followed a common pattern.[26]

But the Orphic poems are different in some significant ways. The Derveni *Theogony* avoids relating Zeus's rise to power directly: instead, it casts it as a flashback. As the poem opens, Zeus – already ruler of the universe – is visiting Night in her cave to consult her as an oracle. The setting makes the poem a piece of wisdom literature, where Night instructs Zeus in the history and nature of the cosmos. One thinks also of Parmenides' poem, where the narrator passes through the gates of Night and Day to receive instruction from an unnamed goddess. In Hesiod, after Cronus castrates Sky, the severed genitals engender the goddess Aphrodite, a personification of playful sexual desire; in the Derveni *Theogony*, Zeus eats Sky's genitals (apparently represented by the Sun) so that he may absorb the identity of all-ancestor and firstborn, establishing himself at once as primal origin, ancestor, and ruler of the cosmos.[27] Zeus has a habit of eating important symbolic entities in these poems. In Hesiod, he devours Metis ('cunning'), in accordance with prophecies from Earth and Sky 'so that the goddess would advise him about good and evil' (*Theog.* 899–900). In the much later Hellenistic poems, Zeus takes the identity of *prōtogonos* ('first ancestor') by eating Phanes, a primordial dragon who hatched from a cosmic egg.[28]

The unique poetic achievement of the Hesiodic *Theogony*, as opposed to its successors, lies in the extraordinary originality of its

[26] Orphica frs. 20.ii, iii, iv Bernabé.
[27] Orphica frs. 8, 9, 12 Bernabé.
[28] Orphica frs. 80.iii, 85, 241 Bernabé. See M. L. West 1983: 198–202 on Phanes' egg. The *Rhapsodies* rationalize the variants by making Phanes and Metis one and the same (frs. 140, 243.9; in frs. 96 and 139 they are two persons of a trinity).

pan-Hellenic perspective.[29] Out of thin air it conjures an umbrella story for a bewildering maze of symbols and myths, piecing together elements chosen to be representative of the heritage of all Greeks. Yet its picture of the divine world is not simply copied from religious traditions: already in Hesiod there are attempts to rationalize the gods' relationships to the cosmos and to one another. When the poem makes a symbolic figure such as Eros the source of its genealogical impetus (*Theog.* 120), that is more than just a tweak to divine genealogy: it is also a statement about the natural forces at work in the universe. Acousilaus and Parmenides understood Hesiod this way, and agreed with him, as Phaedrus points out in Plato's *Symposium.*[30] The *Theogony* belongs as much among the pre-Socratic natural philosophers as among the poets.[31]

Individual episodes within the poem are captivating in their own right. The episode where Cronus castrates his father Sky, and subsequently Aphrodite is born (154–206), lends itself to Freudian interpretation with gleeful abandon. Zeus's fireworks in the battles against the Titans and the monster Typhoeus (617–880) not only provide a dazzling spectacle but also illustrate his divine benevolence. The list of Zeus's wives (886–923) – the main highlight being the scene where Athena is born, leaping forth fully armed from his head – illustrates Zeus's position as universal father, the head of the household for an entire universe.

This last scene brings us to a tricky problem in reading the *Theogony* as a literary text. It is beyond doubt that the last part of the poem is a hanger-on in some way: it was composed either separately from, or later than, the rest of the poem. Exactly how much of the final section is an intrusion is open to debate. Most scholars would place the cut-off point at line 900, some a bit later.[32] The old Loeb edition by H. G. Evelyn-White (1914) confused things further by inserting yet another intrusion after line 929, a nineteen-line passage that duplicates the story of Athena's birth.[33] Several other parts of the poem are also

---

[29] Some recent literary approaches to the *Theogony*: Clay 2003: 12–30 (the poem as a god's-eye perspective on the emergence and articulation of order in the cosmos); Stoddard 2004 (narratological analysis, with chapters on focalization, representation of time, etc.); Pache 2008 (the mortal world's dependence on female divine sexuality hints at erotic aspects of religious experience); Pucci 2009 (the poem's 'concrete, rapid and abstract' style).

[30] Pl. *Symp.* 178b (=*FGrH* 2 F 6a; Parmenides fr. B 13 D–K).

[31] M. L. West 1966: 195–6, on *Theog.* 120, aptly cites parallels in Parmenides, Empedocles, and Plato, as well as more purely literary or religious writers such as 'Orpheus' and Euripides.

[32] See also pp. 113–14 on splicing at the end of the *Theogony*.

[33] A passage in Galen records the nineteen-line passage (Hes. fr. 294=Chrysippus fr. 908) and quotes Chrysippus for an attribution to Hesiod. As West observes (M. L. West 1966: 401–3), a

detachable to some extent: it is possible to read the *Theogony* without its opening hymn, and the authenticity of the Typhoeomachy has often been doubted.[34]

But the text as it stands shows us a poet who has selected his stories carefully to create and reinforce a narrative about the nature of the universe: a story of divine justice, and of how the stability of the cosmos is underpinned by the threat of violence from Zeus. The episode of the separation at Mecone (*Theog.* 535–64) was not an automatic inclusion, for example; the story appears in no other ancient source.[35] The poet chose to include it. Likewise the poet is in full control of the stories of Prometheus and Pandora: he uses them to establish Zeus as the ultimate arbiter of divine and mortal ethics, respectively. The Titanomachy and Typhoeomachy cast the Olympians as a universal police force. And onto this ethical and cosmic constitution the poet superimposes the succession myth, a violent genealogical story-type that we also see in older Near Eastern literature such as the Hurro-Hittite Kumarbi poems and the Babylonian *Enuma elish*. The poet ratifies and justifies Zeus's position using every tool available to him, to make all the cosmos fall within Zeus's purview. We cannot be certain that our *Theogony* was the first Greek poem to draw on so many resources to achieve a grand unified picture of the universe, but it was unquestionably the most successful in doing so.

### 3. The Hesiodic *Catalogue of Women*

The *Catalogue*, in five books, survives only as fragments, but those fragments are extensive: over 1,100 lines are complete or can be restored satisfactorily, representing probably about 25% of the poem. The opening lays out the *Catalogue*'s programme: to tell of famous women from times past, their liaisons with men and gods, and their children (fr. 1.14–18):

τάων ἔσπετέ μ[οι γενεήν τε καὶ ἀγλαὰ τέκνα,
ὅσσ[αι]ς δὴ παρέλ[εκτο πατὴρ ἀνδρῶν τε θεῶν τε

note in the Galen manuscript assigning the passage to the *Theogony* is itself a later addition in a second hand: another intrusion. West suggests the Hesiodic *Melampodia* as a possible source.

[34] See M. L. West 1966: 381–2 on the Typhoeomachy.

[35] There are allusions in sch. vet. Pind. *Nem.* 9.123 (where it is set at Sicyon); Callim. *Aetia* fr. 119 Pfeiffer.

σ̣ιπερμιαίˌνων τὰ ιπρῶτα γένος κυδρῶν βασιλήων
ἧ̣]ς τε̣ Π[ο]σειδάω[ν
ὄσσαισί]ν τ' Ἄρης [

*Of these women tell [me the race and the splendid children:*
*all those with whom lay [the father of men and of gods,*
*begetting at first the race of illustrious kings,*
*and with which ones Poseidon [*
*and [all those with whom] Ares [*

Most of the poem is occupied with legendary genealogies. Starting from Deucalion and Pyrrha (frs. 2–6), it spreads its scope genealogically and geographically through the eponymous ancestors of Greece's main ethnic groups, beginning with the Aeolids (fr. 10 onwards) and working forwards, generation by generation, branch by branch, to the time of the Trojan War. At key points narrative vignettes appear, to spice up the genealogies: Heracles' sack of Pylos and duel with Periclymenus; the tricks of hungry Erysichthon and his cunning daughter Mestra; the foot race of Atalanta and Hippomenes. Some genealogical entries open with the formula *ē' hoiē* ('or like her who'): this has given the poem the alternative title of the *Ehoiae*.

Book 5 is different. The surviving fragments give an extended account of the courtship of Helen, presided over by her brothers, Castor and Polydeuces. Much of the text is filled with a Catalogue of Helen's Suitors from all over Greece and the marriage gifts they bring to woo her; the formal elements of this catalogue follow much the same model as the Catalogue of Ships in *Iliad* Book 2 (see Chapter II on catalogues). The surviving text trails off with an account of Zeus's plan to lower the world's population by causing a great war – the Trojan War – and poetic metaphors for the ceaseless cycle of seasons, hinting at the endless nature of genealogy.[36]

There is no single standard edition. The major edition is that of Merkelbach and West (1967); but new fragments have continued to emerge, and their later minor edition ([3]1990) is just as important. Two more recent editions are also essential: Hirschberger's commentary (2004), and Most's new Loeb edition (2007). It is perhaps frustrating that research on the *Catalogue* requires four books at one's

---

[36] Some recent literary approaches to the *Catalogue of Women*: I. Rutherford 2000 (genre and 'Ehoie' poetry); Hunter 2005 (essays on many topics, including performance context and reception); González 2010 (the end of the heroic age); Ormand 2014 (intertextuality, and aristocratic attitudes to women and marriage).

fingertips, but this also reflects the rapid pace at which our knowledge of the poem has increased.

There is no agreement about the poem's date. Janko's stylometric analysis puts the *Catalogue* roughly contemporary with or slightly earlier than the Hesiodic *Theogony*, in the first part of the seventh century;[37] West interprets a number of supposed references to cult, other poems, and historical events in the poem as collectively pointing to a much later date, between 580 and 520.[38] In both arguments, no weight can be attached to supposed imitative links between the *Catalogue* and other poems, since there is a strong presumption that similarities of that kind represent traditional elements, not allusions to a specific text. If West's later date is correct, still that date must not be interpreted simply: the poem contains much traditional material that goes back at least to the eighth century.[39]

Analysis of the fragments of Book 1 indicates that it must have run to well over 800 lines, perhaps as many as 1,100;[40] so the whole poem would have been somewhat under half the length of the *Odyssey*. On the other hand, Book 5 may have been considerably shorter: it is hard to see what could have filled out the rest of it, unless the surviving fragments come from towards the end of the book.

The *Catalogue* is difficult to study, both because of its fragmentary nature and because of the disparate bibliography. But it is worth studying. In Roman Egypt it was the third most popular of all literary works, after the *Iliad* and *Odyssey*.[41] The *Catalogue* also had an immense impact on Hellenistic mythography, the scholarly trend of producing encyclopaedic summaries of myths, such as the *Library* of pseudo-Apollodorus. This in turn had knock-on effects on writers who made use of such mythographic texts: literary figures such as Ovid, historians like Diodorus, ethnographers such as Pausanias. These influences are often indirect. Even so, the *Catalogue*'s influence on pseudo-Apollodorus was so strong that ps.-Apollodorus has formed the basis for nearly all reconstructions of the poem's structure in the last fifty years.

---

[37] Janko 1982: 85–7, with 248 nn. 38–9.

[38] M. L. West 1985: 130–7.

[39] M. L. West 1985: 164–5; similarly Ormand 2014: 3–6.

[40] M. L. West 1985: 72–6.

[41] The Mehrtens–Pack[3] catalogue (available online through the CEDOPAL database) lists finds of fifty-two copies of the *Catalogue* plus six doubtful cases; compare thirty-six copies of the *Theogony*, thirty of *Works and Days*, and thirty-eight of other Hesiodic works. For comparison, the catalogue also lists 1,420 papyri of the *Iliad*, 252 of the *Odyssey*, 136 of Euripides' entire output, 36 of Sophocles, and 32 of Aeschylus.

Another challenge is that it is sometimes difficult to tell the difference between the *Catalogue* and another poem that seems to have been similar: the *Great Ehoiae* (frs. 185–201 Most, frs. 246–62 Merkelbach–West). Commentaries on the fragments of that poem may be found in Hirschberger (2004) and D'Alessio (2005). With some fragments there is disagreement as to which poem they come from: the assignments in Merkelbach and West, Hirschberger, and Most are all slightly different. Asclepius' parentage (frs. 53–61 and 239–40) is the biggest area of doubt. In one poem his mother was Arsinoe; in the other, Coronis. Merkelbach and West provisionally put all the relevant fragments in the *Catalogue*; Hirschberger assigns Coronis to the *Catalogue* and Arsinoe to the *Great Ehoiae*; Most allocates Arsinoe to the *Catalogue* but leaves the question over Coronis open. The relevant fragments are linked to other fragments throughout the *Catalogue*, so the question is an important one, but insoluble on current evidence. Another problem concerns the Atalanta episode (frs. 47–51), and some other fragments attached to it, which may not belong to the *Catalogue*.

As a guide to the perplexed, an overview of the fragments is given below, based on Most's Loeb edition. This overview is not exhaustive but aims to highlight some of the poem's most interesting episodes, indicated in **bold**. References to recent discussions (other than Hirschberger's full commentary) are also given here and there.

**Proem**: fr. 1
Deucalion: frs. 2 to 8 (see also M. L. West 1985: 50–6)
**Hellen's descendants**; Dorids, Xouthids: fr. 9 to fr. 10.24 (see also M. L. West 1985: 60–76)

AEOLIDS: fr. 10.25 to fr. 71
Thestius' descendants
  Althaea and her children
    Leda and her children (**the *Oresteia***): fr. 19.7 to fr. 21
    Meleager: fr. 22.1–13
    Deianeira; **death and apotheosis of Heracles**: fr. 22.14–33
  Hypermestra and her children: fr. 22.34 to fr. 23.4
Porthaon's daughters; **Heracles sacks Oechalia**: fr. 23.5–37
Salmoneus' descendants
  **Tyro and Poseidon**: fr. 27.24 to fr. 29
  Neleus and Pelias
    **Heracles sacks Pylos; duel with Periclymenus**: frs. 31 to 33
    Neleus' daughter Pero; Melampus and Bias: fr. 35
*(gap)*

Athamas (son of Aeolus): frs. 38 to 40
  Athamas' descendants by Themisto: frs. 41 to 51
    **Atalanta and Hippomenes**: frs. 47 to 51 (see also D'Alessio 2005: 213–16; Ormand 2014: 119–51)
*(gap)*
[*The Arsinoe/Coronis problem*: see above, and also D'Alessio 2005: 208–10]
  Arsinoe; Apollo's servitude to Admetus: frs. 53 to 60
  Coronis (=frs. 59 to 61 Merkelbach–West): see frs. 164, 239, 240
*(gap)*
**Mestra and Erysichthon**; Bellerophon: frs. 69 to 71 (see also Ormand 2014: 85–118)

  INACHIDS: frs. 72 to 109 (see also M. L. West 1985: 76–82)
  Io and her descendants
    Io: frs. 72 to 74
    Proetus, Acrisius, and their children: frs. 77 to 83
    The madness of Proetus' daughters: frs. 80 to 83
  Europa and her son Sarpedon: frs. 89 to 91 (see also M. L. West 1985: 82–5)
  Minos and Pasiphaë: frs. 92 to 95
  Phineus and his **pursuit by the Harpies**: frs. 96 to 105

  PELASGIDS
  Pelasgus; Callisto and her son Arcas; Auge and Heracles, and their son Telephus: frs. 110 to 117 (see also M. L. West 1985: 91–4)

  ATLANTIDS: frs. 118 to 141 (see also M. L. West 1985: 94–9)
  Atlas' daughters and descendants: frs. 118 to 122
  Alcyone, Aethusa, and descendants: frs. 123 to 131
  Pelopids: frs. 132 to 141 (see also M. L. West 1985: 109–14)
    Heracles, **birth**: frs. 138 to 139 (=*Shield* 1–56; see also Ormand 2014: 152–80)
    Heracles, **apotheosis**: fr. 140

  ASOPIDS: frs. 142 to 153
  Aeacus; Peleus sacks Iolcus; Peleus and Thetis: frs. 145 to 153

  BOOK FIVE
  **Catalogue of Helen's suitors**: frs. 154a (or 154b?) to 155.93 (see also M. L. West 1985: 114–19; Cingano 2005; Ormand 2014: 181–202)
  **Twilight of the heroes**: fr. 155.94–143 (see also M. L. West 1985: 119–24; Koenen 1994; Clay 2003: 169–73; Finkelberg 2004; González 2010; Ormand 2014: 202–16)

UNPLACED FRAGMENTS: frs. 157 to 184
Loves of Poseidon and Apollo: fr. 157
Cyrene, Aristaeus, and Actaeon: frs. 158 to 163 (see also M. L. West 1985: 85–9)
Athenian genealogies: frs. 169 to 173
Heracleids: frs. 174, 175
(Dorians, Leleges [=frs. 233, 234 Merkelbach–West]: see frs. 250, 251)

### 4. The Hesiodic *Shield*

The *Shield* – often known by its Greek or Latin titles, the *Aspis* or *Scutum* – is an odd poem, and often derided for its poor literary qualities. But it is our only intact heroic narrative in hexameter verse from between the times of Homer and Apollonius. That by itself is enough to make it important. Martin (2005) has made an attractive argument that the *Shield* should be read as 'pulp' epic: poetry designed around noise and excess, which uses glitzy stylistic effects to exploit its material. It is not compulsory to read the *Shield* through a 'trash aesthetic', as Martin puts it: no-one is obligated to enjoy the poem. But it is important to reject the misguided notion that it is only an adaptation or parody of Homer.[42] The *Shield* may well be a more typical example of early epic than the *Iliad*.

This book follows Most's (2007) text and translation; for a critical edition and commentary, Russo (1950; second edition 1965) is standard.[43] In outline, the poem runs as follows:

| | |
|---|---|
| 1–56 | Birth of Heracles (=*Catalogue* fr. 138.8–63) |
| 57–121 | Prelude to duel between Heracles and Cycnus |
| 122–38 | Heracles' arming scene |
| 139–319 | Rhetorical description (*ekphrasis*) of Heracles' shield |
| 320–480 | Heracles defeats Cycnus and injures the god Ares |

The *Shield*'s origins are obscure. A doubtful report tells us that Stesichorus knew the poem (Hesiod test. 52), which would put it before *c.*560; and it has often been supposed that the fate of Cycnus in the poem's last lines represents the destruction of Crisa in the First

---

[42] See Martin 2005: 154–5 on modern treatments that see the *Shield* as imitative of Homer.

[43] Adrian Kelly informs me that a new critical edition is planned by Henry Mason, currently of Merton College, Oxford.

Sacred War, in retaliation for Crisa's taxation on access to Delphi, referred to in the poem as Pytho (477–80):

τοῦ δὲ τάφον καὶ σῆμ' ἀιδὲς ποίησεν Ἄναυρος
ὄμβρῳ χειμερίῳ πλήθων· τὼς γάρ μιν Ἀπόλλων
Λητοΐδης ἤνωξ', ὅτι ῥα κλειτὰς ἑκατόμβας
ὅστις ἄγοι Πυθοῖδε βίῃ σύλασκε δοκεύων.

But the river Anaurus, full with winter rain, obliterated [Cycnus'] tomb and monument; for Apollo, Leto's son, had ordered it to do so, because, whoever brought famous hecatombs to Pytho, [Cycnus] would observe closely and plunder them with violence.

The trouble is, first, that the duel is set at the shrine of Pagasaean Apollo in Thessaly, not at Crisa, and that an allegory for the First Sacred War really ought to depict a *victory* for a Magnesian hero (Cycnus), not a defeat. Secondly, it is doubtful whether the First Sacred War actually happened. No source prior to 350 gives an explicit sign of having heard of it. The inconsistent accounts of the war that we see after that date may well be 'just so' stories to rationalize control over Delphi by the amphictyony, a council of neighbouring states.[44] Be that as it may, the *Shield* is normally dated to within a few decades of 600: only those who insist on authentic authorship by a historical Hesiod would place it earlier.[45] The poem's geographic origins are also doubtful. It has traditionally been regarded as a Boeotian composition, because (1) the poem celebrates Heracles as a Theban, not Argive, hero, and contains other references to Thebes (104–5, 272); (2) the poem was regarded as Hesiodic in antiquity and Hesiod was Boeotian; (3) the closing lines (see above) may point to a vested interest in the Delphic amphictyony, which included Boeotia.[46] This is not robust evidence. And, again, the theory neglects the Thessalian setting. A final point of obscurity surrounds the opening section of the *Shield* – on Heracles' birth – which also appeared word for word in Book 4 of the *Catalogue of Women* (*Cat.* frs. 138, 139); but exactly what this overlap means for the relationship between the two poems is debated.

---

[44] See Hall 2014: 312–17 for a brief review. Specifically on the *Shield*, see Janko 1986: 40–7 (who accepts both Stesichorus' report and the First Sacred War as genuine). A reference to foreign domination over Delphi in *Hymn. Hom. Ap.* 540–3 reflects the existence of the amphictyony but is not evidence for a war.

[45] Janko 1986 (with review of older discussions) puts the poem between 591 and *c.*570; Zardini 2009: 7–19, between 630 and 600; M. L. West 2011b: 240, *c.*570.

[46] Guillon 1963; Russo 1965: 29–35; Janko 1986: 43–4.

(For further discussion see Chapter VI on 'cropping and stitching' of poems.)

Dense poetic textures and crowded imagery dominate the poem's literary personality.[47] Both in the long *ekphrasis* of Heracles' shield, which forms the centrepiece of the poem, and in the main narrative, the narrator piles detail upon detail. The *ekphrasis* of the shield contains no fewer than twelve personifications of Fear, Strife, Murder, and other dreadful entities; groups of boars and lions; *three* battle scenes – one of the Lapiths and Centaurs (with seventeen named fighters), one of an infantry battle (supervised by Ares, Fear, Rout, and Athena), and one of the siege of a city; a feast of the Olympians; a fishing scene; Perseus running from the Gorgons; a second city with scenes of a wedding, a cavalry parade, farming, sports, and hunting; and the Ocean surrounding everything, symbolically elevating the contents of the shield to a complete world. Myres (1941) makes a noble attempt to reconstruct a possible model where all these scenes could really be squeezed in, and even includes an illustration of his efforts by Joan M. Laing; but, as he points out, no real surviving artwork is nearly as dense and chaotic as this description.

This love of accumulation also appears in the duel of Heracles and Cycnus. The fighting itself occupies only eighteen lines (370–3, 380–5, 413–20). This thin account is filled out by no fewer than six similes (374–9, 386–92, 393–401, 402–4, 405–12, 421–4), four of them without pause; they are followed soon afterwards by a seventh and eighth simile (426–33, 436–42), when Ares attacks Heracles. Taken individually, the similes are perfectly respectable examples of the form, using the natural world to add impact or flavour to the battle:

ἤριπε δ᾽, ὡς ὅτε τις δρῦς ἤριπεν ἢ ὅτε πεύκη
ἠλίβατος, πληγεῖσα Διὸς ψολόεντι κεραυνῷ·
ὡς ἔριπ᾽, ἀμφὶ δέ οἱ βράχε τεύχεα ποικίλα χαλκῷ.

[Cycnus] fell, as when some oak falls, or a great pine, struck by Zeus' smoking thunderbolt: just so he fell, and around him rattled his armor, worked with bronze.

The narrative technique is a familiar Homeric one: when the narrator approaches a climactic moment, he emphasizes its importance by

---

[47] Some recent literary approaches to the *Shield*: Thalmann 1984: 62–4 (Heracles' monstrous shield stands for the ugliness of war); Toohey 1988 (the macabre preoccupation with death in Heracles' shield); Martin 2005 ('pulp epic'); Stamatopoulou 2013 (Heracles' character, and intertextuality with the *Theogony*).

stretching the narrative out – here, with similes. The oddity lies in the way that they are packed together so breathlessly. The poet actually runs out of steam towards the end: the eighth simile, likening two fighters rushing at each other to rocks bouncing down a cliff, is a reprise of the first.

This poem is a fun, and perhaps lurid, curiosity, tantalizing us with its hints at the many poems that we have lost. It should be sobering to think that a genuinely important and influential poem such as the *Cypria* may well have had more in common with the *Shield* than with the *Iliad*.

### 5. The Homeric *Hymns*

The *Hymns* are a collection of thirty-three poems that celebrate and tell stories about various gods of the Greek pantheon. Thirty-one are intact poems of the Archaic period; one, *Hymn* 1 (to Dionysus), survives only as fragments; another, *Hymn* 8 (to Ares), is an intruder in the collection, written over a millennium later.[48] There are other fragmentary poems that we could put on the same shelf as the *Hymns*, such as the hymns attributed to Orpheus and Terpander, but, even so, the 'Homeric' collection shares a set of common generic and stylistic features that unite them as a group.

It is convenient to speak of 'major' and 'minor' hymns. *Hymns* 2 to 5, addressed to Demeter, Apollo, Hermes, and Aphrodite, are substantial compositions, each on a similar scale to the *Shield*. They contain detailed narratives about an important aspect of the relationship between the divine and mortal worlds. It is conventional to cite them by title, without a number. *Hymn* 1, to Dionysus, was also a major hymn, though only snippets survive. The minor hymns are much more modest pieces, though the two longest also contain narratives of great interest (*Hymns* 7 and 19, to Dionysus and Pan). When analysed purely in terms of their formal structure, the 'major' and 'minor' hymns look much less distinct: see the analysis of Janko (1981) and below (pp. 40–2).

This book follows the text and translation of M. L. West (2003b); the standard critical edition is that of Càssola (1986). The major hymns are well served with commentaries, with N. Richardson (1974) on *Demeter* and (2010) on *Apollo*, *Hermes*, and *Aphrodite*; Vergados (2012) on *Hermes*; and Faulkner (2008) and Olson (2012) on *Aphrodite*. Olson

---

[48] See e.g. N. Richardson 2010: 4, with bibliography.

also covers nine of the minor hymns. There is little clear evidence for individual hymns' dates, but the major hymns probably range in date from the mid-600s (*Aphrodite*) to around 500 (*Hermes*).[49]

Alongside the recent crop of commentaries, literary interpretations of the *Hymns* have also been flourishing. A collection of essays edited by Faulkner (2011a) is an essential piece of bibliography. Clay has influentially argued that the major hymns have a cosmogonic flavour, in the sense that they are preoccupied with the institution of the divine order and establishment of individual gods' spheres of interest and positions in the 'politics of Olympus'.[50] Much attention has also been paid to 'epiphanic' moments in the major hymns, where the god's divine nature is revealed to mortals, or to the cosmos; the *Hymn to Hermes* has even been considered anomalous for not containing such a moment.[51]

The *Hymn to Demeter* tells the story of Hades' rape of Persephone (1–41), Demeter's search for her daughter (42–90), and the institution of rites to honour both goddesses and to secure a blessed afterlife for Eleusinian initiates (268–304, 459–89). The poem is remarkable in many ways, not least in its emphasis on women's agency. Women are the main actors in the central episode of the poem, where Demeter takes refuge at Keleos' house in Eleusis. The same episode contains various hints at religious practices: the rite of *Theoxenia*, where the celebrants set a place for a god as an invisible guest at a feast; the origin story of the *kykeōn* potion drunk by Eleusinian initiates (206–11); and the abortive salvation of Demophon, cheated of immortality by his mother's fright (212–74).[52] Even if the poem is not precisely a 'gospel of Demeter', it would be fair to say that this is the closest we get to a 'just so' story about the theology of a Greek religious cult.

The *Hymn to Apollo* is the only hymn to which a named author can be attached – Cynaethus of Chios[53] – but it also poses the most formidable historical problems. The text as it stands relates three substantial narratives in two settings. The first (1–178) focuses on Apollo's cult site on Delos and relates Leto's long struggle to give birth to the god there; the

---

[49] For some mainstream datings see Janko 1982, esp. 200 and 228–31; M. L. West 2011b. West also dates the *Hymn to Dionysus* to the seventh century, though that dating relies on multiple conjectures.

[50] Clay 1989, 1997, 2011.

[51] Vergados 2011 (see 82 nn. 1–2 for further bibliography).

[52] N. Richardson 2010: 50–5 gives an overview of the poem's religious elements and problems in interpreting them.

[53] Sch. Pind. *Nem.* 2.1c.

second and third (179–387, 388–546) focus on Delphi, and tell of
Apollo's slaying of a chaos-dragon (known to later authors as the
'Python', whence the alternative name for Delphi, 'Pytho'), and his
gathering of a group of Cretans to serve as his ministers. The *Hymn*
has most often been understood as a composite of two poems that
were originally separate: hymns to Delian Apollo (1–178) and to
Pythian Apollo (179–546). Burkert and others have argued that
Cynaethus compiled them into a single poem for the combined
Delia–Pythia festival in 523 BCE.[54] But some readers have always wished
to see the entire thing as a single coherent poem. Richardson sees the
poem as a single composition in *three* parts.[55] This is an appealing analysis, especially in view of the three route descriptions distributed across
each section of the poem (Leto's search for a place to give birth, 30–49;
Apollo's journey from Olympus to Delphi, 216–86; the journey of
Apollo's new ministers from Crete to Delphi, 409–39). Even with
Richardson's analysis, however, it remains likely that Cynaethus
made extensive use of a lost *Pythian Apollo* poem, while putting a considerable degree of his own artistry into the final product.

The *Hymn to Hermes* is a humorous story of the exploits and trickery
of Hermes as a baby.[56] Shortly after his birth he steals out of his crib at
night and goes on a cattle raid against his older brother Apollo; along
the way he invents the tortoiseshell lyre, sandals, and kindling, in
quick succession (17–183). Apollo discovers the theft and confronts
him, and the two gods try to outwit each other (184–321) but eventu-
ally go to Zeus for arbitration (322–96). Afterwards Apollo becomes
entranced by Hermes' lyre (397–502) and, with the gift of the lyre,
the two are reconciled before Zeus (503–78). The story is entertaining
not just for Hermes' numerous deceptions but also for the irony of his
disingenuous performance as a baby: ironic, since of course he genuinely is a baby. The poem's use of body language (laughter, farting,
sneezing) suggests an element of farce that is reminiscent of Old
Comedy. This poem is probably the latest of the major hymns, but recent
studies have shown that it draws on some very archaic elements: the
motif of a cattle raid as an initiatory act is of great antiquity, and is all
the more striking since the poem does not seem to have been designed

[54] Burkert 1979; Janko 1982: 112–15; M. L. West 1999: 368–72, 2003a: 11–12. See Chappell
2011 for a survey.
[55] N. Richardson 2010: 9–13.
[56] On the reception of this *Hymn* see Vergados 2012: 76–124.

for any kind of initiatory function; and the abortive sacrifice scene where Hermes slaughters two of Apollo's oxen but does not eat them has parallels in an early Sumerian story about the hero Lugalbanda.[57]

The *Hymn to Aphrodite*, the shortest and probably the earliest of the major hymns, relates Aphrodite's love affair with the Trojan hero Anchises, and a lengthy prophecy made by Aphrodite about the birth of Aeneas. The most tantalizing points in this poem, apart from its archaic style, relate to Aphrodite's declaration about Aeneas' descendants (196–7):

σοὶ δ' ἔσται φίλος, υἱός, ὃς ἐν Τρώεσσιν ἀνάξει
καὶ παῖδες παίδεσσι διαμπερὲς ἐκγεγάοντες...

You are to have a dear son who will rule among the Trojans, as will the children born to his children continually...

Ancient writers sometimes took these lines as a reference to a supposed contemporary dynasty of Aeneadae who held power in the seventh-century Troad. The truth of the matter is obscure and continues to be debated.[58] The poem ties itself to Trojan material in other ways too: when Aphrodite reassures Anchises, she draws parallels to his great-uncle Ganymede (202–17) and to Tithonus, brother of Priam and father of Memnon (218–38).

## 6. The Epic Cycle

Of all lost hexameter poems, the ones most often lamented by modern enthusiasts are those constituting the Epic Cycle. This was a group of eight early epics, including the two Homeric epics, which when spliced together formed a complete continuous account of the Trojan War: in sequence, the *Cypria, Iliad, Aethiopis, Little Iliad, Sack of Ilion, Returns, Odyssey,* and *Telegony.* Alongside West's translated edition of the fragments (M. L. West 2003b) we have the critical editions of Bernabé (1996 [first published 1987]) and Davies (1988), and several commentaries and analyses of the fragments.[59]

---

[57] On initiation see Johnston 2002. For parallels in *Lugalbanda in the Mountain Cave* see Larson 2005.

[58] For contrasting views and bibliography see Faulkner 2008: 3–18; Olson 2012: 1–9.

[59] Severyns 1928: 245–425; Bethe 1929: 149–204; Huxley 1969: 123–73; Davies 2001; M. L. West 2013; Fantuzzi and Tsagalis 2015a.

The bulk of our knowledge of the six lost epics comes from a set of summaries in the *Chrestomathy* ascribed to 'Proclus'. The identity of this Proclus is uncertain – it may be the famous Neoplatonist philosopher – but immaterial, as Proclus' summaries are in turn extracts from a mythographic source dating to the Hellenistic or early Roman period.[60] There is considerable evidence that the epics originally extended further than Proclus indicates: for example, Burgess sees evidence that the *Cypria* was originally an *Iliaca* that covered the entire war.[61] We shall return to Burgess' 'cropping hypothesis' in Chapter VI. For now, we shall focus on the story as told by Proclus, since it is in that form that the epics made up a continuous 'cycle':

**Cypria**, 11 books, usually attributed to Cyprias of Halicarnassus or Stasinus of Cyprus.[62] The lead-up to the Trojan War and first nine years of the war, starting from the dispute of the goddesses at Peleus' and Thetis' wedding feast, extending through the judgment of Paris, the rape of Helen, the gathering of the fleet at Aulis, the landing at Troy, and events leading into Book 1 of the *Iliad*.

**Iliad**, 24 books, attributed to Homer. Achilles' wrath against Agamemnon and Hector; the deaths of Sarpedon, Patroclus, and Hector; funeral games for Patroclus; the ransom and burial of Hector's body.

**Aethiopis**, 5 books, usually attributed to Arctinus. The arrival of the Amazons and the death of Penthesileia (the so-called 'Amazonis'); the arrival of the Aethiopes led by Memnon; the deaths of Antilochus, Memnon, and Achilles; funeral games for Achilles; the beginning of the quarrel over Achilles' arms.

**Little Iliad**, 4 books, usually attributed to Lesches of Mytilene. The judgment of the arms; the capture of Helenus, and his prophecies; the fetching of Neoptolemus and Philoctetes; the building of the wooden horse and its introduction into the walls of Troy.

**Sack of Ilion**, 2 books, attributed to Arctinus. The Trojans' debate over the wooden horse; the death of Laocoön; the sack of Troy, with deeds of Neoptolemus, Menelaus, the lesser Ajax, and Odysseus; the sacrifice of Polyxena.

[60] As entry points into the bibliography on Proclus and the mythographic tradition, see Davies 1986: 100–9; M. L. West 2013: 4–16.

[61] Burgess 1996, 2002. The main pieces of evidence are *Cypria* frs. 33, 34 Bernabé (West rejects the latter), which belong to an account of the sack of Troy; and a second-century-BCE Halicarnassian inscription (*Cypria* test. West) identifying Cyprias as the author of an *Iliaca*.

[62] Burgess 2002 (arguing for Cyprias); M. L. West 2013: 32–4 (Stasinus).

***Returns***, 5 books, usually attributed to Agias. The dispute of Agamemnon and Menelaus; the departure of the Greeks; Menelaus' arrival in Egypt; the wrath of Athena and death of the lesser Ajax; the return of Neoptolemus; the murder of Agamemnon; the return of Menelaus.

***Odyssey***, 24 books, attributed to Homer. Telemachus' expedition to search for his father; Odysseus' departure from Calypso's island, sojourn among the Phaeacians, and account of his wanderings; the returns of Odysseus and Telemachus; the slaughter of Penelope's suitors.

***Telegony***, 2 books, usually attributed to Eugammon of Cyrene. Odysseus' voyage to Elis; his sojourn in Thesprotia; Telegonus' expedition to search for his father, and killing of Odysseus; the establishment of Odysseus' family as cult figures.

Isolated pieces of testimony attach other poems to a 'cycle': a theogony, Eumelus' *Titanomachy*, the *Danais*, Cinaethon's *Oedipodea*, the Homeric *Thebaid* and *Epigoni*, and the *Alcmeonis*.[63] In terms of mythological content, a single cycle containing all of these plus the Trojan epics would be a hopeless mess. The only way to imagine a coherent longer cycle is to cherry-pick the ancient testimony. West suggests instead that there were multiple cycles, of which the Trojan Cycle was one. Scholars sometimes refer to the *Oedipodea, Thebaid, Epigoni*, and *Alcmeonis* as a 'Theban cycle', but they were not grouped together in antiquity.[64] The Trojan epics, by contrast, do form a coherent group in Proclus' surviving summaries, and when modern scholars refer to the 'Epic Cycle' it is normally the Trojan epics that they are talking about.

We have no good evidence of any of the six lost epics being read after the time of Pausanias in the second century CE.[65] Quotations and references transmitted in later sources are typically distilled from earlier scholarship, not based directly on the poems. One reference suggests

---

[63] Cyclus test. 2 Bernabé (=*Tab. Iliac.* 10K§h Sadurska, the Borgia plaque), 14, 15; Cyclic *Theogony* test., fr. 1 Bernabé; Eumelus fr. 14 West; *Epigoni* fr. 3\* West (attribution uncertain); *Alcmeonis* fr. 6 West. M. L. West 2013: 13–14 speculatively suggests adding the *Naupactia* to the Borgia plaque's list.

[64] The Borgia plaque links the *Oedipodea* and *Thebaid* in a 'cycle', but also includes the *Danais* and a *Titanomachy*, so it is not a 'Theban' cycle. The only other potential evidence for a grouping is that Herodotus and Alcidamas regarded the *Thebaid* and *Epigoni* as both Homeric (*Epigoni* test. 1, 5).

[65] Pausanias knew the *Cypria* and *Little Iliad* directly (10.31.2, 10.26.1), and probably also the *Returns* (10.29.6, 10.30.5). Athenaeus may also have read some of the poems.

that Porphyry (mid-to-late third century) may have known the *Little Iliad* personally;[66] but in some cases (*Aethiopis, Telegony*) we have no evidence that the poems survived beyond the time of Augustus.[67] They were certainly lost before the sixth century.[68]

The Cycle is of enormous importance for the history of the development of the Trojan War legend and for the study of Hellenistic mythographic traditions. Purely in terms of literary merit, though, it is fair to question whether we are missing out on very much. Ancient writers often contrast the Cyclic epics with Homer, with the implication that they are inferior. Aristotle famously criticizes the *Cypria* and *Little Iliad* for their episodic character, lacking an overarching plot-shape or unity.[69] He does not extend the contrast to the other Cyclic epics, but he does tell us that they also contained much less direct speech than Homer.[70] For Hellenistic literary critics, 'cyclic' became a general derogatory term meaning 'banal, conventional'.[71] Horace, criticizing 'the cyclic writer of old' (*scriptor cyclicus olim*), prefers Homer's rushing 'into the midst of things' (*in medias res*) to the practice of narrating the Trojan War from its very beginnings (*gemino...ab ovo*).[72] An epigram by Pollianus rages against the Cycle for plagiarizing Homer, and for droning on repeating 'and then...and then...'.[73] And Proclus' *Chrestomathy* tells us that literary standards of the day – the era of Proclus' Hellenistic source, that is – did not prize the Cycle for its poetic qualities but for its thorough and continuous narration of the legends.[74]

To an extent, however, these charges are themselves only a convention. Ancient testimony is not unanimous in drawing contrasts between Homer and the Cycle: the ancients assigned the *Thebaid* and *Epigoni* to Homer, and sometimes also the *Cypria, Little Iliad*, and *Returns*. And the *Little Iliad* probably possessed more unity than Aristotle lets on:

---

[66] *Little Il.* fr. 3.

[67] The latest evidence of the *Aethiopis'* survival is the Capitoline tablet, dating to Augustus' reign (*Tab. Iliac.* 1A Sadurska); for the *Telegony*, the Hellenistic-era summary in Proclus is the only testimony we can be sure is based directly on the poem, unless Pausanias' reference to the *Thesprotis* (8.12.5=*Teleg.* fr. 3) actually refers to the *Telegony*.

[68] John Philoponus, *In Arist. An. post.* 157.14–17 Wallies, reports that the poems could no longer be found.

[69] Arist. *Poet.* 1459a.30–b.7 (M. L. West 2003b: 118–19).

[70] Arist. *Poet.* 1460a.5–11.

[71] Most famously Callim. *Epigr.* 28 (ἐχθαίρω τὸ ποίημα τὸ κυκλικόν, 'I despise the cyclic poem', etc.). See also Monro 1883: 328–34; Severyns 1928: 155–9; Fantuzzi and Tsagalis 2015b.

[72] Hor. *Ars P.* 146–9.

[73] *Anth. Pal.* 11.130.

[74] Phot. *Myr.* cod. 239, 319.i.30–3 (Procl. *Chrest.* 20 Severyns), citing τὴν ἀκολουθίαν τῶν ἐν αὐτῷ πραγμάτων ('the continuity of the material in [the Cycle]').

Helenus' prophecies almost certainly provided a framing device for the other incidents in the poem. A good deal of thought appears to have gone into the composition of the *Aethiopis* and *Telegony*, in particular. Both poems are framed around, not a unity, but a *duality* of action: each consists of two major episodes that counterpoint each other. In the *Aethiopis*, the episode of Penthesileia and the 'Amazonis' balances the episode of Memnon and Achilles' death: in the first part, Achilles' victory over the Amazons is undermined by Thersites' rumours and murder at Achilles' hands; in the second part, the deaths of Antilochus and Achilles are partially redeemed by the rescue of Achilles' body. As for the *Telegony*, modern critics usually deride the poem for its inconsistencies with the *Odyssey* and the odd marriages between stepsons and stepmothers at the end of the poem. But the two halves of the poem appear to celebrate competing claims to Odysseus' grave site: one in Thesprotia, the other in central Italy (the traditional site of Circe's island and Telegonus' home).[75] Sammons identifies both of these as large-scale cases of 'narrative doublets', a storytelling technique that is common in Homer and which Sammons shows to be common in the Cycle too; still, it is striking to see entire poems framed around this structure.[76]

Our sources cast each of the authors of the Cyclic epics as distinct figures. In other words, the Cycle was not a single monumental creation based on a predetermined design. The poems were originally independent and were only later compiled into a single continuous 'cycle'. But how, when, and why this compilation happened is very uncertain. It makes most sense to imagine that the compilation happened after the word 'cycle' (*kyklos*, literally 'circle') had acquired a literary meaning. That must have appeared earlier than Aristotle, who cites a previous argument where a logician had given *kyklos* as an example of a word with a figurative sense, namely 'an epic poem'.[77] Elsewhere Aristotle mentions an obscure figure, Phayllus, who it seems had given a condensed summary of a 'cycle' (but we do not know what was in Phayllus' cycle).[78] So we are looking at the

---

[75] Livy 1.56.3 and Dion. Hal. 4.63.1 report the sixth-century Roman colonization of Circeii, probably already a cult site to Circe; Aesch. fr. eleg. 2 alludes to Circe's teaching of pharmacology to the native Italians (see also Plin. *HN* 7.15, 25.11); later allusions place Circe in Italy still more explicitly, e.g. Ap. Rhod. *Argon.* 3.310–13.

[76] Sammons 2013.

[77] Cyclus test. 1, 8 Bernabé (=Arist. *An. post.* 77b.2, *Soph. el.* 171a.10).

[78] Arist. *Rhet.* 1712a.12. M. L. West 2013: 23–6 speculates that Phayllus compiled the Epic Cycle, *c.*350–320 BCE.

mid-fourth century at the latest. There may be some basis for pushing
the date back further: ancient commentators on Horace's *Art of Poetry*,
where Horace refers to 'the cyclic writer of old', connect the word 'cyclic' with Antimachus' *Thebaid* (*c.*400 BCE).[79] Antimachus was a byword
for longwindedness, and supposedly went in circles before getting to
the point. However, Horace's commentators are very muddled: one
is under the impression that Antimachus meandered for twenty-four
books before the plot got under way, and the other somehow manages
to take Horace's line 'I shall sing of Priam's fortune' as a quotation
from the *Thebaid*. Still, there may possibly be a kernel of truth in
their idea that the literary sense of *kyklos* goes back to Antimachus in
some way.[80]


## 7. Oracle collectors (*chresmologoi*)

Think of prophecies in hexameter verse, and most people will think of
the Delphic Oracle. Both in antiquity and in the modern era, Apollo's
Pythia at Delphi has had a reputation for obscurity and ambiguity. This
stereotype comes from the arcane quotations that Herodotus and
Pausanias give us.[81] But it is an error. And not a doubtful or a slight
error: it is drastically wrong. Historical pronouncements of the Pythia
were almost never in verse;[82] they were normally clear and explicit;[83]
and nearly all attested verse oracles were invented after the fact for
the sake of telling a good story. (It would, in any case, be the default
presumption that most oracles are *ex eventu* compositions, written in
hindsight of the events they 'foretell'. Inauthenticity is especially clear
in cases such as the oracles that Pausanias links to the Messenian

---

[79] Porphyrio sch. Hor. *Ars P.* 146 (=Antimachus test. 12a Wyss, 26b Matthews); ps.-Acro sch.
Hor. *Ars P.* 136 (=Antimachus test. 12b Wyss).

[80] Cf. Matthews 1996: 21–2, 73, that these scholia are 'essentially worthless'. Pseudo-Acro
reports a variant theory that 'cyclic' referred to wandering poets, going around from city to city;
no corroboration exists for this theory either.

[81] Parke and Wormell 1956 give the text of all Delphic oracles with context and sorted by date;
L. Andersen 1987 selects from these the oracles in hexameter, along with a concordance.
Fontenrose 1978 gives another complete catalogue (240–416), without text, and adds oracles
from Didyma (417–29).

[82] Fontenrose 1978: 186–95; Bowden 2005: 21–4, 33–8. A few oracles may have been delivered
in verse; others may have been rewritten as verse oracles – perhaps, as Bowden suggests, on the
model of *chresmologoi* (see below).

[83] Fontenrose 1978: 21–2, 42–4, 233–8; Bowden 2005: 49–51.

Wars of the eighth and seventh centuries: his entire account is pure fiction.[84])

The stereotypical obscure verse oracle is much more in tune with what we know of the *chresmologoi*, oracle collectors, of the sixth and fifth centuries.[85] We possess only fragments. Epimenides and Musaeus are the best known names in the genre; testimony about their lost poems appears in Bernabé's edition of the Orphic fragments.[86] Also significant are Abaris of Hyperborea, Bacis of Eleon, and Onomacritus of Athens; then there are minor figures such as Amphilytus, Diopeithes, Euclus, and various individuals called Sibyls. Modern critical editions serve these figures poorly: only the Onomacritus fragments have an adequate edition.[87]

The Athenians of the Archaic period, at least, took oracle collectors seriously. According to Herodotus (7.6), Onomacritus was banished for introducing an oracle of his own into his edition of Musaeus' oracles – evidently he was the real author of the poem in question, writing in the persona of Musaeus. Later on, oracle collectors had a mixed reputation both in public forums and in historiography. Aristophanes viciously satirizes Bacis in his *Knights*, *Birds*, and *Peace*; Herodotus is contemptuous of Abaris (4.36); Thucydides reports on Athenian fury at the oracle collectors after the disaster of the Sicilian expedition (8.1.1). But some oracle collectors continued to enjoy favour on a case-by-case basis: Herodotus will not hear a word said against Bacis (8.77; see also 8.20, 8.96, etc.); Musaeus also seems to have retained his popularity (Hdt. 8.96, 9.43; Ar. *Ran.* 1033); Thucydides reports on popular faith in oracles (2.8.2, 2.54) and himself approves of an oracle at one point (5.26.3); and the Athenians took their loss in the battle of Aegospotami as confirmation of oracles by the Sibyl and Musaeus (Paus. 10.9.11). It is intuitively likely, though unprovable, that many famous oracles supposedly from Delphi actually came from oracle collectors. It is very difficult to sustain a Delphic origin for something like the prophecy of the 'wooden wall' that supposedly influenced Themistocles' naval policy, for example.[88]

---

[84] See Fontenrose 1978: 103–7 on these oracles.
[85] Fontenrose 1978: 145–65; Bowden 2005: 33–8.
[86] Bernabé 2004–7: iii.32–4 (Musaeus frs. 62–71), 143–52 (Epimenides frs. 40–5).
[87] See Appendix.
[88] Hdt. 7.140–3, etc. (oracles 94–5 Parke-Wormell, Q146–7 Fontenrose). Tzetz. *Hist.* 9.796–805 ascribes the 'wooden wall' oracle to Bacis. See further Fontenrose 1978: 124–8.

Stylistically, the extant fragments make heavy use of metonymy; animal imagery;[89] and instructions laid out in a conditional 'If/when X happens, Y will happen' form.[90] A few seem to contain elements of theogonic material.[91] They have some points in common with legendary seers: the same tropes appear in the prophecies of Calchas, Teiresias, and Theoclymenus in Homeric epic.[92] Clement of Alexandria compiles a list of oracle collectors that includes real authors alongside purely legendary figures such as Calchas, Boio, Manto, and the Argonaut Mopsus; he goes on to attribute a *Divination of Mopsus* poem to Battus, the founder of Cyrene.[93]

A typical example of the genre is the following quotation from Bacis, which Herodotus connects to Xerxes' invasion (Hdt. 8.20):

> φράζεο, βαρβαρόφωνος ὅταν ζυγὸν εἰς ἅλα βάλλῃ
> βύβλινον, Εὐβοίης ἀπέχειν πολυμηκάδας αἶγας.

*Pay heed: when a barbarian-voiced one casts a papyrus yoke
on the sea, keep the bleating goats away from Euboea.*

Supposedly these lines meant that the Euboeans should take Xerxes' bridging the Hellespont as a sign to evacuate the island. The conditional structure, and the metonymy in *papyrus = boats, goats = property*, are typical features.

A fourth-century Attic inscription quotes an oracle that was originally designed to fit Xerxes' invasion of Greece in 480 (*IG* II² 4968.15–21):

> ...ἠδὲ φυλάττεσθαι], μὴ σοί τις ἔχις ἀλίπλανκτο[ς
> ἐκ βυθίου πόντου] κρυπτὸς μετὰ πήματος ἐλθώ[ν
> προ]θει ἀκτῆς ἑρπέθ' ἄμ' αὐτῶι
> , τὰ] θεοὶ στυγέουσι βροτοί τε·

---

[89] *IG* II² 4968.12–23 (see below); Amphilytus in Hdt. 1.62; Hipparchus' dream in Hdt. 5.56; Bacis in Hdt. 8.20; satires of Bacis in Ar. *Av.* 967–8 and Lucian, *De mort. Peregr.* 30. Animal imagery in oracles spuriously attributed to Delphi: Hdt. 1.47, 1.55, 5.92b, 6.77 (tentatively assigned to Bacis by Fontenrose), 7.220; Paus. 4.20.1.

[90] Hdt. 8.20, 8.77; Paus. 9.17.5. Also in satires and forgeries of Bacis: Ar. *Av.* 967–79; Paus. 4.27.4 (apodosis only); Lucian, *De mort. Peregr.* 30. An extreme case is Teiresias' prophecy, *Od.* 11.100–37, with a string of five conditional and temporal clauses (see Peradotto 1990: 63–75). Few oracles attributed to Delphi, whether real or legendary, use conditionals: see Fontenrose 1978: 166–70.

[91] Abaris, *New Jacoby* 34 F 1 (Philodemus, *On piety*, 4688–4707 Obbink); cf. *Theogonies* attributed to Musaeus and Epimenides.

[92] Calchas on the omen of the snake and the birds, *Il.* 2.301–30; Teiresias on Odysseus' homecoming, *Od.* 11.100–37; Theoclymenus on the Suitors' fate, *Od.* 20.351–7. As an exception, cf. Calchas' lucid oracle at *Il.* 1.93–100.

[93] Clem. Al. *Strom.* 1.21.132.3–133.1.

μηδ' ὀνύχεσσι φέρων τανυσίπ]τερος ἥσσονα μάρψας
ἴρηξ ἀμφιβαλὼν κ]ούφαις πτερύγεσσι νεοσσόν,
λιμὸν ἀκειόμενος φ]οινὴν εἰς γαστέρα θῆται·...

*...and beware,] in case some viper roaming the sea*
*may come hidden [from its place in the deep] with pain for you*
*                    ]crawl forth from the shore with it*
*                    , which] both gods and mortals loathe:*
*and in case a long-]winged bird may snatch a weaker bird,*
*a hawk grasping] its young prey in its nimble [claws,*
*and place it, bloody, in its stomach [to cure its hunger...*

Originally the hawk represented Xerxes; at the time of the inscription, it became Philip of Macedon. Parke's analysis of this oracle shows that the oracle collectors were still being quoted and reinterpreted in the mid-fourth century.[94]

## 8. Epigraphy

Hexameter inscriptions do not share a clearly defined genre with literary hexameter poetry, on the whole. They are normally very short and lack tropes such as similes. But themes familiar from literary verse do appear, and occasionally metrical formulae too. Regrettably, the most thorough editions lack a metrical index, so I present a catalogue below. The most important single edition is *CEG*, Hansen's *Carmina Epigraphica Graeca* (1983). Wachter's *Non-Attic Greek Vase Inscriptions* (2001) gives improved texts in places, and adds several new inscriptions. A few are supplied from other sources, including ancient witnesses.

- Four inscriptions from 700 BCE or earlier: Wachter ITH 1 (~*CEG* 453); *CEG* 432, 433, 454.
- Twenty from 600 BCE or earlier: Wachter COP 2A, COP 2B, COP 3(b), COP 11(b), DOC 3, IOD 4A; *CEG* 109, 132, 137, 143, 144, 145, 152, 287, 288, 326, 352, 353, 403, 404.
- Ninety-two from 500 BCE or earlier: Wachter BOI 3 (=*CEG* 327), BOI 4C (=*CEG* 445), COP 1A (=*CEG* 360), COP 1B (=*CEG* 358), COP 1C (=*CEG* 359), COP 1D, COP 4, COR 17b (=*CEG* 452), NAU 1B; *CEG* 15, 16, 23, 35, 36.ii, 40, 47.i, 53, 55, 59, 62, 65, 71, 110,

---

[94] Parke 1985. Parke suggests an ascription to Musaeus or Bacis; Bernabé assigns it to Epimenides (fr. 45).

129, 138, 139, 146, 157, 166, 181, 182, 183+184+185, 186, 187, 188, 189, 191, 193.i, 195, 198.ii, 203, 204, 206, 211, 215.ii, 217, 281, 282, 290, 291, 294, 299, 301, 333, 334, 335, 337, 338, 344, 345, 348, 354, 355, 363, 368, 369, 370, 371, 372, 374, 375, 376, 391, 398, 405, 406, 412.i, 422, 423, 424+425, 426, 427, 434, 435.ii, 438, 444.i, 456, 459, 462; Immerwahr 2009 no. 847; Pausanias 5.17–19 (=chest of Kypselos), 6.19.6.

- Sixty-seven from 400 BCE or earlier: Wachter DOC 6; *CEG* 73, 83, 84, 88, 100, 116, 119, 122, 124, 125, 126, 130, 133, 141, 150.i, 224, 226, 227, 239, 240, 250, 256, 259, 260.i, 265.ii, 267, 271.ii, 273.i, 277, 278.i, 283, 295, 296, 297, 298, 318, 323, 325, 328, 329, 339, 340, 341, 356, 361.i, 364, 377, 378, 384, 388.i, 397, 400, 417, 441, 464, 465; *Inscriptiones Graecae* I³ 754, 865; *Supplementum Epigraphicum Graecum* 20: 294; Immerwahr 2009 nos. 1641, 2330; Herodotus 5.59, 5.60, 5.61; *Contest of Homer and Hesiod* 15, 18 (cf. alternate texts in *Life of Homer* 2.11, 2.36).
- Six of uncertain, but early, date: Wachter COP 5, COP 6, COP 50; *Inscriptiones Graecae* XII.3 543; *Palatine Anthology* 7.177; *IG* XIV 1293.b.1–3 (i.e. the Tabula Albana; second-hand quotation; =*FGrH* 40 F 1b; cf. Paus. 9.10.4).
- Twenty-six damaged and of questionable metre: Wachter COP App. 1A(c), COR GR 26(1), NAU 1G; *CEG* 17, 29, 30, 63, 64, 107, 114, 128, 223, 249, 255, 257, 289, 292, 300, 303, 310, 319, 402.ii, 408, 419, 420; Immerwahr 2009 no. 1668.

Inscriptions can be a shock for an unwary student trained in Attic and Homeric Greek. Most are in alphabets that use ε and ο where a conventionally trained student would expect η/ει and ω/ου. Vowels that are elided for metrical purposes are usually written rather than omitted (an extreme case is καταέθēκε for κατέθηκε, *CEG* 137). Many retain archaic letters for the sounds *h*, *k*, and *w*; and the last of these, ϝ digamma, often appears with unfamiliar surrounding vowels (e.g. πρόξενϝος for πρόξεινος, *CEG* 143).[95]

The two largest groups are grave epitaphs and dedications. Grave epitaphs are mostly in the elegiac metre, with only a minority in hexameter. In dedicatory and other inscriptions, there is a roughly fifty–fifty split between hexameter and elegiac verse, and a small share set aside for other metres. A few inscriptions do not fit in these two groups, and mark private possessions or celebrations of personal achievements.

---

[95] Friedländer 1948: 7–64 gives a selection of fifty-nine hexameter inscriptions rewritten in Hellenistic orthography, with notes.

Grave epitaphs show the most variety, and occasionally draw on themes familiar from epic to celebrate the deceased. The remarkable epitaph for Deinias is impressively concise (*CEG* 132; Corinth, *c.*650):

Δϝενία τόδε [σᾶμα], τὸν ὄλεσε πόντος ἀναι[δές].

This [monument] belongs to Deinias. The sh[ame]less sea killed him.

With a single word, 'shameless', the poet encapsulates the frustration and grief felt by Deinias' survivors, and the indignity that his family cannot grieve for him at his actual grave. The anthropomorphization of the sea even hints at epic scenes, such as Poseidon wrathfully stirring up a storm in *Odyssey* Book 5. Some other particularly striking grave inscriptions are the epitaphs for Menecrates, the Oeanthean *proxenos* on Cercyra (*CEG* 143, *c.*625–600); a touching memorial for Gnathius, dedicated by his young beloved (*CEG* 47; Attica, *c.*525–500?); and epitaphs in full-blown heroic style for Arniadas (*CEG* 145, Cercyra, late seventh or early sixth century) and Pythion of Megara (*CEG* 83; Athens, 446–425?).

Dedicatory inscriptions are often one- or two-line formulae that vary only in the name of the donor. But they also include two of the most famous of all early inscriptions: the early verse inscription on the Mantiklos Apollo (*CEG* 326; Thebes, *c.*700–675), and the 'Nikandre inscription' (*CEG* 403; Delos, *c.*650). A few of these, too, contain echoes of the epic tradition. One Phaueristos (or Phaneristos?), dedicating a set of vessels to Athena, drew on the age-old heroic trope of 'unfading fame', κλέϝος ἄπθιτον (*CEG* 344, lost; Crisa, *c.*600–550?). Athletes and lovers sometimes commemorated their conquests with a verse or two, and one Exoida dedicated a discus with an epigram that has resonances in the *Iliad* and the *Hymn to the Dioscuri* (*CEG* 391; Cephallenia, *c.*550–525?).[96]

---

[96] Κεφαλᾶνας μεγαθύμōς ~ *Il.* 2.631: Κεφαλλῆνας μεγαθύμους; Διϝὸς ϙόϙοιν μεγάλοιο ~ *Hymn. Hom.* 33.9: Διὸς κούρους μεγάλοιο.

# II GENRE

Is early hexameter poetry a single genre? Would it be useful to refer to the entire corpus as 'epic'?[1] The answer depends on context. The word 'epic' poses problems. This becomes a little clearer if we consider the *Oxford English Dictionary* definition:

**A.** *adj.* **1.** Pertaining to that species of poetical composition (see EPOS *n.*), represented typically by the Iliad and Odyssey, which celebrates in the form of a continuous narrative the achievements of one or more heroic personages of history or tradition.[2]

Question: what defines Homeric epic as 'epic'? Answer: the fact that it is like Homer. This is a circular definition. That does not make it a bad one; in fact it is a stunningly accurate representation of how the word gets used. But, if we are looking at other poems, it makes no sense to start out with the assumption that they are peripheral.

Is Parmenides' poem somehow less 'hexameterish' than the *Iliad?* Parmenides knew perfectly well how to string six dactyls together. But his poem is less traditional, and for many readers that alone makes it less 'epic'.[3] Quite apart from terminology, it is dangerous to extrapolate from Homer. Ancient literary critics such as Aristotle, Horace, and Proclus draw *contrasts* between Homer and other heroic epics more often than not.[4] Inevitably the *Iliad* and *Odyssey* will be a yardstick in some ways, but we cannot take Homer as the sole archetype for all Archaic epic: it is dangerous to start with Homer and only afterwards transfer our findings to other poems.[5] What is characteristic of Homer is not necessarily characteristic of hexameter poetry taken as a whole.

There are different groups and types of hexameter poetry, but no *firm* boundaries between them, no tidy categories without overlaps. So we have two basic approaches open to us. One is *top-down*: identifying a given poem or idea as archetypal for each 'sub-genre', as the *OED*

---

[1] Hainsworth 1991: 1–10 gives a superb and undogmatic overview of the various meanings of the word 'epic'; see also Hutchinson 2013: 20–1 on 'hexameters' as a superordinate genre.

[2] Oxford University Press, 2015.

[3] Cf. Arist. *Poet.* 1447b.17–20, treating Empedocles as a φυσιολόγος rather than a ποιητής because his poetry is not imitative.

[4] See pp. 26–7 above.

[5] Cf. Martin 2005, arguing that the *Shield* is more typical of early hexameter poetry than Homer.

definition does. The other is *bottom-up*: cataloguing the constitutive elements of hexameter poetry. Both have their place. The top-down approach is useful for discussing big ideas. It tends to result in sharp boundaries between sub-genres, since it nudges us towards ignoring grey areas (intermediate types of poetry mess up the nice clean archetypes). The bottom-up approach relates more to compositional techniques and to the cues that ancient audiences used to engage with the poems; it tends to blur different sub-genres together, since it emphasizes a common pool of traditional conventions and stylistic elements.[6]

We have already considered the first of these in the Introduction, where we looked at ancient distinctions between 'Homeric' and 'Hesiodic' poetry as cultural property. In this chapter, we shall take the bottom-up approach: we shall catalogue some common ingredients of hexameter poetry. Tropes that are characteristic of Homer will only be cited if they also appear outside Homer.

## 1. Large-scale: overarching topics and themes

The following are broad themes that pervade entire poems. They cannot easily be analysed in terms of a formal sequence of motifs; if they have structural constraints, they are not strict ones. It is entirely reasonable to treat these themes as genres in their own right. Equally, they can be regarded as 'sub-genres', with hexameter as a superordinate genre.

### (a) Heroic narrative

Stories of legendary heroic deeds are the theme most typically associated with 'epic'. This sub-genre includes the *Iliad*, the *Odyssey*, the *Shield*, and many fragmentary exemplars: the Epic Cycle; the Theban epics; various Heracles epics, including the *Capture of Oichalia*, and epics by Panyassis, Pisander, and perhaps Cinaethon; perhaps multiple Theseids;[7] and probably the *Minyas*, *Wedding of Ceyx*, *Descent of Peirithous*, and *Aegimius*. Ancient writers describe the *Naupactia* as a genealogical poem 'about women', but most surviving fragments relate

---

[6] For an exemplar of the bottom-up approach see Thalmann 1984; for the top-down approach, Ford 1992 (on Homer), 1997: 399–408 (more general).

[7] Arist. *Poet.* 1451a.20 appears to refer to multiple Theseids, but only two extant fragments are linked to the title.

to an *Argonautica* narrative.[8] Choerilus' historical epic the *Persica* should also be shelved in this sub-genre.

Aristotle considered the character of heroic narrative to be basically akin to that of tragedy. Some modern literary criticism has followed him in this, seeing in Homer an underlying seriousness, or sense of inexorability, or tragic irony.[9] But many other modern critics have argued that heroic narrative is a descendant of a much older tradition of 'praise poetry', a form of poetry found in diverse cultures, which typically celebrates a living individual or a god.[10] In this view, the true central theme and purpose of heroic narrative is *kleos*, 'fame' or 'renown';[11] and poetry is not just a celebration of a hero's reputation but also a vehicle for reports of the hero, *creating* the hero's reputation. This is most famously illustrated by two Homeric scenes where Achilles (a non-professional singer) and Demodocus (a professional) sing of the *klea andrōn*, the 'glories of men'; the phrase also gets used of one story that is spoken, not sung;[12] and several studies have attached great importance to the use of *kleos* in poetic phrases that may be traceable back to Indo-European roots.[13] However, this interpretation does not always transfer easily to heroic narratives outside Homer. A poem such as the *Shield* is, of course, a vehicle for its hero's reputation in a trivial sense, and the *Theogony* and the *Hymns* are sung in praise of gods and so serve as *kleos*, bringing reports about the divine realm to mortal audiences.[14] But, in Homer, *kleos* is closely intertwined with tragic themes such as mortality, personal identity, and tension between the hero and a surrounding community. That kind of intertwining is not often apparent elsewhere.

Epic poets of the Hellenistic and later ages imitated many Homeric formal elements (invocations to a Muse, similes, combat scenes, and sacrifice scenes), but in the Archaic period there is no reason to assume that any of these was actually obligatory. The most consistent formal

---

[8] *Argonautica* narrative: frs. 3–9. Genealogical poem 'about women': test. and fr. 11.

[9] Arist. *Poet.* 1449b. See also Kirk 1962: 372–85; Redfield 1975; Griffin 1980; R. Rutherford 1982.

[10] See M. L. West 2007: 63–8, 396–410 on Indo-European praise poetry and heroic narrative.

[11] Nagy 1979: 16–17; Thalmann 1984: 124–31. For contrary views see Ford 1992: 59–67; Olson 1995: 1–23.

[12] *Il.* 9.189–91 (Achilles); *Od.* 8.72–5 (Demodocus); *Il.* 9.524–5 (Phoenix's spoken story of Meleager).

[13] Nagy 1974: 229–65; Watkins 1995: 173–8; Finkelberg 2007. Nagy 1990: 146–52 argues that Homeric epic (κλέος-poetry) and Pindar's epinician verse (αἶνος-poetry) are cognate genres, both descended distantly from praise poetry.

[14] Thus Nagy 1979: 94–7 (on *Theog.*), 181–7 (on *Hymn. Hom. Dem.*).

feature is the use of third-person narrative, interspersed with direct quotation when characters speak.[15] Only rarely does a narrator make his presence felt in the story, speaking with his own voice, or blurring the distinction between his own voice and that of a character.[16] In the case of Homer, this creates an effect of distance which has often led readers to perceive the narrative as *naïf*, impersonal, and unmediated, even if that *naïveté* is self-conscious and studied.[17] Numerous studies in the last few decades have qualified this interpretation, showing that Archaic poets selected and adopted identifiable personas.[18] Homer, in particular, actively exercises a finely nuanced control over the way in which scenes develop;[19] but it is reasonable to question whether all heroic poets demonstrated the same degree of finesse, or in the same way.

### (b) Wisdom poetry

In wisdom poetry a speaker directly imparts insights, instructions, or knowledge, usually to an addressee who is clearly identified. When discussed with a perspective looking to later Greco-Roman poetry such as Aratus or Virgil's *Georgics*, it is more often known as 'didactic poetry'; 'wisdom poetry' looks backwards, to a cross-cultural backdrop of many Near Eastern parallels.[20] Our main exemplar is the Hesiodic *Works and Days*. Several lost Hesiodic poems also fall into this category: the *Precepts of Chiron*, the *Great Works*, the *Bird Omens* (or *Ornithomancy*), and, focusing more on the natural world, the *Astronomy*. When elements of wisdom poetry pop up in other genres, they tend to be in the form of parables and aphorisms (on which see below).

It seems that, in the sixth century, in the hands of poet-philosophers such as Solon and Theognis, moral and political teaching gradually

[15] The seminal analysis is Pl. *Resp.* iii.392c–394c; see also Arist. *Poet.* 1448a.19–29, 1448b.34–8, 1460a.5–11.

[16] See especially S. Richardson 1990: 167–96 on 'self-consciousness' and fourth-wall-breaking in Homer (e.g. when the poet directly addresses a Muse, a character in the story, or the audience; comments on plot developments; etc.).

[17] Lewis 1942: 19–25; Auerbach 2003: 3–23; Ledbetter 2003: 9–39; Beecroft 2010: 61–105.

[18] See pp. vi–x on 'Homer' and 'Hesiod' as personas and their relationship to the narratorial voice.

[19] See especially De Jong 1987, 2001; Minchin 2001. De Jong 2006 argues (*contra* Ford 1992) that Homeric epic creates κλέος for the poet as well as for the heroes.

[20] M. L. West 1997: 306–33; I. Rutherford 2009: 14–19. On the reception of Hesiodic 'didactic poetry' see Hunter 2014: 40–122.

shifted into elegiac metre. But hexameter remained the metre of choice for discussing the nature of the physical world, most notably for the pre-Socratic poets Parmenides and Empedocles. Xenophanes straddled both genres.[21] Both the elegiac and hexameter offshoots retained the poetic conceit of addressing the poem to a recipient or student. This recipient (in narratological terms, an 'implied narratee') acts as a proxy for the poem's actual (or 'external') audience, allowing them to receive the teachings at the same time as the character in the poem.[22] Thus the *Works and Days* is addressed to Perses, and the *Precepts of Chiron* to Achilles; Theognis instructs his boy beloved Cyrnus; Empedocles addresses *On Nature* to Pausanias (fr. B 1), and another fragment addresses the people of Acragas (fr. B 112). The Derveni *Theogony*, though primarily a cosmogonic poem, has Night instructing Zeus, declaring oracles in her cave (fr. 6 Bernabé). Parmenides adapts this motif from the Hesiodic *Theogony* but reverses the relationship: Hesiod was visited by the Muses and instructed in poetry (*Theog.* 22–34), but Parmenides travels beyond the gate of Day and Night to receive teachings from an unnamed goddess (fr. B 1).

Few historians of ancient philosophy make the mistake of treating Hesiod as something wholly separate from the pre-Socratics. But students of Hesiod sometimes do. Certainly the later philosopher-poets focus more consistently on applying reason to the world around them; but, from a purely poetic perspective, philosophical and literary verse draw on the same tradition. Ancient critics felt the same way. Heracleitus (fr. B 40) categorizes Hesiod as a philosopher along with Pythagoras, Xenophanes, and Hecataeus; and Plato interprets earlier poets as using mythology to represent natural forces, even to the extent of describing Homer, Hesiod, and Simonides as proto-sophists.[23]

### (c) Cosmogony

Cosmogonic poetry tells of the origins of the universe, of the establishment of the present cosmic order, and of how the gods use the threat of

---

[21] M. L. West 1978: 22–5 presents a more detailed overview of Archaic Greek wisdom poetry (but omitting the pre-Socratics).

[22] This can be challenged in specific cases: for example, Schmidt 1986 sees the Perses of the *Works and Days* as a proxy for the kings whom Hesiod criticizes.

[23] For poets as proto-sophists see Pl. *Prt.* 316d. Homer uses divinities to represent natural forces: e.g. *Theaet.* 152e.

violence to maintain that order. In this sub-genre, parallels from the Near East are especially close: the Babylonian *Enuma Elish*, the Ugaritic Baal cycle, and the Hurro-Hittite poems about Kumarbi.[24]

In the Greek tradition, regularly recurring themes include the birth and genealogy of the gods (that is, 'theogony' proper);[25] the apportioning of divine prerogatives; and various battles between gods or against demonic powers so as to establish a stable divine order. Especially prominent are the battles against the monster Typhoeus (or Typhaon) and the Titans (the Titanomachy).

Our main exemplar is the Hesiodic *Theogony*. We have fragments of various other theogonies, usually grouped as 'Orphic' poems: the theogonies of Musaeus and Epimenides, and the Derveni and Eudemian theogonies. These are framed around the Near Eastern succession myth as strongly as Hesiod's, though they are very different in both style and tenets. We also know of various Titanomachies, especially the one attributed to Eumelus. Cosmogonic elements also appear in narrative digressions in the *Works and Days*;[26] the major *Hymns*;[27] and many allusions and echoes throughout Homer. In the *Hymn to Hermes* 417–33, the second ever performance of kitharoidic poetry is a theogony sung by Hermes. And Empedocles' poetry is at least as closely attached to this category as to wisdom literature: he is deeply concerned with the origin and generation of natural forces, often personified, especially Love and Strife; one fragment (B 123) rattles off a list of 'Titans' (Birth, Death, Sleep, etc.) that could easily sit in a theogony.

It has been alleged that Homeric epic has no interest in cosmogony.[28] In fact, the *Iliad* is pervasively flavoured with cosmogonic elements, especially in those parts of the story set on Olympus. A few passages refer to the birth of the gods or apportionment of divine prerogatives;[29] others refer to divine battles and rebellions, including the battle with Typhoeus;[30] and the scenes on Olympus contain frequent reminders

---

[24] See further M. L. West 1997: 276–305; I. Rutherford 2009: 9–14, 22–35.

[25] Ziegler, in Roscher 1884–1937: v.1469–1554, gives the most detailed account of early Greek theogonic literature, including prose sources.

[26] The births of the Strifes, *WD* 11–26; Prometheus and Pandora, 47–105; the Myth of the Races, 106–201.

[27] See especially Clay 1989 on the major *Hymns*' preoccupation with the establishment of a stable divine order.

[28] Lane Fox 2008: 350.

[29] *Il.* 14.200–4 (cf. 14.246 and 14.302), 15.187–99, 18.394–409.

[30] *Il.* 1.396–406, 2.781–3 (Typhoeomachy), 5.392–4. *Il.* 20.19–74 may echo a Titanomachy or Gigantomachy. See also *Od.* 11.305–20 and *Cat.* frs. 16–17 on the Aloeadae attempting to conquer Olympus.

of Zeus's maintenance of the divine order by threat of violence, as in the Hesiodic *Theogony*.[31]

## 2. Medium-scale: sub-themes and major structural features

When smaller-scale features are repeated in more than one poem, scholars – especially specialists in Homer – are often tempted to regard one poem as consciously imitating the other. We have no way of ruling out this inference, but in general it is unwarranted, at least prior to the classical period. Elements in this section are best regarded as, not precisely formulaic, but regularized organizational tools that were potentially at any poet's command, whether oral or literate.

For this reason, structural patterns at the 'medium' scale are more obviously characterized by regular sequences of motifs. Attention to motif sequences requires two important caveats. First, formal features are never rigid, and many studies have shown how poets shuffle and adapt seemingly regular patterns in creative ways.[32] Second, there is no one correct way of dissecting such patterns.[33] As such, there is no way of assessing the predictive power of these patterns; they are poor tools for determining authorship or date, for example.

### (a) Hymn or hymnic prelude

Poets would regularly begin performances of hexameter poetry – of any kind – with a hymn to one or more gods. This is shown by the testimony of the *Hymn to Hermes*, Pindar, Thucydides, and pseudo-Plutarch,[34] as well as by the closing formulae in many of the *Hymns*, which refer to poems to be performed after the hymn. Pindar and Thucydides call this prelude a *prooimion*. In English it is best to avoid that term, because it creates confusion with the English word

---

[31] *Il.* 1.565–7, 1.580–1, 1.590–4, 8.7–27, 15.16–24, 15.178–86, 19.126–31. See also *Od.* 5.121–8.

[32] As a recent example see Kelly 2012 (on recognition scenes in *Odyssey* 23).

[33] See Hainsworth 1990: 250 on the *Odyssey*: 'In the most favourable circumstances, when a scene is of a very frequent kind...it is possible to discern the poet's units of composition. Closer analysis, however, is apt to lose its objective character...Analysis into themes, therefore, may legitimately vary from one critic to another.'

[34] *Hymn. Hom. Herm.* 429–30; Pind. *Nem.* 2.1–3; Thuc. 3.104.4; ps.-Plut. *De mus.* 1133c. Cf. *Od.* 8.499, Demodocus beginning his song 'from the god'; see Clay 2011: 238 for discussion.

'proem', which has deep roots and is conventionally used for opening paragraphs even of modern epics.[35]

We find exemplars not only in the *Hymns* but also in the *Theogony* (a hymn, or rather a pair of hymns, to the Muses, 1–34 and 35–105); *Works and Days* 1–10 (to Zeus); and, in a modified form modelled on the *Theogony*, Parmenides fr. B 1. Hymnic preludes are depicted indirectly in *Odyssey* 8.499–500 (Demodocus' third song) and *Hymn to Hermes* 427–33 (Hermes' hymn-within-a-hymn to Mnemosyne, followed by a theogony). There are only three surviving examples of a hymn that is still attached to its subsequent poem: the two Hesiodic exemplars, and in elegiac verse Simonides' Plataea ode, frs. eleg. 10 and 11.1–20 (a hymn to Achilles).

As we saw in Chapter I, in the Homeric *Hymns* it is traditional to distinguish a group of longer hymns (numbers 1–5), of which the shortest is 293 lines, from the shorter hymns (numbers 6–33), of which the longest is 59 lines. A formal analysis by Janko suggests instead a fourfold grouping: hymns that are based solely on mythical narrative ('purely mythic' hymns); hymns that enumerate the god's attributes without narrative ('attributive'); an intermediate group called 'composite mythic', which contains both attributive and mythic sections; and 'composite prolonged', where there are attributive sections both before and after the mythic section, and where the standard 'farewell' to the god is extended to become in effect a third attributive section. Each group displays a distinct sequence of motifs, in a manner similar to type scenes. The purely mythic, composite, and prolonged groups account for the major hymns. The minor hymns are evenly distributed between the purely mythic and purely attributive groups, though a couple are defective in terms of formal structure.[36]

It is plausible, though uncertain, that at least the shorter hymns served as a corpus of set pieces that any poet could draw on to preface an epic performance. There is some indication that the hymns in the

---

[35] Προοίμιον also had more than one meaning in antiquity: in Ar. *Eq.* 1343 and Arist. *Rh.* iii.1414b.19–26 it means the opening of a show speech; in Crates of Mallos fr. 1 Broggiato (=*Life of Homer* 10.B.1 West) it means the same as English 'proem'. See also Nagy 2009: 230, who takes -οιμ- < *soim-, hence προοίμιον = 'pre-threading'.

[36] Janko 1981. Mythic: *Hymns* 2, 4, 6, 7, 15, 16, 17, 18, 20, 26, 28, 31, 33; composite: *Hymns* 1, 3.179–546, 5, 19, *Theog.* 1–34; prolonged: *Hymn* 3.1–178, *Theog.* 35–105, and add Simonides' hymn to Achilles (frs. eleg. 10 and 11, provided that fr. 10 comes from an attributive section); attributive: *Hymns* 9–12, 14, 21–5, 27, 29, 30, 32, *W&D* 1–10; defective: *Hymns* 12, 13. (See above p. 20 on *Hymn* 8, written over a millennium later.)

*Theogony* and *Works and Days* were also used this way.[37] The major Homeric *Hymns* are so big that it is doubtful whether they could have been used as preludes, in spite of Thucydides' reference to the *Hymn to Apollo* as a *prooimion*.[38] But that is not to say that the preludic function of hymns had died out: Pindar and Simonides show that this function persisted until at least the 470s.[39]

### (b) Type scenes

Type scenes – set-piece episodes with a regular sequence of motifs – are very prominent in Homer, and have been extensively studied.[40] It is generally thought that they have their origins as components in the cognitive toolkit of pre-Homeric oral bards, aiding them in improvisation by providing a continuous flow of cues.[41] In non-Homeric hexameter, type scenes are thinner on the ground and they seem to be motivated more by an awareness of codified forms than by an improvisational function. Some clear exemplars are Heracles' arming scene (*Shield* 122–43);[42] the hospitality scene when Demeter arrives at Keleos' house (*Hymn to Demeter* 105–211);[43] the adornment scenes in *Theogony* 573–84, *Cypria* frs. 5–6, *Hymn to Aphrodite* 60–74, and *Hymn* 6.5–13;[44] and the sacrifice scene in *Hymn to Hermes* 115–37. Divine epiphanies in the *Hymns* also follow patterns that are familiar from Homer.

Although we identify type scenes by their formal structure, they are far from formulaic. Ancient poets routinely adapted them in many ways. For example: in Homeric arming scenes a hero normally dons his gear in the sequence greaves–breastplate–sword–shield–helmet–spear; but, in the *Shield*, Heracles leaves his shield until last, so as to create a clean transition to the extended description of it that dominates

[37] Crates of Mallos fr. 78 Broggiato (Hes. test. 50). See M. L. West 1966: 136–7 on ancient obelization of the *Theogony* and *Works and Days* proems.

[38] Similarly Clay 1997: 498.

[39] Aloni 1980 argues that hymns' preludic function extended into the Hellenistic period.

[40] Arend 1933 is the seminal discussion; Edwards 1992 gives an overview in English, with extensive bibliography.

[41] Minchin 2001: 32–72 discusses type scenes in relation to a performer's cognitive competences.

[42] On arming scenes see Arend 1933: 92–8; Kirk 1985: 313–16.

[43] Reece 1993: 5–46 discusses formal patterns in hospitality scenes, with analysis of *Hymn. Hom. Dem.* at 229–30.

[44] On adornment or beautification scenes see Arend 1933: 97–8 and Table 7.

the poem. In the *Hymn to Demeter*, where the host would normally provide the guest with a meal, Demeter instead instructs her host on how to prepare a ritual potion, the *kykeōn*, in her honour. And the sacrifice scene in the *Hymn to Hermes* is distorted for humorous effect: Hermes effectively offers a sacrifice to himself (!), and runs into trouble when (in his capacity as sacrificer) he wants to eat the roasted meat but (in his capacity as dedicatee) refuses to swallow it.

*(c) Genealogy*

Characters in Homer are frequently identified with reference to their parents; but there are also several thorough genealogies, which typically serve to bolster a character's status.[45] In the *Theogony* and *Catalogue of Women* they are more important still. Pausanias informs us that genealogy was also prominent in the *Naupactia*.[46]

The branching nature of genealogy poses a challenge to a poet's narrative strategy. Homer and the *Catalogue* normally begin by reporting all the children of one individual; these children are followed by their descendants, one child at a time, dealing with each genealogical branch fully to the third or fourth generation. West has shown that the *Catalogue* organizes genealogy in manageable chunks, steering a middle course between 'vertical' and 'horizontal' approaches.[47] Homeric genealogies show the same tendency, dealing with genealogical chunks of about the same size. The *Theogony*'s genealogies come in smaller chunks and are less systematic, but still have various organizing principles.[48]

In all of these cases it is normal to find narrative vignettes, containing heroic or divine/cosmogonic material, peppered among the genealogies. The *Iliad* seasons Glaucus' genealogy with the story of Bellerophon, for example; and among the genealogies in the *Catalogue* are sprinkled various deeds of Heracles and the stories of Atalanta, Mestra, and so on.[49] Of the relationship between narrative

---

[45] Major Homeric genealogies: *Il.* 6.150–211 (Glaucus), 14.110–27 (Diomedes), 20.213–41 (Aeneas); *Od.* 15.225–55 (Theoclymenus). Briefer examples: *Il.* 13.448–54 (Idomeneus), 21.186–91 (Achilles); *Od.* 7.56–66 (Alcinous), 16.115–20 (Odysseus).

[46] *Naupactia* test. and fr. 11.

[47] M. L. West 1985: 46–7.

[48] On these principles see M. L. West 1966: 34–9.

[49] *Il.* 6.156–202 (Bellerophon); *Cat.* frs. 22.20–33, 31.13–33.9, 139–141 (Heracles), frs. 47–51 (Atalanta), frs. 69–71 (Mestra).

and genealogy, West writes: 'If the Succession Myth is the backbone of the *Theogony*, the genealogies are its flesh and blood'. Muellner, drawing on Vernant, writes of genealogy as itself a form of narrative, while the vignettes are 'nongenealogical [narrative] on the way to becoming genealogical again'.[50]

## (d) Catalogue

Catalogues have been extensively studied, largely because of the historical importance of the Iliadic Catalogue of Ships.[51] We can distinguish at least three varieties: 'formal' catalogues, with detailed catalogue entries that follow fairly regular formulae;[52] 'casual' catalogues, simple lists with little ornamentation;[53] and a type that has been called the 'Ehoie tradition' (after the *ē᾽ hoiē* formula used in the *Catalogue of Women*), which consists of catalogues of legendary women and the genealogical relationships between them.[54]

Entries in 'formal' catalogues are linked to specific geographic locations and follow well-defined routes through the landscape of Greece (see below on route descriptions). Our exemplars are, in the *Iliad*, the great Catalogue of Ships, the Trojan Catalogue, and a renewal of the Catalogue of Ships when the Myrmidons enter battle for the first time;[55] and the Catalogue of Helen's Suitors in the *Catalogue of Women* Book 5 (frs. 154, 155.1–75, 156). The catalogue of Trojan allies that appeared in the Cyclic *Cypria* (arg. 12) probably fitted this type. It is also likely that the *Naupactia* had a formal catalogue of Argonauts, which would have served as a model for the one in Apollonius' *Argonautica* (Apollonius' catalogue imitates the 'formal' style).[56] These are major virtuosic set pieces and come with a great deal of dramatic build-up.[57] They also play a preludic role: the catalogues of *Iliad* 2

[50] M. L. West 1966: 31; Muellner 1996: 56.

[51] See especially Visser 1997. See also Sammons 2010, arguing that Homeric catalogues are designed to compete with Hesiodic and Cyclic ones.

[52] On typical elements see especially Edwards 1980; see also Kirk 1985: 170–7 (on the Catalogue of Ships).

[53] On this class of catalogues see Tsagalis 2010.

[54] I. Rutherford 2000.

[55] Catalogue of Ships: *Il.* 2.484–779; Trojan Catalogue: 2.815–77; Myrmidons: 16.112–13 (invocation of Muse) and 168–97 (full catalogue entry).

[56] *Naupactia* fr. 4 states that the poet 'lists all the heroes recognized[?] by him' (πάντας ἀριθμεῖ τοὺς ὑπ᾽ αὐτοῦ φερομένους ἀριστεῖς). ὑπ᾽ αὐτοῦ is an emendation, and the meaning of φερομένους is uncertain. Cf. Ap. Rhod. *Argon.* 1.20–233.

[57] On the artistic character of the Catalogue of Ships see especially Minchin 2001: 73–99.

act as a kind of ceremonial opening of war, the Myrmidon entry in *Iliad* 16 introduces Patroclus' display of heroism, and the list of Helen's suitors announces the contest for her hand in marriage and a subsequent slide into the Trojan War.

Among 'casual' catalogues we have Zeus's list of his former lovers (*Il.* 14.315–28); lists of Nereids (*Il.* 18.39–49; *Theog.* 240–64); the ghosts of dead heroes seen in the underworld (*Od.* 11.566–635; *Returns* frs. 3–9; *Minyas* frs. 2–6); and a few other, briefer, roll calls. Empedocles' list of 'Titans' (fr. B 123) also fits this model well.

The 'Ehoie' type is really a cross between catalogue and genealogy. Like genealogy, it is preoccupied with procreation and the movement from one generation to the next;[58] and it routinely contains vignettes of heroic narrative. The 'Ehoie' type is represented by the bulk of the *Catalogue of Women*; Odysseus' catalogue of dead heroines (*Od.* 11.225–330); and the *Great Ehoiae*. Much of the *Naupactia* also seems to have been occupied with a catalogue of the 'Ehoie' type.[59]

### 3. Small-scale: tropes and stylistic features

*(a) Proem and invocation of Muse(s)*

'Proem' is used here with its conventional English sense: a brief preface, especially the introductory paragraph to a heroic narrative epic. Following the practice of *The Homer Encyclopedia*, I keep it distinct from the device of the hymnic prelude (see above).[60] Regular formal features of a proem are: (1) introduction of one or more major themes in the first line (e.g. 'anger' in the *Iliad*; 'a man' in the *Odyssey*); (2) an address to the divine Muse(s), praying for inspiration; (3) a relative clause that expands on (1) and leads into a discursive (but not thorough) exploration of the poem's contents. Often a second invocation (4) renews the focus on the highlighted theme, with a further

---

[58] Northrup 1980: 152 notes the frequent references to children in the *Odyssey*'s catalogue of heroines.

[59] *Naupactia* test. and fr. 11.

[60] On epic proems generally see Bassett 1934; G. Wheeler 2002; Harden and Kelly 2013, with a formal analysis similar to the one given here. To avoid terminological problems Bassett uses the term 'induction', while Wheeler uses 'introit'. There are also many studies especially of the *Odyssey* proem (see Wheeler for bibliography). Confusion arises when hymns are called 'proems', especially in poems that have both, such as the *Theogony*: in the senses used here, the *Theogony*'s opening hymn occupies lines 1–104, while the proem is at 104–15.

dependent relative clause (5) that leads into the main body of the poem. Most extant poems feature some or all of these elements.[61] But formal proems were not obligatory: the *Works and Days* and *Shield* possess no proems.

Proems of this form are naturally intimately connected to the trope of invoking a Muse. Muse invocations appear in other contexts too, but where they do appear they are still typically introductory, and they often touch on the problem of the relationship between the performer and his poetic persona – the poet's voice as opposed to the Muse's voice.[62] The trope of the Muse invocation is a uniquely Greek invention. It is in turn closely tied to the trope of 'two types of knowledge' (see below).

For most post-Archaic epics the *Iliad* and *Odyssey* proems served as models. But in Archaic poetry, the fullest examples of the pattern are the *Catalogue of Women* fr. 1.1–15:

> **(1)** νῦν δὲ γυναικῶν φῦλον ἀείσατε, **(2)** ἡδυέπειαι
> Μοῦσαι Ὀλυμπιάδες, κοῦραι Διὸς αἰγιόχοιο,
> **(3)** αἳ τότ' ἄρισται ἔσαν [...
> [...]
> **(4)** τάων ἔσπετε μ[οι γενεήν τε καὶ ἀγλαὰ τέκνα,
> **(5)** ὄσσ[αι]ς δὴ παρελ[εκτο πατὴρ ἀνδρῶν τε θεῶν τε...

> **(1)** *And now sing of the tribe of women,* **(2)** *sweet-voiced Olympian Muses, daughters of aegis-holding Zeus,*
> **(3)** *those who were the best at that time...*
> [...]
> **(4)** *Of these women tell [me the race and the splendid children:*
> **(5)** *all those with whom lay [the father of men and of gods...*

*Theogony* 104–15:

> **(2)** χαίρετε τέκνα Διός, δότε δ' ἱμερόεσσαν ἀοιδήν·
> **(1)** κλείετε δ' ἀθανάτων ἱερὸν γένος αἰὲν ἐόντων,
> **(3)** οἳ Γῆς ἐξεγένοντο καὶ Οὐρανοῦ ἀστερόεντος...
> [...]

---

[61] Surviving exemplars are: *Il.* 1.1–10ff. (it would be wrong to specify a definite end point because of the way in which the relative clauses expand gradually into the main narrative); *Od.* 1.1–11ff.; *Cat.* fr. 1.1–15ff.; *Theog.* 104–15; *Epigoni* fr. 1; *Little Iliad* frs. 1 and 28 Bernabé (the latter=fr. 1 West); Choerilus, *Persica* frs. 1 and 2 Bernabé. On the *Little Iliad* proem see Scafoglio 2006; on the *Persica* proem see MacFarlane 2009. Harden and Kelly 2013 also interpret Odysseus' request to Demodocus (*Od.* 8.492–9ff.) as a proem of sorts, and Hermes' first song (*Hymn. Hom. Herm.* 52–62) as a blend of hymn and proem.

[62] See especially Pedrick 1992 (on the *Odyssey* proem); G. Wheeler 2002.

**(4)** ταῦτά μοι ἔσπετε Μοῦσαι Ὀλύμπια δώματ' ἔχουσαι
ἐξ ἀρχῆς, καὶ εἴπαθ', **(5)** ὅτι πρῶτον γένετ' αὐτῶν.


**(2)** Hail, children of Zeus, and give me lovely song; **(1)** glorify the sacred race of the immortals who always are, **(3)** those who were born from Earth and starry Sky...
[...]
**(4)** These things tell me from the beginning, Muses who have your mansions on Olympus, and tell **(5)** which of them was born first. ...

and *Odyssey* 1.1–10:

**(1)** ἄνδρα μοι ἔννεπε, **(2)** Μοῦσα, πολύτροπον, **(3)** ὃς μάλα πολλὰ
πλάγχθη, ἐπεὶ Τροίης ἱερὸν πτολίεθρον ἔπερσε·
πολλῶν δ' ἀνθρώπων ἴδεν ἄστεα καὶ νόον ἔγνω...
[...]
**(4)** τῶν ἁμόθεν γε, θεά, θύγατερ Διός, εἰπὲ καὶ ἡμῖν.


**(1)** *Tell me of the man,* **(2)** *Muse, so versatile,* **(3)** *who travelled
far and wide, after he sacked the sacred city of Troy;
many were the men whose cities he saw and whose minds he knew...*
[...]
**(4)** *Pick a starting point, goddess, daughter of Zeus, and tell us this too.*

The *Iliad* has only a shadow of **(4)** and **(5)**, with a rhetorical question at line 8 and expansion in the relative clause in the following line. Another doubled invocation has been convincingly identified in the fragments of the *Little Iliad* proem.[63] Alongside the fragment given as fr. 1 in West's and Davies' editions ('Of Ilios I sing, and Dardania land of fine colts...'), another line, fr. 1 Bernabé, also contains a Muse invocation ('Muse, tell me of those things that never happened before / and never will again'). Bernabé concluded that the two come from separate poems; Scafoglio rejects this, and draws attention to an imitation in Virgil's *Aeneid*, 1.1–11. But the double invocations in the *Odyssey*, *Theogony*, and *Catalogue of Women* provide even closer parallels.

A proem is closely linked to a hymnic prelude, but the two must not be conflated. Their functional and formal distinctness is especially clear in the way they are joined in Simonides' elegiac Plataea ode. At the end of his hymn to Achilles, Simonides switches to his main narrative as follows (fr. eleg. 11.19–24):

---

[63] Scafoglio 2006.

ἀλλὰ σὺ μὲ]ν νῦν χαῖρε, θεᾶς ἐρικυ[δέος υἱέ
   κούρης εἰν]αλίου Νηρέος· αὐτὰρ ἐγὼ [
κικλήισκω] σ' ἐπίκουρον ἐμοί, π[ολυώνυμ]ε Μοῦσα,
   εἴ περ γ' ἀν]θρώπων εὐχομένω[ν μέλεαι·
ἔντυνο]ν καὶ τόνδ[ε μελ]ίφρονα κ[όσμον ἀο]ιδῆς
   ἡμετ]έρης...

[But] farewell to you now, [son] of a very famous goddess,
   [the daughter] of the sea-god Nereus; and I
[summon] you as my ally, [famous] Muse,
   [if] mortal prayers [are of any concern:]
[prepare] this sweet ornament, too, of our
   song...

The 'farewell' in 19–20 is a standard closing for hymns; the summon-
ing in 20–1 signals the transition into a proem; the last phrase, with its
reference to the coming song, has the air of a doubled invocation.[64] The
*Theogony*'s transition is even more compressed, where Hesiod's farewell
to the Muses (*Theog.* 104) also serves as his invocation for the proem.
The one other case where a hymnic prelude survives attached to a
poem, *Works and Days* 1–10, moves directly from the hymn to the
main content without a formal proem. Simonides' poem, though it is
elegiac, provides our clearest evidence that proems like those in the
*Iliad* and *Odyssey* could be preceded by formal hymnic closes. Hymns
can themselves open with brief invocations to the Muse: the major
*Hymns to Hermes* and *Aphrodite* do so, and so do about a third of the
minor hymns.[65]

### (b) Two types of knowledge: 'truth' vs. 'report'

In the *Theogony*'s opening hymn the Muses famously declare (*Theog.*
27–8):[66]

ἴδμεν ψεύδεα πολλὰ λέγειν ἐτύμοισιν ὁμοῖα,
ἴδμεν δ' εὖτ' ἐθέλωμεν ἀληθέα γηρύσασθαι.

[W]e know how to say many false things similar to genuine ones, but we know, when
we wish, how to proclaim true things.

---

[64] On this transition see especially I. Rutherford 2001: 44–5.
[65] *Hymns* 9, 14, 17, 19, 20, 31, 32, 33.
[66] For detailed discussion see Clay 2003: 58–67.

This sentiment is not isolated. It belongs to a tradition of poetic utter-
ances cast in terms of two types of knowledge: one true, the other false;
one divine, the other mortal; one authentic, the other mere opinion.[67]

Thus in *Iliad* 2.484–6 the Muses possess divine knowledge which is
accurate, while mortal knowledge is mere *kleos* ('report' or 'rumour'),
prone to inaccuracy and untruth. A performer or narrator who is div-
inely favoured may have access to the first type of knowledge: so
Odysseus tells the story of his wanderings 'expertly, as a singer would
do' and not 'making up lying stories, from which no-one could learn
anything' (*Od.* 11.363–9). Penelope's account of the two gates through
which dreams come plays on the same trope at a more symbolic level:
dreams that come through the gate of ivory are false, while the gate of
horn produces dreams that are fulfilled (*Od.* 19.560–9). And this
dichotomy is not only about knowledge that is reserved to the gods.
Hesiod attributes to the Muses his ability to transmit accurate information about navigation at sea, something of which he has – or claims he
has – no first-hand knowledge (*WD* 660–2): here again, the distinction
is between direct access to truth and indirect report. When Apollo pro-
claims his prerogative over oracular knowledge, he warns that some
omens are true and some false, and only with self-restraint can a mortal
tell which is which (*Hymn. Hom. Herm.* 533–49).

A zenith of abstraction is reached in Parmenides' poem, which relies
heavily on a dichotomy between divine *alētheia* ('truth') and mortal
*doxa* ('opinion'). In his proem Parmenides evokes both Homeric and
Hesiodic models: the gates of Night and Day through which the narrator passes (but in which direction?) echo Penelope's gates of dreams,
while the divine instruction he receives from an unnamed goddess
evokes the *Theogony*'s visitation of the Muses. The poem goes on to
repeat similar imagery elsewhere: truth 'is', and is represented by
light or ethereal fire; opinion 'is not', and is represented by dense
night (frs. B 8.50–61, B 9.1–5); but, Parmenides argues, both are
worthy of study. The themes are philosophical but the tradition is a
poetic one. The trope extends through hexameter poetry continuously
from Homer to Parmenides. It is a distant ancestor to many philosophical sentiments in Plato: Socrates is surely thinking of it when he asks,
in the *Phaedo* (65b), 'Does human sight and hearing possess any truth?

---

[67] See also Snell 1953: 136–52, who outlines the development of this dichotomy from Homer to
Parmenides, adducing Heracleitus and Xenophanes in addition to the texts mentioned here.

Or is it like the poets are always babbling: that we neither hear nor see anything accurately?'

## (c) Simile

It is the Homeric simile that is most familiar to readers of early hexameter, and that served as a model for later epic poets. But they were used independently in other poems too, though typically not very frequently.[68] Similes have an especially prominent role in the *Shield* and in the fragments of Empedocles; and there are a few exemplars in some of the major *Hymns*. A couple of examples will illustrate the basic format. *Hymn to Hermes* 43–6:

> ὡς δ᾽ ὁπότ᾽ ὠκὺ νόημα διὰ στέρνοιο περήσηι
> ἀνέρος ὅν τε θαμειναὶ ἐπιστρωφῶσι μέριμναι,
> ἢ ὅτε δινηθῶσιν ἀπ᾽ ὀφθαλμῶν ἀμαρυγαί,
> ὡς ἅμ᾽ ἔπος τε καὶ ἔργον ἐμήδετο κύδιμος Ἑρμῆς.

And as when a sudden notion passes through the breast of a man who is constantly visited by thoughts, or when sparkling glances spin from someone's eyes, so glorious Hermes made his action as quick as his word.

And *Shield* 437–42:

> ὡς δ᾽ ὅτ᾽ ἀπὸ μεγάλου πέτρη πρηῶνος ὀρούσῃ,
> μακρὰ δ᾽ ἐπιθρῴσκουσα κυλίνδεται, ἣ δέ τε ἠχῇ
> ἔρχεται ἐμμεμαυῖα· πάγος δέ οἱ ἀντεβόλησεν
> ὑψηλός, τῷ δὴ συνενείκεται, ἔνθα μιν ἴσχει·
> τὼς <ἄρ'> ὁ μὲν ἰαχῇ βρισάρματος οὔλιος Ἄρης
> κεκληγὼς ἐπόρουσεν...

Just as when from a great cliff a boulder rushes and rolls down, bouncing mightily, and with an echo it goes eagerly along; but it encounters a lofty hill and dashes against it, and it is stopped there; so too chariot-weighting, dire Ares, shouting with a roar, rushed forward...

Similes add layers of meaning. When Heracles and Ares face each other, we already expect their confrontation to be fierce and cataclysmic; by adding the simile, with its imagery of the bouncing boulder, the poet superimposes less direct suggestions of speed, weight, noise,

---

[68] See M. L. West 2007: 95–9 on the Indo-European background to the Greek simile.

and a terrific momentum stoppable only by an immovable object. In Hermes' case, the added layers are the whirlwind activity of a volatile mind: the lightning speed of a glance moving from one object to another, or a thought from one place to another.

Similes often appear in isolation, but they may also be used systematically, to add even more significance, in ways that will be familiar to readers of Homer. In the *Iliad*, comparisons of people and phenomena to stars (brightness, burning intensity) or lions (ferocity, violence, strength) indicate development of an ongoing theme (the escalation of violence throughout the *Iliad*). Parallels sometimes pop up in other poems. The pile-up of eight similes in *Shield* 374–442, marking the collisions of Heracles with Cycnus and Ares, embodies that poem's fascination with dense, crowded poetic textures and imagery. In the *Hymn to Demeter*, when Keleos' daughters run to meet Demeter, two similes compare them to deer frisking through a meadow (174–5) and their flying hair to a saffron flower (177–8): juxtaposed, these images evoke the opening of the hymn, where Demeter's daughter Persephone frolics in a meadow gathering flowers, before being kidnapped by Hades. And similes in the *Hymn to Hermes* repeatedly compare Hermes to a baby (151–2, 163–4, 241); ordinarily these would just be platitudes, but since they are literally true (Hermes actually *is* a baby) they become ironic comments, alerting us to Hermes' self-conscious attempts to disarm others by putting on a *show* of being a mere baby.

Comparisons may be more than a stylistic device. Beall argues that ploughing in the *Works and Days* acts as a metaphor for the human condition. Snell sees the history of similes as an integral part of the history of analogical thought.[69] In the fifth century the history of the simile culminates with Empedocles, who uses similes not only to add poetic depth but also as explanatory tools. He often explains one physical process by comparing it to another, as in this passage where he explains the idea of vision rays emitted from the human eye (fr. B 84.1–8):[70]

ὡς δ' ὅτε τις πρόοδον νοέων ὡπλίσσατο λύχνον
χειμερίην διὰ νύκτα, πυρὸς σέλας αἰθομένοιο,
ἅψας παντοίων ἀνέμων λαμπτῆρας ἀμοργούς,
οἵ τ' ἀνέμων μὲν πνεῦμα διασκιδνᾶσιν ἀέντων,
φῶς δ' ἔξω διαθρῶισκον, ὅσον ταναώτερον ἦεν,

---

[69] Beall 2004, esp. 27–9; Snell 1953: 191–226.
[70] See also frs. B 23.1–10 (mixing of paints as an analogy for the blending of the elements), B 100.8–22 (suction in a water clock as an analogy for blood vessels).

λάμπεσκεν κατὰ βηλὸν ἀτειρέσιν ἀκτίνεσσιν·
ὡς δὲ τότ᾽ ἐν μήνιγξιν ἐεργμένον ὠγύγιον πῦρ
λεπτῇσίν <τ᾽> ὀθόνῃσι λοχάζετο κύκλωπα κούρην...

*As when someone, intending a journey, prepares a lamp,*
*a flame of flashing fire through the winter night,*
*fastening the lantern sides as protection against any winds*
*(they divert the breeze when the winds blow),*
*yet the light leaps through outside, inasmuch as it is finer-textured,*
*and illuminates the ground with its tireless rays:*
*just so then the ancient fire, guarded in the membranes*
*and fine tissues, lies in wait in the round pupil...*

### (d) Other miscellaneous features

There is not space to cover every poetic device that is characteristic of early hexameter – at least, not as fully as the accounts given above. So this chapter ends with briefer notes on some further recurring features.

**Oracle.** Oracles are a genre unto themselves with their own set of formal features, whether they are the short poems spuriously attributed to the Delphic Oracle, the surviving fragments of oracle collectors, or prophecies made by legendary figures. The major studies of the Delphic Oracle provide good guides to oracles generally.[71] Fontenrose's formal study characterizes oracles as giving commands, warnings, or factual statements about past, present, and future, either simply or with some condition that has yet to be met.[72] He goes on to analyse oracles as being composed of up to six independent motifs, which may be combined in a manner similar to a type scene: A, a salutation to the person addressed; B, a restatement of the question posed; C, an assertion of mantic authority; D, a condition to be met; E, the core message; and F, a clarification of the message's context.[73] The same analysis can be applied to the oracles in oracle collectors and in purely legendary stories. In Homer, for example, Calchas' oracle to Achilles declaring the reasons for the plague (*Il.* 1.93–100) comprises a message ('here is why Apollo is angry; here is how to appease him') and a condition to be met ('provided we give Chryseis back to

---

[71] Especially Fontenrose 1978: 11–57, 166–95; also Parke and Wormell 1956: xxi–xxxvi (neither discussion attempts to tie characteristics to specific eras).
[72] Fontenrose 1978: 13–20.
[73] Fontenrose 1978: 177–9.

her father, and offer a sacrifice'): that is, the motifs ED. By contrast, Teiresias' prophecy to Odysseus (*Od.* 11.100–37) is a long string of conditions and predictions, in the sequence BAFEDEDEDEDECDEC.[74]

The obscurity and animal imagery of oracle collectors such as Epimenides, Musaeus, and Bacis link their oracles closely to the device of the competitive riddle. However, we have only a few riddles couched in hexameter: the famous riddle of the Sphinx (*Oedipodea* fr. 2); Calchas' riddle to Mopsus in the *Melampodia* (Hesiodica fr. 214); a riddle about the lifespan of the Naeads (Hesiodica fr. 254); and the riddle of the lice that presages Homer's death in the *Contest of Homer and Hesiod* (*Contest* 18).

**Parable and exemplum.** Aesop's *Fables* are the popular archetype of the Archaic parable, though they do not survive in their original form. But moralizing tales also appear in hexameter in wisdom poetry, and as exempla or mythological paradigms in narrative poetry. The most famous is the parable of the hawk and the nightingale in *Works and Days* 202–12, where the hawk justifies its killing of the nightingale by right of strength: the story uses the hawk's manifest injustice to question the principle of 'might makes right'.[75] Closely related is the device of the mythological paradigm, where a character in a narrative poem tells a story from the past as a model for behaviour in the present: some especially famous examples in Homer are when Phoenix tells the story of Meleager to try and persuade Achilles to relent from his anger, and when Achilles tells the story of Niobe to persuade Priam to eat in spite of his grief.[76] Outside Homer our most extended example comes from the fragments of Panyassis' *Heraclea*, where King Eurytus of Oichalia first encourages his guest Heracles to drink heartily, only to become more hesitant as his guest becomes more drunk and dangerous (fr. 20.1–9):[77]

> ‘πρῶται μὲν Χάριτές τ᾽ ἔλαχον καὶ ἐύφρονες Ὧραι
> μοῖραν καὶ Διόνυσος ἐρίβρομος, οἵ περ ἔτευξαν·

[74] On the conditionals in Teiresias' prophecy see especially Peradotto 1985: 438–43.

[75] See recently Steiner 2012, with bibliography. Epimenides fr. 45 Bernabé also draws on this fable.

[76] *Il.* 9.527–605, 24.601–20. On parables in Homer generally see Pelliccia in Finkelberg 2011b: ii.622–4; on mythical paradigms or 'para-narratives' see Alden 2000.

[77] Panyassis frs. 19–22. West takes frs. 20–2 as Heracles replying prudently to Eurytus' reckless encouragement. More plausible is Huxley's view (1969: 178–9) that the fragments are all spoken by Eurytus, who begins by enthusing about wine but becomes hesitant as he sees his guest becoming more drunk and more dangerous. On this reading the most likely sequence is: 19, 21, 20, 22 (the pairs 19, 21 and 20, 22 are in any case suggested by their grouping in Athenaeus, our source for the fragments, ii.36d–37d).

τοῖς δ' ἔπι Κυπρογένεια θεὰ λάχε καὶ Διόνυσος, ...
...εἴ τις μέ<τρα> πίοι καὶ ἀπότροπος οἴκαδ' ἀπέλθοι
δαιτὸς ἀπὸ γλυκερῆς, οὐκ ἄν ποτε πήματι κύρσαι·
ἀλλ' ὅτε τις μοίρης τριτάτης πρὸς μέτρον ἐλαύνοι
πίνων ἀβλεμέως, τότε δ' Ὕβριος αἶσα καὶ Ἄτης
γίγνεται ἀργαλέη, κακὰ δ' ἀνθρώποισιν ὀπάζει.'

'The Graces and the cheerful Horai take the first portion, and Dionysus the mighty roarer, the ones who created it. After them the goddess born in Cyprus takes her share, and Dionysus...But when someone drinks heavily and presses to the limit of the third round, then Hybris and Ate take their unlovely turn, which brings trouble.'

Recently a new exemplar was found in an elegiac poem of Archilochus, rediscovered and published in 2005, where an unknown speaker cites the Achaeans' flight from Telephus as a paradigm for giving way to necessity.[78]

**Route description.** Poetry cannot easily portray geography in a two-dimensional map. Early Greek poetry resorts to describing linear routes through a landscape: point A to point B to point C and so on. This poetic device includes not only physical journeys but also the way-points traced by catalogues. The most elaborate map of this kind is the Catalogue of Ships in *Iliad* 2.494–759, which follows a route in three parts: first winding clockwise around central and southern Greece, then eastwards through the Dorian islands of the south Aegean, and finally from Phthia northwards through Thessaly.[79] The *Hymn to Apollo* has three journeys: Leto's path clockwise around the Aegean looking for a place to give birth to Apollo (30–49), Apollo's journey from Olympus to Delphi (216–86), and the journey of Apollo's new ministers from Crete to Delphi (409–39).[80] Other, less clear, routes are outlined or implied in the *Odyssey*'s catalogue of dead heroines, the *Catalogue of Women*'s catalogue of Helen's suitors, and the journeys in the *Hymn to Hermes*.[81] Detailed 'maps' also appear in other poetic genres, in Simonides' Plataea ode and Aeschylus' *Agamemnon*.[82]

**Ekphrasis (rhetorical description).** This device is best known from examples in Homer, especially the description of Hephaestus

---

[78] P.Oxy. 4708; on the new Archilochus as exemplum see especially Swift 2012.

[79] On the route see Kirk 1985: 183–6.

[80] See further N. Richardson 2010: 10–13.

[81] *Od.* 11.225–330 (on the route see Northrup 1980); *Cat.* frs. 154b to 155.64 (M. L. West 1985: 114–19); *Hymn. Hom. Herm.* 68–145, Hermes' odd route from Pieria to Mount Cyllene (Arcadia) via Onchestus (Boeotia) and the river Alpheios (Elis).

[82] Simon. fr. eleg. 11.29–43 (the march from Sparta northward to Plataea); Aesch. *Ag.* 281–311 (Clytemnestra's beacons across the Aegean).

forging Achilles' new shield (*Il.* 18.478–608). Most of our non-Homeric examples are fragmentary; the great exception is the colossal description of Heracles' eponymous shield in *Shield* 144–319, also made by Hephaestus. Heracles' shield is described in a systematic fashion, starting from a central section filled with monstrous personifications such as Fear, Tumult, and Murder, and working outwards with orientalizing animal motifs, scenes of gods and humans, and finally the river Ocean surrounding everything.[83] It is not simply a cheap copy of the Homeric shield, though it certainly draws on the same set of tropes. Like Achilles' shield it juxtaposes scenes of war and peace, a siege and a wedding; but it gives greater emphasis to divine figures and it appears that a few lines in the Iliadic *ekphrasis* were actually interpolated from the *Shield*.[84]

We have indications of several other *ekphraseis*. (1) Francis argues persuasively that the gods' creation of Pandora (*Theog.* 570–89; *WD* 60–82) is an *ekphrasis* of an artefact, which is subsequently imbued with life.[85] (2) Lesches, *Little Iliad* fr. 5: a description of Achilles' spear (see also *Cypria* fr. 4?), a gift from the gods like his more famous shield. (3) Eugammon, *Telegony* arg. 1: a mixing bowl depicting the story of Trophonius, Agamedes, and Augeas.[86] (4) *Telegony* fr. 5: Hephaestus forges Telegonus' spear from the barb of a stingray (found in Phorcys' lake, near Circe's home in Italy), a tip of adamant, a butt-spike of gold, and a haft of goat's horn.[87] (5) Eumelus, *Titanomachy* fr. 14: probably from a description of a metal cup or jug, featuring as part of its decoration a group of golden-faced mute (or 'scaly'?) fish (χρυσώπιδες ἰχθύες ἐλλοί).[88] (6) It is possible to interpret *Hymn* 7 (to Dionysus) as a narrative based on a pictorial representation: the story of Dionysus turning the Etruscan sailors into dolphins was a popular theme in sixth-century art.[89]

[83] See Myres 1941 for a detailed reconstruction with illustrations. On symbolism in this *ekphrasis* see especially Thalmann 1984: 62–4; Becker 1992.

[84] Lynn-George 1978 makes a compelling argument that *Il.* 18.535–40 is interpolated from *Shield* 156–60.

[85] Francis 2009: 13–17.

[86] The full story appears in Charax *FGrH* 103 fr. 5; see also M. L. West 2003a: 167 n. 69.

[87] *Pace* West, στύραξ='butt-spike' (cf. Xen. *Hell.* 6.2.19; Pl. *Lach.* 184a; Hesych. σ.2092). The detail of the haft appears in sch. Opp. *Hal.* 2.497.

[88] See Davies 2001: 17. The bronze ἔλλοπας ἰχθῦς ('mute fish') in *Shield* 212–13 indicate that this phrase is from an *ekphrasis*; see also M. L. West 2003a: 233 n. 14, arguing that Eumelus' fish are real ones in a lake.

[89] M. L. West 2003b: 16–17.

**Poet's 'seal' (*sphragis*).** The *sphragis*, or signature left by the poet, is a rare device in hexameter. Where it appears, it usually takes the form of the narrator explicitly adopting a specific persona. At *Theogony* 22–34 the poet explicitly adopts the persona of Hesiod, telling the story of how the Muses personally inspired him with the gift of poetry; the poet of *Works and Days* 646–62 claims to have won a poetry contest at the funeral games of Amphidamas in Euboea, also (implicitly) adopting the persona of Hesiod; and at *Hymn to Apollo* 165–76 Cynaethus famously adopts the persona of Homer as a blind poet from Chios whose songs 'remain supreme'. The device is more common in other genres, with important examples in Archilochus, Sappho, Solon, and Pindar. A notable example in a 'heroic' narrative is the end of Timotheus' *Persae*, fr. 791.229–33 *PMG*, where the narrator compares himself to two semi-mythical hexameter poets, Orpheus and Terpander. This trope tends to gravitate towards the beginning or end of a poem.

**Miscellaneous stylistic devices.** Many features of narrative arrangement, word order, and language that are characteristic of Homer also appear in non-Homeric hexameter. Thalmann gives a good review of some of these, documenting them copiously with non-Homeric examples: parataxis (avoidance of subordinate clauses); *hysteron prōton* (where the chronologically latest event is mentioned first; or an AB–BA arrangement where the first element in one phrase appears last in the answering phrase); ring composition (a more elaborate version of *hysteron prōton*, with multiple concentric layers ABCD...DCBA); 'spiral' composition (like ring composition but the rings interlock with one another); and parallelism (ABC...ABC...).[90] The formulaic style is also a key element of non-Homeric hexameter. It becomes progressively less prominent in fifth-century poetry but some non-Homeric poems display a creative use of the formulaic system, as we shall see in the following chapter.

---

[90] Thalmann 1984: 4–28. From a narratological perspective see also Minchin 2007: 102–16 on *hysteron prōton*, Minchin 2001: 181–202 on ring composition.

# III TRADITION AND LEGEND

Some of the generic elements we looked at in the last chapter were the-matic, some stylistic, and some purely formal. An exhaustive catalogue would be impractical – not to mention tedious. But, taken together, generic elements like these constitute the traditional side of hexameter poetry. Typical features are the ones that define the tradition as a trad-ition: if poets repeat a feature, then it propagates successfully, survives, and becomes a traditional element of hexameter poetry. Or, to put it more aphoristically: repetition is tradition.

The tradition in question spans several centuries, so there are some obvious follow-up questions. How did the hexameter tradition develop after Hesiod and Homer? What did it look like beforehand? How far back does the hexameter tradition go? But also a less obvious question: how do we take into account elements which were traditional but, by chance or otherwise, happen not to be attested in the surviving evi-dence? For example, there is a real question over how much extant mythical narratives are determined and influenced by hexameter poetry. Is it justifiable to talk about hexameter poems and the broader mythical tradition as though they were the same thing?

## 1. Unrecorded traditions

All Greek hexameter poetry was performance poetry. It was not designed for private reading or for analysis in classrooms: it was a thing of live poets and live audiences. We shall look at the circum-stances of performance in Chapter IV. For now, it is most urgent to emphasize that the surviving written tradition is only a very poor reflec-tion of the material that was available to poets of the time.

In the very earliest oral hexameter poetry, traditional motifs and gen-eric forms acted as a kind of stockpile that a poet could draw on for improvisatory, or semi-improvisatory, purposes.[1] At the same time, since the existence of traditional elements depends on those elements' suitability for repetition, the elements exerted a creative force of their own. Poetry in that environment was a collaboration between bard

---

[1] Lord 1960: 68–98 provides a seminal treatment.

and tradition: bards selected traditional elements for their poetic purposes, while traditional elements evolved to be suitable for those purposes. Performing a pre-existing poem was not a matter of verbatim copying but of composing the poem anew. This is usually called 'recomposition'.

As time passed, reiteration became more important than recomposition. The development of the hexameter tradition, from its earliest stages through to the fifth century, is the story of a gradual transition between at least three performance models:[2]

- 'Recomposition': story outlines are traditional, but details and verbal expression may be improvised or innovated using a toolkit of traditional set pieces and motifs.
- 'Recaptured' performance: re-performance of existing poems with stricter constraints on reproduction determined by stricter social conditions, with an emphasis on the social nature of performance, in religious festivals, symposia, and so on.
- 'Recited' performance: replication of an authoritative recorded version, with an insistence on verbatim repetition.

There is naturally disagreement over where to place any specific poem on this spectrum. It is no longer possible to imagine that any Greek poem that has survived in writing belongs solely to the first of these categories. But the underlying point is secure: traditional set pieces such as type scenes, proems, and the hymnic form served both improvisatory and mnemonic functions. As performance shifted towards recapture and repetition, these elements came to be more valuable as mnemonic devices than as improvisatory building blocks, and their role in the composition of new poems became more indirect. For later hexameter poets such as Choerilus and Panyassis, these elements were not compositional aids so much as genre markers for their poetry, echoing and evoking classic models of the past.

Poets never stopped innovating on traditional material, of course. In Chapter II we saw how the *Shield* poet innovates within the traditional format of the arming scene. But the pool of available material shifted from a stock of traditional devices towards a stock of specific texts. In the *Theogony*, when the Muses instruct Hesiod in poetry, we should think of it as a traditional motif. But when Parmenides uses the same

---

[2] More elaborate models are envisaged by Kirk 1962: 95–8 (four phases); Nagy 1996: 29–63 (five phases).

idea, we should be thinking of allusions to specific works (fr. B 1.11–12, 22–6):

ἔνθα πύλαι Νυκτός τε καὶ Ἥματός εἰσι κελεύθων,
καί σφας ὑπέρθυρον ἀμφὶς ἔχει καὶ λάινος οὐδός· ...
...καί με θεὰ πρόφρων ὑπεδέξατο, χεῖρα δὲ χειρί
δεξιτερὴν ἕλεν, ὧδε δ' ἔπος φάτο καί με προσηύδα·
ὦ κοῦρ' ἀθανάτοισι συνάορος ἡνιόχοισιν,
ἵπποις ταί σε φέρουσιν ἱκάνων ἡμέτερον δῶ,
χαῖρ'...

*In that place are the gates of the paths of Night and Day,*
*and a lintel and a polished threshold enclose them...*
*...And the goddess welcomed me kindly, took my right*
*hand in hers, and she spoke and addressed me as follows:*
*'My son, accompanied by immortal charioteers*
*and mares who bear you to my house,*
*welcome...'*

Parmenides' unnamed goddess is not just a stock motif. Her didactic role specifically echoes that of the Hesiodic Muses, who 'know how to say many false things similar to genuine ones': the allusion frames a central theme in Parmenides' poem, the dichotomy of truth versus belief. The reference to the gates of Night and Day echoes the didactic and oracular role played by Night in the Derveni *Theogony* (or another similar poem): this frames Parmenides' poem as a mystic initiation into hidden knowledge.[3] Later hexameter poets echo Parmenides in their turn. Empedocles borrows his imagery of a highway (*hamaxiton*) as a metaphor for learning, and the proem of Choerilus' *Persica* borrows the image of a chariot as a metaphor for poetry.[4]

Poets' use of source material that is now lost, or was never written down, is a deep-seated problem in studying early hexameter. Even experienced scholars sometimes make the mistake of assuming that a reference to a myth is automatically a reference to a poem: if a vase represents a Trojan War scene, it must be a homage to a hexameter poem; if a legendary figure has some kind of cult at the site of his or her grave, the stories told about him or her must be epic narratives. This goes even for material within the poems themselves: if the *Works and Days* refers to 'Strife', it must supposedly be a response to

---

[3] For other verbal echoes in Parmenides fr. B 1, see the commentary of Coxon 2009.
[4] Empedocles fr. B 133; Choerilus fr. 2 Bernabé (=fr. 316 *SH*).

a specific text, namely the Strife of the *Theogony*; if the *Iliad* relates the genealogy of Diomedes and his father, Tydeus, that must supposedly be borrowed from a Theban epic. The nature of the surviving evidence feeds this habit. Our early evidence for myths and their transmission consists solely of poetic narratives and pictorial representations, so it is naturally tempting to think of these two media when we think about myth-making.

Scholars of the pictorial tradition, by contrast, are keenly aware that this conclusion is nonsense. Many studies in the last three decades have decisively and consistently rejected the notion that pictorial representations are to be interpreted as illustrations of poetic accounts.[5] The most pointed counter-examples are the Gigantomachy and the story of Troilus: both legends were colossally popular in pictorial arts but, so far as we can tell, no hexameter poems ever gave them anything more than a passing mention.[6]

The Gigantomachy is the battle of the Olympian gods against the Giants, where Heracles saves the day. In the classical period the most authoritative 'accounts' of the Gigantomachy were pictorial: the decorations of the Alcmaeonid temple of Apollo at Delphi, and the metopes on the east side of the Parthenon at Athens. Homer and Hesiod mention the Giants only in passing; Pindar gives slightly more information; but a full report of the story does not appear in any surviving textual source until pseudo-Apollodorus, in the first century BCE.[7] The absence of the Gigantomachy from the poetic record is so glaring that ancient writers often confused it with the Titanomachy,[8] and Clay has wondered whether an older form of the *Theogony* might once have had a Gigantomachy where the Prometheus episode now is.[9]

The story of the Trojan prince Troilus, ambushed and pursued by Achilles and murdered at the altar of Thymbraean Apollo, accounts

---

[5] Kannicht 1982; Lowenstam 1992, 2008: 1–12; Snodgrass 1998: 127–50; Burgess 2001: 35–44, 53–114; Junker 2012: 1–95.

[6] For a summary of ancient testimony see Gantz 1993: 445–54 (Gigantomachy), 597–603 (Troilus).

[7] Gigantomachy: *Cat.* fr. 69.89; Pind. *Nem.* 1.67–9, 7.90, *Pyth.* 8.12–18; Eur. *Ion* 205–18 (the temple of Apollo at Delphi), *HF* 177–80; various later sources, e.g. ps.-Apollod. 1.6.1–2, sch. on Pind. *Nem.* 1.101, *Isthm.* 6.47; possibly *Theog.* 954, *Cat.* fr. 138.35–6 (=*Shield* 28–9). Giants (no reference to Gigantomachy): *Od.* 7.58–9, 206, 10.120; *Theog.* 50, 185–6. For pre-400 BCE pictorial evidence see *LIMC*, 'Gigantes' nos. 1–21, 32–43, 95–388, and (Etruscan) 405–20, 425.

[8] E.g. Eumelus, *Titanomachy* fr. 3 (West's reading Τιτανομαχίαι is an emendation from Γιγαντομαχίαι); Eur. *Hec.* 466–74 and scholia ad loc., *IT* 224; sch. *Hec.* 471 glosses 'Titans' as 'Giants beneath the earth' (ὑποχθονίων Γιγάντων). See further Gantz 1993: 447.

[9] Clay 2003: 113–15.

for a staggering twenty per cent of all Greek depictions of Achilles. The pictorial record shows a remarkably uniform storyline, with numerous shared details and only occasional inconsistencies.[10] But not a single contemporary poem gave a detailed account of the story, so far as we can tell. The *Iliad* mentions Troilus' name once (24.257). The *Cypria* at least reported the story (arg. 11), but the sheer quantity of material assigned to that eleven-book epic means that it must have been a relatively brief report: it is certainly very difficult to imagine it as the inspiration for one-fifth of all depictions of Achilles.[11] The *Cypria* is hardly likely to have been more striking than a comparable episode in the *Iliad*, Achilles' encounter with another Trojan prince, Lycaon (*Il.* 21.34–135), which provides the occasion for some of the most powerful dialogue in all epic, but of which not a single pictorial treatment survives from the Archaic period.[12] Other poetic treatments are too late, and too marginal, to be responsible for the story's towering popularity throughout the Archaic era.[13]

This is not to say that pictorial representations of myths are totally unconnected to poetic traditions; that would be swinging the pendulum too far the other way. The current consensus is that artists could creatively engage with poems when they wanted to, though this is best understood as beginning only in the late sixth century.[14] There are even a few depictions that appear to have been modelled on a specific poetic source: West cites three vases from 540–490 BCE which imitate the binary structure of Arctinus' *Aethiopis*, one side depicting the 'Amazonis', the other the 'Memnonis'.[15] But that kind of privileging of a poem is extremely rare.

---

[10] See especially Kossatz-Deissmann, in *LIMC* s.v. 'Achilleus' nos. 206–388 and s.v. 'Troilos'; *LIMC* s.v. 'Achle' nos. 11–84 (Etruscan).

[11] Proclus allots three words to the Troilus episode in his 610-word summary of the *Cypria*. Unambiguous pictorial treatments of the Troilus episode go back to 700 BCE (*LIMC* s.v. 'Achilleus' no. 332a; perhaps 'Troilos' no. 7); the date of the *Cypria* is unknown. In the surviving fragments Janko 1982: 176 sees a stylometric affinity to *Hymn. Hom. Aphr.* M. L. West 2011b: 232–3, 240 dates it to *c.*520 BCE on linguistic considerations; at 2013: 63–5 he changes his mind and dates 'older, pre-Cyclic poem(s)' to the late 600s BCE, but the Cyclic epic to *c.*580–550. Finkelberg 2000 argues for a position broadly consistent with that taken here: that legendary material associated with the *Cypria* always remained multiform and was never pinned to an authoritative text.

[12] Lowenstam 2008: 114–19, discussing possible fourth-century Italian depictions of Lycaon, doubts that even artists of that time were very familiar with the *Iliad*.

[13] Ibyc. frs. S151.40–5, S224 Page; Phrynichus fr. 13 Snell; the fragments of Sophocles' and Strattis' *Troilus* plays.

[14] See bibliography in n. 5 above.

[15] M. L. West 2013: 130.

So to account for the potential range of media for the transmission of myths, we need a broader perspective. A reference to a myth could be alluding to any of the following:

**1. Specific hexameter poems**: the Homeric epics, the poems discussed in this book, and other poems that circulated in writing but which no longer survive.

**2. Oral epos legend**: in other words, purely oral epic. This category refers to narratives traditionally related in hexameter, but which never made it into the written record. The existence of such poems may be reasonably inferred if a narrative shows definite signs of being shaped by traditional hexameter features such as those outlined in Chapter II. A good candidate is the story of Jason and the Argonauts: the story had a heavy impact on the *Odyssey*,[16] but, since we have no attestation of any dedicated epic on the subject, there is a presumption that no specific written poem was known in the classical period.[17]

**3. Other poetic genres**: mythological elements appear frequently in the surviving remnants of other poetic genres, and lyric poets sometimes used different material from what we see in hexameter poems. For example, the story of Hermes' cattle raid against Apollo in the *Hymn to Hermes* had previously been used in a lost poem by Alcaeus. Alcaeus had Hermes also steal Apollo's bow and arrows, but in the *Hymn* this is only mentioned as a possibility.[18] However, it is relatively uncommon for a lyric poem to be devoted specifically to a mythical narrative; Stesichorus' lost poems are the main examples.[19] There may also have been purely oral exemplars but, since lyric poetry is not so dominated by traditional set pieces as hexameter, we have no way of detecting their existence.

**4. Oral non-poetic legend**: there can be no doubt that material in this category existed in great quantity, but we have no access to it, since the surviving evidence is poetic and pictorial. Oral non-poetic legend presumably overlapped with the poetic and pictorial traditions to some extent, but we cannot know how great the overlap was.

---

[16] Danek 1998, esp. 197–201, 251–7.

[17] Similarly M. L. West 2005: 40: an Argonautic poem 'was current only in oral form, or, if it was ever fixed in writing, it disappeared before the Hellenistic age'. We only know of an obscure poem on the building of the Argo ascribed to Epimenides (frs. 57a–59 Bernabé); and Argonautic material used in the *Naupactia* (frs. 2–10), in Eumelus' *Corinthiaca* (frs. 17–23), and in melic poetry (e.g. Pind. *Pyth.* 4).

[18] Alcaeus fr. 308(d); *Hymn. Hom. Herm.* 514–15. See further Vergados 2012: 553 on line 515.

[19] See the new edition of Davies and Finglass 2015.

**5. Pictorial tradition**: we must assume that pictorial artists could engage with any of the above categories if they wished, and could even – though only rarely, and late – evoke specific poems. But the pictorial tradition had its own set of well-defined themes and tropes; in some cases it may well have had its own stories too.

The Gigantomachy and Troilus are good candidates for categories 4 and 5. Their popularity lies squarely in the pictorial tradition and not at all in the poetic tradition. If they had an earlier origin, that origin must lie in oral non-poetic legend.

There is an enormous quantity and diversity of material to which we have no access. Because of that, it is an extravagance ever to imagine that a story, or a character, or even a scene, must point to a specific poem. Oral epos legend is nearly always going to be a more parsimonious interpretation than imagining a reference to a specific poem; oral non-poetic legend will be more parsimonious still. An allusion never proves a poem.

## 2. Hexameter and the formula

Some aspects of the prehistory of the epic tradition can be deduced from language and metre. The most striking characteristic of early hexameter poetry is its extensive and sophisticated system of metrical formulae, and it is widely thought that these formulae were a key part of the toolset that allowed the very earliest, pre-Homeric, epic poets to improvise.

Dactylic hexameter consists of a strict quantitative rhythm of twelve beats, or *hemipedes*:[20]

$$\| - \smile\smile - \smile\smile - \smile\smile - \smile\smile - \smile\smile - \times \|$$

(Here $\|$ indicates the start or end of a line.) These symbols represent long and short notes, so in musical terms this notation equates to

♩ ♫ ♩ ♫ ♩ ♫ ♩ ♫ ♩ ♫ ♩ ♩

except that in most cases ♫ can be replaced by ♩.[21] Each line has a tendency to divide into two or more cola, or 'prosodic phrases': partly syntactical, partly rhythmic entities. The most common cola are 5 + 7 hemipedes

---

[20] The name 'hexameter' implies 'six feet': feet are however an abstraction created by later analysis of the metre, and not the historical basis of the metre.

[21] On a possible irregularity in this rhythm see pp. 77–8.

and $5\frac{1}{2} + 6\frac{1}{2}$.[22] There are other, lesser divisions after hemipedes 2, 3, 7, and 8, which can be combined with each other and with the major divisions in regular ways to produce a line of three or more cola: thus some common divisions are $2 + 6 + 4$, $3 + 2\frac{1}{2} + 6\frac{1}{2}$, and $5 + 2 + 5$.

The formulaic system consists of many traditional phrases – formulae – that can be slotted into each of these cola, in such a way that the rhythm of the line as a whole emerges perfectly. In this way, it is thought, a pre-Homeric improvising bard could hypothetically reel off hexameters *ad lib*. Some formulae are used strictly, others less so. Here are some formulae corresponding to the $5 + 2 + 5$ division:

| Five hemipedes: | Two hemipedes: | Five hemipedes: |
|---|---|---|
| ‖ τὸν δ᾽ ἁπαλὸν γελάσας | | Διὸς υἱὸς Ἀπόλλων ‖ |
| ‖ τοὺς δ᾽ ἐπιμειδήσας | προσέφη | ἑκάεργος Ἀπόλλων ‖ |
| ‖ τὸν δὲ μέγ᾽ ὀχθήσας | | νεφεληγερέτα Ζεύς ‖ |
| ‖ τὸν δὲ χολωσάμενος | | κρατὺς Ἀργειφόντης ‖ |
| | | |
| laughing gently | | Zeus's son Apollo |
| smiling at them | X spoke to him | far-shooter Apollo |
| greatly angered | | cloud-gathering Zeus |
| in anger | | the strong Argus-slayer |

Mixing and matching these will always produce a perfectly formed hexameter. Incidentally, it would be a mistake to think of this system of formulae as a *restriction* on a poet; rather it is one of many tools that our hypothetical improviser has at his disposal.[23]

It is usually understood that, as time passed and oral improvisation gave way to literary poetics, the usefulness of formulae as compositional tools gave way to their usefulness as mnemonic devices. As with larger-scale generic elements, metrical formulae moved from being aids in improvisation towards being markers of genre. Certainly there are only slender traces of the formulaic system in fifth-century hexameter poetry, such as Parmenides' poem or the shorter *Hymn to Dionysus* (but formulae play an important role in later parodies and imitations, such as the Hellenistic *Battle of the Frogs and Mice*).

But Homer did not have a monopoly on the system's versatility. Hoekstra has analysed a set of Homeric formulae that developed to

---

[22] These divisions are responsible for the main mid-line word break, or caesura: $5 + 7$ produces a penthemimeral ('masculine') caesura, $5\frac{1}{2} + 6\frac{1}{2}$ gives a tritotrochaic ('feminine') caesura.

[23] On the system's versatility, and authorial control over it (in Homeric epic), see Hainsworth 1968; Friedrich 2007.

fit both the 5 + 7 and the 5½ + 6½ colometry (that is, both penthemimeral and trochaic caesuras).[24] Some of these formulae gain the extra
short syllable through grammatical inflection:

'men fierce in battle'
‖ ἀνδρῶν δυσμενέων...          (5 + 7; 6× Homer)
‖ ἀνδράσι δυσμενέεσσι...        (5½ + 6½; 4× Hom.)

Other pairs are equivalent in both sense and grammatical case:

'well-built city'
...εὖ ναιόμενον πτολίεθρον ‖     (5 + 7; 6× Hom.)
...ἐϋκτίμενον πτολίεθρον ‖      (5½ + 6½; 10× Hom., 2× non-Hom.)[25]

Hoekstra sees this kind of formula as a very archaic type, since none of
his exemplars shows very recent linguistic developments.

However, this technique for building versatility into the formulaic
system continued to see innovations in post-Homeric poetry. Here
are several more pairs that exist in 5 + 7 and 5½ + 6½ variants:

'as the years rolled past'
...περιτελλομένων ἐνιαυτῶν ‖    (3× Hom., 1× non-Hom.)
...περιπλομένων ἐνιαυτῶν ‖      (3× Hom., 3× non-Hom.)[26]

'the mind of *aegis*-bearing Zeus'
...Ζηνὸς νόος αἰγιόχοιο ‖        (4× non-Hom.)
...Διὸς νόος αἰγιόχοιο ‖         (6× Hom., 1× *Hymn. Hom. Herm.*)[27]

'[women] skilled in fine works'
...περικαλλέα ἔργ' εἰδυῖαι ‖     (3× *Cat.* incl. 2× supplemented)
...ἀμύμονα ἔργ' εἰδυίαι ‖        (5× Hom., 1× *Theog.*, 1× *Cat.*)

'[a woman] possessing a lovely form'
...πολυήρατον εἶδος ἔχουσα ‖     (5× non-Hom., incl. 2× suppl.)
...ἐπήρατον εἶδος ἔχουσα ‖       (3× *Cat.* incl. 1× suppl.)[28]

---

[24] Hoekstra 1981: 40–53. Note also Hoekstra's earlier (1957) analysis of the Hesiodic formulaic system.

[25] Also ἀλιστέφανον πτολίεθρον (*Hymn. Hom. Ap.* 410).

[26] Also περιτροπέων ἐνιαυτός (*Il.* 2.295); ἐπιπλομένων ἐνιαυτῶν (*Shield* 87).

[27] This count excludes a supplement at *Cat.* fr. 69.100.

[28] The ἐπήρατον variant also appears at fr. 242.2; Most 2007 rejects that fragment from the *Catalogue,* but this analysis may add a little weight in favour of its authenticity.

'before the clear-voiced Hesperides'

...πρόπαρ' Ἑσπερίδων λιγυφώνων ‖          (1× *Theog.*)

...ἵν' Ἑσπερίδες λιγύφωνοι ‖          (1× *Theog.*)

These formula pairs are of mixed age, to judge from their linguistic character. The first pair relies on having one variant with an Aeolic form περιπ(ε)λ-, the other with Ionic περιτελλ-; the second pair relies on Διός and the late Ionic innovation Ζηνός.[29] The third pair relies on a fossilized rhythmic irregularity caused by a lost *w* sound, or digamma (hiatus before *ϝέργα ϝιδυίαι); but the fourth and fifth rely on digamma *not* being observed (short -ον before εἶδος, elision before Ἑσπερίδες; in Homer, digamma is always observed on *ϝέσπερ-). For all pairs other than the first we have to turn to non-Homeric poetry to see both variants put into practice.

The continuing development of such versatile variants after the formation of the Homeric epics points to continuing development in the tradition. To be clear, it is *not* proof that the surviving poems were themselves oral productions, or subject to oral improvisation to any particular extent. But it does show that, at the time when the *Catalogue of Women* and some of the major *Hymns* were being produced, the epic style was not just a matter of imitating older models. It was a living, evolving tradition with continuity that may well have reached back to the late Bronze Age.


### 3. Prehistory of the epic tradition

Occasionally it is possible to dig deeper into old linguistic elements of the epic tradition and detect strands of earlier traditions. So to some extent, it is possible to speak about a prehistory of the epic tradition. The most abundant evidence for this prehistory comes from Homer. It is conjectural in many respects, and there is ongoing debate over how to interpret the evidence.

Extant hexameter poetry is primarily in the Ionic dialect, with a sprinkling of other dialectal forms. These dialects are conventionally imagined as influencing the epic tradition as follows:

- Arcado-Cypriot dialect: earliest stratum; few traces, but common
- Aeolic: also prehistoric; very many metrical formulae rely on Aeolisms

---

[29] On the age of Ζηνός see Janko 1982: 62–3, 87–8.

- Ionic: core dialect of extant hexameter
- Doric: uncertain date; very rare in Homer, more common in the *Theogony*[30]
- Attic: latest stratum; traces only, perhaps introduced by Athenian editing and adaptation of older Ionic texts

Other than the core Ionic dialect, the most important are the Arcado-Cypriot and Aeolic elements. Arcado-Cypriotisms are few in number but account for some exceptionally common words in the epic dialect, such as αὐτάρ ('then'), δῶμα ('house'), ἵερος ('sacred'), and κέλευθος ('path'): these all appear frequently in non-Homeric hexameter too. Linguists sometimes conflate Arcado-Cypriot elements with the Mycenaean dialect, since its closest known relative is Arcado-Cypriot, and so they interpret these elements as a supposed 'Achaian' phase derived from Mycenaean.[31]

Aeolisms are more common because they are deeply embedded in many systems of metrical formulae. The general impression is that Ionian poets incorporated Aeolic formulae into their own poetry and would typically 'translate' them into Ionic where possible. But sometimes they preserved the Aeolic originals, if their rhythms were different from those of the Ionic equivalents: poets had more versatility if they kept both forms around. For example, a poet could choose between Ionic πρός and Aeolic πότι (and, in Homer, also πρότι) for the idea 'towards', depending on whether he wanted a one- or a two-syllable word; for 'to be' he could choose between Ionic εἶναι and Aeolic ἔμμεναι, ἔμεν, and other variants; and we saw above how he could choose between Ionic περιτελλομένων or Aeolic περιπλομένων. There are very many more examples.[32]

Some cases are less clear-cut. In Classical Ionic and Attic, *o*-stem (second declension) nouns took the ending *-ou* in the genitive case. In hexameter we find *-ou* alongside a more archaic form *-oio*, which is probably Aeolic in origin;[33] but often *-oio* is a false archaism, used in imitation of genuine Aeolic formulae, as in Ζηνὸς ἐριγδούποιο ('of

---

[30] See M. L. West 1966: 79–89 on dialectal elements in the *Theogony*.
[31] Thus Ruijgh 2011, with a catalogue of Arcado-Cypriotisms at 262–7.
[32] See M. L. West 1988: 159–65; Haug 2002: 70–106; Tsagalis 2014.
[33] Haug 2002: 106, 146, 160.

Zeus the loud-booming', 2× non-Homeric), where Ζηνός is a late Ionic form.

Masculine *a*-stem (first declension) nouns also have dialectal variants in the genitive. These include all patronymics ending in -*ēs* (*Atreïdēs* ['Atreus' son'], *Laertiadēs* ['Laertes' son']). Usually they retain the two-syllable ending -*āo*, but sometimes they take -*eō* pronounced as a single syllable. Conventionally, these forms are understood as Aeolic and Ionic, respectively. Where -*eō* appears before a vowel, it may well be a stand-in for the older form with a syllable elided: for example, Λαερτιάδεω Ὀδυσῆος ('of Laertes' son Odysseus') and Ἀτρεΐδεω Ἀγαμέμνονος ('of Atreus' son Agamemnon') might be rewritten forms of hypothetical older Aeolic formulae, *Λαϝερτιάδα' Ὀδυσῆϝος and *Ἀτρεϝίδα' Ἀγαμέμνονος, with only cosmetic changes to make them look like Ionic. Several considerations support the intuition that these are often archaisms in disguise.[34]

The principle that older formulae, including Aeolic formulae, were often adapted simply by modernizing or Ionizing their pronunciation, is a well-accepted one among linguists. In this way poets were able to draw on older formulae and on the Aeolic formulaic system while also acquiring the extra versatility offered by contemporary Ionic.

What is debated is the relationship between the two traditions: whether we should think of a *diffusion model*, where the Aeolic and Ionic traditions coexisted at least partially, and Ionian poets adapted Aeolic formulae while both traditions flourished; or a *phase model*, where the Aeolic tradition preceded the Ionic tradition, and Ionian poets adopted the Aeolic tradition wholesale to create a new Ionic tradition from scratch.[35] In the phase model, archaisms and Aeolisms are one and the same thing.

---

[34] First: though -εω does appear in Homer in places where it is impossible to reconstruct *-ᾱ' (11× before a consonant, 8× at line-end), more often it appears before a vowel, where *-ᾱ' is possible (38×). These counts exclude occurrences before trace consonants such as *w* or *s*, and bisyllabic -εω on Βορέω/βορέω < *βορέαο. Second: unlike the elided form *-ᾱ', Ionic -εω could in principle be treated as a short syllable by correption (shortening before a vowel in the following word); yet correpted -εω appears only once in extant hexameter, at *Hymn. Hom. Aphr.* 148: Ἑρμέω ἐμὴ (there Ἑρμέω must be interpreted as a relatively recent adaptation of Ἑρμείω). Third: though the possibility of reconstructing *-ᾱ' is moderately common in Homeric formulae, in non-Homeric hexameter -εω continues to appear but *-ᾱ' can *never* be reconstructed; this suggests that cases of possible *-ᾱ' in Homer are relatively archaic contexts.

[35] For the phase model: Janko 1982: 89–93; Haug 2002: 151–8. Diffusion model: Horrocks 1997: 212–17; Jones 2011; Nikolaev 2013.

### Excursus: a-stem genitives and the phase model

This debate is esoteric, but we shall look at one problem here, as a taster for readers interested in going down the rabbit hole. Readers whose eyes are already glazing over may want to jump ahead to page 71.

One key piece of evidence that is frequently cited in favour of the phase model is the treatment of *a*-stem genitive endings, mentioned above. The original proto-Greek ending was *-ā(h)o*, and Aeolic *-āo* is close to this. In early Ionic, however, *-ā(h)o* came to be pronounced *-ǣo*; over time *ǣ* merged with *ē*, producing the ending *-ēo*; and the vowel lengths were transposed – a process called quantitative metathesis – resulting in the form we see attested, monosyllabic *-eō*. If an Ionian epic tradition had existed at the time when Ionic still had *-ǣo/*-ēo*, then we should expect extant hexameter to display some remnants of that period in the form of formulae with the ending written *-ēo* (*-ηo). But only *-āo* and the post-metathesis Ionic form *-eō* appear. This implies the existence of a period when there was no epic tradition in Ionic, only in Aeolic: the Aeolic phase.

This argument has been challenged in various ways. Horrocks and Jones point out that some old pre-metathesis Ionic forms do appear in Homer in other contexts: we see στείομεν (< *στᾱ́ομεν) and νηός (< *νᾱϝός) alongside the metathesized forms στέωμεν and νεός/-νεως.[36] Jones also demonstrates inconsistencies in the treatment of other Aeolic *ā* vowels: sometimes they are left as α, as in the ending on νεφεληγερέταο 'cloud-gatherer'; at other times they are updated to η, as in νεφελη- in the same word, or in some Aeolic verb forms such as συλήτην.[37]

Jones's argument raises the worrying prospect that the whole business might be more a matter of orthographic conventions than of dialects. The letters η (eta) and ω (omega) did not exist in Archaic and early Classical Athens: prior to 404 BCE, Athenian copies of the *Iliad* would have begun

*μενιν αειδε, θεα, Πελειαδεο Αχιλεος

*Sing, goddess, of the wrath of Peleus' son Achilles*

In this predicted orthography there is no visible difference between the vowels in the *a*-stem ending on Πελειαδεο and the *e*-stem ending on Αχιλεος. There is also no difference between a metathesized Ionic ending and a modernized Aeolism: *Πελειαδεο could represent either Πηληϊάδεω (the text as transmitted) or the older form *Πηληϊάδηo.[38] Orthodox opinion has it that the εω/ηo distinction existed in the 'original' Ionic texts of Homer. But it is sometimes suspected that our text of the Homeric epics – and,

---

[36] Haug, in Finkelberg 2011b: i.9, rejects these examples on the grounds that the vowels sit astride the boundary between stem and ending, and this might have delayed the metathesis.

[37] As Jones 2011 observes, dual forms of alpha-contracted verbs are regularly treated this way. Alpha-contracted duals do not appear at all in non-Homeric early hexameter.

[38] If the ending was originally *-η' with the omicron elided, the omicron would still have been written: prior to the Hellenistic era elided vowels were normally written explicitly.

perhaps, other hexameter poems – is the product of a systematic transliteration from the most prestigious copies from the classical period, the Athenian texts.[39] This hypothesis is known as the 'metagrammatism' or 'metacharacterism' theory. It is conjectural in Homer's case, but we can guarantee that this process did take place with Attic authors such as Aeschylus and Sophocles. It is possible that the εω/ηο distinction came about as a result of such a transliteration; and that the distinction was not introduced with the aim of distinguishing between different *dialects* but between different *syllabifications*.

On this hypothesis, where older Athenian texts had *εο, later editors systematized the orthography depending on the poetic rhythm. On bisyllabic ◡◡, εο was retained. On monosyllabic —, the orthography was changed to εω by analogy with monosyllabic –εω in contemporary Ionic.[40] And on bisyllabic — ◡, -αο was adopted, using Aeolic orthography where possible because *-ηο no longer existed in Ionic.[41]

Yet –ηο did not die out everywhere. The Central Ionic dialect of Naxos preserved a distinction between *ǣ* and *ē* up until the late sixth century BCE, without metathesis: the Naxians used η for *ǣ*, and ε for both *ē* and *ĕ*. One famous verse inscription, the 'Nikandre inscription', has as its second line (*CEG* 403, *c.*600 BCE)

ϙόρη Δεινοδίϰηο τō Νᾱhσίō ἐhσοχος ἀλήōν

*daughter of Deinodikes of Naxos, far above the others*

This gives two instances of monosyllabic -ηο-, exactly the missing link that ought not to exist in the phase model. In 'standard' epic orthography the line would run

*κούρη Δεινοδίϰεω τοῦ Ναξίου ἔξοχος ἀλλῶν

Another verse inscription, *CEG* 405, shows that this orthography was retained into the late 500s. So a Naxian text of the *Iliad* would have written the first line

*μενιν αειδε, θεη, Πελειαδηο Αχιλεος

*Iliad* 21.86 is a good candidate for this standardization theory:

Ἄλτεω, ὃς Λελέγεσσι φιλοπτολέμοισιν ἀνάσσει

*of Altes, who rules over the war-loving Lelegians*

---

[39] Reece in Finkelberg 2011b: ii.514–15.

[40] Incidentally, this would also destroy all evidence of bisyllabic *-ηο where the omicron was written but elided (see also n. 36 above).

[41] The biggest exception is the word ἕως 'while, until'; but ἕως is anomalous no matter how we look at it. Its spelling implies iambic ◡ — (1× Homer), yet its actual rhythm is usually trochaic — ◡ (21× Homer; 1× non-Homeric at *Little Il.* fr. 32.13 Bernabé); cf. ἕως monosyllabic — (3× Homer), εἵως spondaic — — (23× Homer; 2× non-Homeric at *Hymn. Hom. Aphr.* 225, *Shield* 378). *ἦος only appears as a modern emendation. In sixth- and fifth-century Athens, ἕως, εἵως, and *ἦος would all have been written *heος. One wonders whether ἕως was adopted rather than *ἦος so as to avoid confusion with hος (Athenian for ὅς); both are common at line beginnings. See also Janko 1994: 17–18.

Conventionally the -εω of Ἄλτεω is regarded as a metathesized Ionism: it cannot represent an elided \*-α᾽ since it is followed by a trace consonant (\*ϳός). But the manuscripts show variation between Ἄλτεω, Ἄλταο, Ἄλταω (!), and Ἄλτεο;[42] line 85 has Ἄλταο (— — ⌣); and 86 has a cluster of other Aeolisms (-εσσι, πτολέμο-). This is an ideal place for conjecturing an Athenian orthography of -εο, representing bisyllabic \*-άεο in 85, monosyllabic \*-άεο in 86, and where confusion over the most appropriate orthography led to inconsistency in Hellenistic editions.

Note also the following cases, all with difficult syllabification for Hellenistic editors: *Il.* 5.60 (Ἁρμονίδεω; -αο in one manuscript), 5.534 (Αἰνείεω vulgate; frequent variants -είω, -είαο; -εία᾽ Leaf), 8.16 (Ἀΐδεω; -αο Plutarch and one manuscript), 20.484 (Πείρεω; -εως Zenodotus and several manuscripts; -εος in two manuscripts), *Od.* 3.181 (Τυδείδεω; -αο, -εως in one manuscript each), all difficult because followed by trace consonants such as *w*; and *Il.* 16.554 (Μενοιτιάδεω; -αο vulgate), difficult because of the ambiguous metrical value of the following syllable.[43] These variants are distributed across multiple critical editions.[44]

A conjecture is not proof, of course, and the treatment of *a*-stem genitives is not the only pillar supporting the phase model (though it is an important one). The theory that poems in Ionic were transliterated from the Athenian alphabet is disputed. West strongly rejects the idea that orthographic standardization in the Hellenistic Period was 'a hazardous throw in which any ε or o was liable to be mistaken for η or ω';[45] still, the orthographic alterations suggested here are not haphazard, but an extremely systematic standardization.[46] Horrocks regards the Naxian treatment of η in *CEG* 403 as evidence of conservative orthography, not of conservative pronunciation;[47] yet it is hard to imagine conservatism in orthography at such an early date. Either way, however much we trust or doubt the extant spelling conventions, there is continuing debate on the question of the phase model versus the diffusion model.

Linguists believe that in a few phrases it is possible to see glimpses of formulae even older than the Aeolic and Arcado-Cypriot layers. The phrase *kleos aphthiton* ('unfading glory') was mentioned in Chapter II. That could possibly go back to Indo-European origins: if so, it is a piece of poetry from the Neolithic Age. That is a very exceptional case.

More proximate, though still very ancient, is a group of phrases which are thought to date to a time when an early form of the Greek language still retained a syllabic *r̥* sound, that is, *r* treated as a vowel. This phoneme existed in Proto-Indo-European, but died out in most Indo-European languages except for Sanskrit and the Slavic languages.

[42] Leaf 1902: 391 (Leaf chooses Ἄλτα᾽).
[43] Janko 1994: 385.
[44] *Iliad*: Leaf 1902; Monro and Allen 1920; M. L. West 1998–2000. *Odyssey*: Allen 1917–19.
[45] M. L. West 1978: 61, with a bibliography of other suggestions relating to early orthography.
[46] See also Haug, in Finkelberg 2011b: i.117–18, on sporadic vs. systematic Atticisms.
[47] Horrocks 2010: 39.

The Homeric phrases in question are either unmetrical or metrical only by an extraordinary analysis, such as Ἐνυαλίῳ ἀνδρειφόντῃ '(like) man-slaughtering Enyalios' (5× *Iliad*); or else 'corrected' versions of phrases that would be unmetrical if pronounced normally, such as νὺξ ἀβρότη 'immortal night' (1× *Iliad*) for the more standard, but unmetrical, pronunciation *νὺξ ἀμβρότη. In their original forms these would have been perfectly metrical:

Ἐνυαλίῳ ἀνδρειφόντῃ        < *Enūwaliōi anṛk$^{hw}$ontāi ($\smile$ — $\smile\smile$ — $\smile\smile$ — —)
νὺξ ἀβρότη < *νὺξ ἀμβρότη     < *nux amṛtā (—$\smile\smile$ —)

with ṛ serving as a short vowel in both phrases. These reconstructions are guaranteed by other considerations: for example, the -*mṛt*- of *amṛtā* 'immortal' is cognate with Latin *mort*- ('death').

These archaic phrases do not appear in early hexameter outside Homer. They are probably pre-Mycenaean in origin: syllabic ṛ had already been lost in the Mycenaean dialect attested in Linear B tablets from the Late Bronze Age.[48] In principle, syllabic ṛ might have survived longer in a proto-Aeolic dialect independent of Mycenaean: though Mycenaean is the only Greek dialect attested from the Bronze Age, it was not the only dialect being spoken. The ancestor dialect(s) of both Aeolic and Ionic must have co-existed with Mycenaean. However, the balance of probabilities favours linking Mycenaean and proto-Aeolic in this case, since we see the transformation *ṛ > *or, ro* (as in *amṛt- > *ἀμβρότ-) in both Mycenaean and Aeolic. In Ionic the transformation was *ṛ > *ar, ra*, so we can guarantee that formulae with those spellings were never used in Mycenaean, and must have come from Ionic or proto-Ionic: for example ἧπαρ ὑπὸ πραπίδων 'in his liver beneath the midriff' (3× *Iliad*; perhaps < *ēk$^w$ṛ supai k$^w$ṛpidōm?).

The origin of the hexameter itself, as a verse form, is another matter of ongoing debate. This topic is even more obscure and intractable. One area of disagreement is whether or not the hexameter has its origins in Indo-European metre. Indo-European metres are characteristically *isosyllabic*: that is, they rely on a particular number of syllables per line. This describes Aeolic poetry nicely. But the hexameter is

---

[48] M. L. West 1988: 156–9; Horrocks 1997: 201–3; Latacz 2004: 259–67.

*isochronic*, with pervasive use of contraction: that is, the practice of substituting — for ⏑⏑.

West and Nagy have nonetheless suggested isosyllabic origins: West, in a combination of two cola, a hemiepes and a paroemiac (— ⏑⏑ — ⏑⏑ — plus ⏒ — ⏑⏑ — ⏑⏑ — ⏒); Nagy, in a pherecratic with dactylic expansion (⏒ ⏒ — ⏑⏑ — ⏑⏑ — ⏑⏑ — ⏑⏑ — ⏒). Both are based ultimately on the Aeolian glyconic metre. West's model, with its versatile ⏒ after the break, successfully predicts formulae of the kind we saw earlier, adapted to both the 5 + 7 and 5½ + 6½ colometries, but does not predict the other common colometries that we see in hexameter, nor the development of bridges (positions in the line where colon-end, and therefore word-end, is avoided); Nagy's model arguably accommodates many colometries and bridges that we see in Homer, but is not so comfortable in explaining why the same features are not preserved in the lyric metres that he cites as parallels. Neither explains the origin of contraction very elegantly (that is, — for ⏑⏑). Barnes follows Fränkel and Porter in favouring a four-colon model, which is undoubtedly the most general way of describing the pattern of colometries that we see in hexameter, but is so general and versatile that it is purely descriptive: it has no power to explain the origins of those cola or the forces driving their development. Hoekstra advocates abandoning research on the hexameter's origin altogether, and insists that only synchronic analysis makes sense. Ruijgh interprets the intractable nature of the problem as evidence that the hexameter must not originate in isosyllabic metres after all: it must have come to the Mycenaeans from a non-Greek isochronic poetic tradition, perhaps poetry of the Minoan culture of Bronze Age Crete.[49]

That is hardly the last word on the subject. The more common view is that the hexameter was originally isosyllabic, though the process of its derivation is disputed. This topic is devilled by the complexity of the formulaic system and the versatility of the colometric system. It is all too easy for a theory to gloss over inconvenient details. Purely statistical or automated analysis of metrical formulae and colometry should be the basis for a genuinely objective discussion; to date, however, only

---

[49] M. L. West 1973a; Nagy 1974: 49–102; Barnes 1986; Hoekstra 1981: 33–45, esp. 38–9; Ruijgh 2011: 257–8. See also Edwards 1986: 174–88 for a review of older literature on Fränkel's four-colon model.

a handful of attempts at automated analysis have been made, most of them very narrow in scope or deeply flawed.[50] For the time being the prehistory of the epic tradition is, if not totally obscure, at least very much open to doubt and debate.

---

[50] Successful: Andrews 2005: 15–19. Less successful: Mansilla and Bush 2002; Eder 2007; Papakitsos 2011.

## IV PERFORMANCE

Archaic hexameter poetry could be declaimed by a rhapsode; in some circumstances it could also be sung or chanted to the accompaniment of a lyre. Beyond that we know disappointingly little about performance practices or about the social context of performance. Even Homer is only a partial exception. We know that Homeric epic was performed competitively at the Great Panathenaea festival in Athens, but that was not its only possible setting and we have no reliable evidence at all about its original setting. With Hesiod we know even less. We must make do with isolated snippets of information and hints. This chapter cannot offer many answers: only present what relevant information is available and indicate which kinds of guesses are reasonable ones.

### 1. Musical instruments

Within the poems themselves, performers are normally portrayed singing and accompanying themselves on a lyre. A singer is an *aoidos*. The instrument is referred to interchangeably as either a *kitharis* or a *phorminx*, or, on one occasion, a *lyrē* (*Hymn. Hom. Herm.* 423). The verb for playing the instrument is usually *kitharisdō* (1× Homer, 12× non-Homeric), sometimes *phormisdō* (4× Homer, 1× non-Homeric). The mythic archetype for all these instruments is the tortoiseshell lyre invented by Hermes in the *Hymn to Hermes* (24–54). The *Hymn*, probably dating to *c.*500 BCE, describes it as having a soundbox fashioned from a tortoise shell supported by reeds and a leather backing, two outstretched arms with a crossbar, and seven sheep-gut strings; it is played with a plectrum.

By the classical era these terms consistently referred to distinct instruments. The *kithara* was the most prestigious, a large lyre used by professionals in competitive performance. The *phorminx* was a smaller bowl-lyre, associated with leisure and the revel (*kōmos*); by the classical period it was considered antiquated and was being superseded by the *barbitos*, a newer lyre with longer arms and a deeper tone. The tortoiseshell *chelys* or *lyra*, with its small, jury-rigged soundbox, would have had a soft tone and was associated with amateur aristocrats; like the *barbitos*, it was used by women as well as men.[1] In each case the instrument was held in the left hand and played with the right, using the left to mute strings as needed. Musicians may also have used the left hand to create higher-pitched notes, as is common on modern string instruments, with a light touch at harmonic positions along the strings.[2] The *kithara* was played in a standing position because of its size, secured against the shoulder by a strap around the left wrist; the others could be played sitting or standing. Each instrument was regularly used for a wide variety of genres.

Stylized pictorial evidence from the eighth century shows lyres with only three or four strings. That may be only an artistic convention: certainly by the seventh century lyres regularly had seven strings. At that time, according to later (and inconsistent) traditions, the semilegendary musician Terpander supposedly increased the number of strings from four to seven.[3] Later innovations added more strings.

In the earliest period the instrument played more or less in unison with the singer, reinforcing the voice and clarifying the melodic line;[4] the voice would presumably take on the burden of ornamentation. We are told that instrumental passages without singing were first introduced by the dithyrambic poet Crexus, probably a contemporary of Philoxenus and Timotheus (that is to say, in the late fifth century BCE).[5] Our sole surviving musical score for a hexameter poem, a Hellenistic-era hymn from Epidaurus addressed to (probably) Asclepius, shows that in later times instrumental passages could be played between hexameter lines.[6]

Performances of Homeric poetry at the Great Panathenaea, by contrast, were the province of rhapsodes, who are shown with no musical instrument in sight and instead hold a staff (*rhabdos*; the word is not related to *rhapsōidia* ['song-stitching'] but associated by wordplay).[7] It

---

[1] For more details on these instruments see M. L. West 1992: 49–59; Landels 1999: 47–68; Bundrick 2005: 14–26.

[2] On technique see M. L. West 1992: 64–70; Landels 1999: 55–61.

[3] Terpander test. 1, test. 16, fr. 6 Campbell; Plin. *HN* 7.204. But cf. test. 14 (Terpander changed the tuning, not the number of strings); test. 17 (Terpander added only one string); ps.-Plut. *De mus.* 1137b (Terpander's music had only three notes).

[4] Ps.-Arist. *Pr.* xix.918b.7–8 weighs against the idea that the lyre played at a different octave: as an example of an instrument playing at the (lower) octave he cites the φοῖνιξ, rather than one of the standard lyres.

[5] Ps.-Plut. *De mus.* 1141b.

[6] M. L. West 1992: 279, 287–8.

[7] Ps.-Pl. *Hipparch.* 228b–c; Lycurg. *Leoc.* 102; Dionysius of Argos *FGrH* 308 F 2; Dieuchidas of Megara *FGrH* 485 F 6. See Burgess 2004 on possible rhapsodic performance of the Epic Cycle.

follows that we cannot be confident that any particular poem was originally sung. In Homer, performances are always musical, but in Hesiod the narrator holds a staff, unmistakeably a rhapsode (*Theog.* 30–1): yet both use the same verb for what the performer does, *aeidein* ('sing'). Pindar lumps rhapsodes and singers together, calling the Homeridae *rhaptōn epeōn…aoidoi* ('singers of stitched hexameters'; *Nem.* 2.2). Later sources tend to confine sung hexameter to hymnic poetry, especially that of Terpander. Heracleides of Pontus mentions that Terpander set Homeric poetry to music for competitions, implying that he thought it was not sung previously; Plato calls Homer's character Phemius a rhapsode, even though Phemius uses a lyre.[8] Xenophanes composed not only hexameter but also elegiac and iambic poetry, yet we are told that he performed his own work rhapsodically.[9] There is a significant possibility that the musician-performers whom we see in Homer are just a poetic convention, representing an imaginary past that never really existed.

## 2. Rhythm

We know the basic rhythm of hexameter performance thanks to the evidence of the hexameter itself (see p. 63): it is a march-like rhythm with six beats and a regular *dum-diddy-dum-diddy* riff. Ancient theorists called the alternate hemipedes *thesis–arsis* ('placement–lifting') or *katō–anō* ('downward–upward'). These terms refer quite literally to downward and upward movement, a performer beating time with his feet, to judge from descriptions of musicians doing exactly that in Quintilian and other ancient sources.[10] For rhapsodes, the obvious way of establishing a regular beat would be the traditional staff. In modern terms, *thesis* and *arsis* translate to downbeat and upbeat.

In some performance contexts – we do not know which – there may have been a rhythmic irregularity that ancient theorists referred to as 'irrational' (*alogon*). This term did not indicate a truly mathematically irrational ratio of note lengths, but just that a rhythm did not fit

---

[8] Heracleid. fr. 157 Wehrli (ps.-Plut. *De mus.* 1132b–c); Pl. *Ion* 553c.

[9] Xenoph. fr. A 1 §18 (ἐρραψῴδει τὰ ἑαυτοῦ).

[10] Quint. *Inst.* 1.12.3 ('even the foot is busy with keeping a regular time'), 9.4.55 ('the beat of fingers and feet'). See M. L. West 1992: 133–7, esp. 133 nn. 13, 14. Terentianus Maurus 1345 is more metaphorical ('[a metrical foot] lifts the sound in one part, puts it down in the other').

comfortably into the most commonly recognized types.[11] Dionysius of Halicarnassus, citing unnamed rhythmicians on the subject, tells us that in dactylic rhythm two short syllables occupy a slightly longer time than one long, and that the ratio between them is 'irrational'.[12] But other ancient testimony is against him. The fourth-century-BCE theorist Aristoxenus categorizes dactylic rhythm as *en isōi logōi* ('in equal ratio'), as do other sources;[13] and Dionysius contradicts himself elsewhere, speaking of 'irrational' dactyls as a rushing of tempo, not a slowing.[14] Moreover, Dionysius' initial observation is confined to just two rhythmic units, the dactyl (— ⌣⌣) and an obscure foot called the 'cyclic anapaest'. It follows that 'irrational' time in dactylic rhythm was hardly universal. So Dionysius' comment about the 'irrational' dactyl probably refers to an unevenness caused by semi-musical chanting as opposed to natural language or formal song: in English, too, quasi-spoken musical forms such as Anglican chant or hip-hop have strongly characteristic rhythms, different both from spoken language and from one another.

We can be confident that there were breaks in rhythm between lines, as in modern improvised verse forms.[15] Some pieces of evidence for this are the indifferent length of the last note in each line; the fact that there are no hypermetric metrical features (that is to say, sound combinations at line-end); and the (late) testimony of the Epidaurian hymn to Asclepius, mentioned above, which has an instrumental phrase between each line.

But it is debated whether there were any breaks between cola within a line. On the one hand, pauses between cola would (1) violate the regularity of the dactylic beat (on which see above); (2) create hypermetric instability because of the shifting placement of pauses in successive lines; (3) obstruct all metrical features based on sound combinations between adjacent words, namely elisions, correptions, and closed syllables; and (4) be physically unnecessary, since trained singers are accustomed to much longer phrases on a single breath than untrained

---

[11] Aristox. *Rhythm.* 22.27–8 Pighi (2.20 Barker): irrational time is between 1 : 1 and 2 : 1 time; Aristid. Quint. 1.(§14).34: irrational rhythms 'do not fit comfortably into any of the ratios specified above'.

[12] Dion. Hal. *Comp.* 17 (71.4–72.2 Usener–Rademacher).

[13] Aristox. *Rhythm.* 24.16 Pighi (2.30 Barker); Maurus 1409 (the dactyl 'balances the time in the *arsis* with the *thesis*'; similarly 1350 of the spondee); Aristid. Quint. 1.(§15).35 (rhythms called dactylic because of their ἰσότης ['equality']).

[14] Dion. Hal. *Comp.* 20 (93.6–16 Usener–Rademacher).

[15] Daitz 1991: 151–3; Danek and Hagel 1995: 6–8.

singers. On the other hand, Andrews has shown that 'overlength' (an excess of phonemes) is more common in syllables at colon-end than elsewhere, implying a slightly more protracted phonation.[16] Ancient testimony is mixed. Quintilian tells us that rests occur 'within metre', *inania...in metris*; but he also speaks of a continuous flow of *arsis* and *thesis* (Latin *sublatio* and *positio*) until the end of each line.[17] The earliest surviving account of caesuras in hexameter – that of the Roman-era theorist Aristides Quintilianus – gives no hint about their impact on performance practice.[18] Then there is the bizarre system of punctuation devised for Homer by the second-century-CE grammarian Nicanor (nicknamed *stigmatias*, 'the punctuator'): Nicanor mandates pauses of varying lengths after nearly every phrase, including quadruple-length pauses after every sentence end, vocative, or interjection.[19] Protracted silences of that kind are unrealistic, especially in view of the 'equal' time that Aristoxenus and other theorists associate with dactylic rhythm. However, it is perfectly reasonable to imagine a moderate rubato in accordance with Andrews' findings.


### 3. Pitch and melody

If hexameter poetry was performed musically – and that is a big 'if' – then the sound of its music becomes a legitimate object of inquiry. Our evidence on the tuning of ancient Greek music is very fragmentary prior to Aristoxenus in the late fourth century BCE.[20] In extant Greek musical theory the basic unit of tuning was not the octave (as in modern Western music) but the tetrachord, a group of four notes with an interval between the outer notes that we would call a perfect fourth (a frequency ratio of $4:3$). There were various different systems for tuning the inner notes of each tetrachord, depending on both mode (Lydian, Dorian, Phrygian, and so on) and temperament, or tuning. Aristoxenus distinguished three temperaments: 'diatonic', 'enharmonic', and 'chromatic'. These systems were not confined to the pitches used in modern Western music but made heavy use of what we would call microtones,

---

[16] Andrews 2005: 9–24.
[17] Quint. *Inst.* 9.4.51, 9.4.55. Quintilian's *inania* probably refer to strict caesuras in non-hexameter metres, such as in the middle of the pentameter: thus Landels 1999: 115.
[18] Aristid. Quint. 1.(§24).47.
[19] Sch. on Dion. Thrax, 26–8 Hilgard; see also Daitz 1991: 150.
[20] See Barker 2007: 19–104 on what may be inferred about Aristoxenus' predecessors.

especially in the enharmonic and chromatic tunings favoured by fifth-century musicians. Fifth-century music made many other innovations too, but we cannot delve into that complex subject here.[21]

Aristoxenus believed that the enharmonic was the most recent temperament, invented by the semi-mythical melic poet Olympus, and that earlier music was diatonic or chromatic.[22] Modern musicologists tend to believe that the diatonic was originally the norm.[23] But ancient diatonic tuning was not the same as in modern tonal music. If we trust the detailed report in Claudius Ptolemy's *Harmonics*, we can plot the exact intervals in the diatonic tetrachord as tuned by several ancient theorists.[24] The earliest of Ptolemy's theorists is Archytas, a Pythagorean and a contemporary of Plato. Table 1 converts these intervals to the corresponding number of semitones in the modern equal temperament system. If Aristoxenus is right, and Olympus' music was indeed based on the notes *mesē*, *parhypatē*, and *hypatē* tuned diatonically, still the interval between the lower two notes may have been anywhere between half a semitone and well over a semitone.

As mentioned above, our only musical score for hexameter poetry comes from a Hellenistic-era hymn, after the musical revolution of the fifth century. For what it is worth, in that score the same melody is repeated in each line, and there is an instrumental phrase between each line. We cannot know how far back these practices go. There may possibly be clues in the nature of the language itself. All words in Archaic Greek, except clitics, had a pitch accent: that is, one vowel pronounced at a higher pitch than the rest of the word. In written Greek from the Hellenistic period onwards, base pitch is shown either unaccented or with a *bareia* ('grave') diacritic; high pitch, with an *oxeia* ('acute'); and, on some long vowels, a high pitch descending towards base pitch, marked with a *perispōmenē* ('circumflex').

A study by Danek and Hagel (1995) uses the pitch accent of the spoken language to attempt to reconstruct melodic contours in poetry. Their first starting observation is that, in normal voice production in languages with a pitch accent, pitch does not change instantaneously but climbs and descends over the course of a word, phrase, and sentence. The pitch of successive high-pitched syllables tends to descend

[21] For recent treatments see Landels 1999: 86–109; Barker 2007; Hagel 2009.
[22] Ps.-Plut. *De mus.* 1134f–1135b.
[23] Hagel 2009: 10, with n. 35.
[24] For commentary on Ptol. *Harm.* 2 see especially Mathiesen 1999: 451–77.

Table 1. Intervals in the ancient diatonic tetrachord

| | Archytas | Aristoxenus, 'soft' | Aristoxenus, 'tense' | Eratosthenes | Didymus | Ptolemy, 'soft' | Ptolemy, 'tense' | Ptolemy, 'even' |
|---|---|---|---|---|---|---|---|---|
| *mesē* to *lichanos* | 2.039 | 2.490 | 1.992 | 2.039 | 2.039 | 2.312 | 1.824 | 1.824 |
| *lichanos* to *parhypatē* | 2.312 | 1.494 | 1.992 | 2.039 | 1.824 | 1.824 | 2.039 | 1.650 |
| *parhypatē* to *hypatē* | 0.630 | 0.996 | 0.996 | 0.902 | 1.117 | 0.845 | 1.117 | 1.506 |

Intervals are expressed in equal-temperament semitones to three decimal places. Derived from Ptol. *Harm.* 2. (§14).73–4. Two of Ptolemy's own temperaments ('tonic' and 'ditonic') are omitted because they duplicate others shown here. *Mesē, lichanos, parhypatē,* and *hypatē* are the names of four notes in a tetrachord, going from high frequency to low frequency. Each tetrachord adds up to 4.980 semitones, not 5, because a true perfect fourth corresponds to 4.980 equal-temperament semitones.

over the course of a phrase. This means that melodic contours can be conjectured for musical phrases longer than a single word. Their second observation is that some extant Greek musical scores – but not all – show a good correspondence between pitch accent and musical pitch. They adopt the following additional assumptions: (1) the lyre had four strings; (2) the *perispōmenē* is a melisma sung on two notes, the second lower than the first; and (3) a word's natural pitch-contour persists even when it has the *bareia* accent, with the result that the *bareia* is not a total cancellation of high pitch but rather a reduction, intermediate between base pitch and high pitch. Based on these, their reconstruction of a basic outline of a four-note melody follows naturally and systematically.[25]

Danek and Hagel do however point out that this type of reconstruction is heavily stylized: it is a skeletal structural analysis, not an *obbligato* melody. They are also agnostic about the tuning of the strings. There are a few additional caveats to bear in mind. First is the four-stringed lyre: by the seventh century, seven strings were standard. Another is that Dionysius of Halicarnassus famously reports at one point that the *oxeia* accent is typically about a fifth higher than base pitch,[26] but that interval does not fit into a single tetrachord. Lastly, while some extant musical scores observe pitch accent carefully, that is hardly universal. Dionysius states that 'words are subordinate to melodies, not melodies to words', and cites an example in Euripides (*Orestes* 140–2) where the melody runs counter to the natural pitch accents; many extant musical scores do the same.[27] In the Epidaurian hymn to Asclepius, pitch accent was simply ignored: every hexameter has the same melody. The study of the relationship between pitch accent and colon boundaries is of great interest and is likely to yield further results, but even a systematic reconstruction like that of Danek and Hagel has to be treated as mostly speculative.

---

[25] Andrews 2005: 2–9 makes many similar observations, but does not attempt to pin pitch contours down to a musical melody.

[26] Dion. Hal. *Comp.* 11 (40.17–41.1 Usener–Rademacher).

[27] Dion. Hal. *Comp.* 11 (41.18–42.14 Usener–Rademacher); for extant scores, see M. L. West 1992: 283–326. Some egregious early examples: no. 3 West (Eur. *Or.* 338–44), a low note on the second syllable of ματέρος; no. 4 (Eur. *IA* 784–92), a descent of nearly an octave onto the second syllable of πατρίας; and possibly no. 7 (p.Cair.Zen. 59533), descending lines on ἑτάρων and γονάτων. The main exemplars where melody and pitch accent do go hand in hand are late: nos. 12–13 West, second century (these also include melismata on syllables with *perispōmenē*).

## 4. Performance context

For some readers, the romantic icon of the early hexameter poet is Achilles singing of the 'glories of men' in front of his tent (*Iliad* 9.185–91). According to this view, the earliest performances were private, an aristocrat singing to himself or to an intimate companion. But that is just one possibility: we can hardly take it as typical.

Starting in the sixth century BCE, competitive performance of Homeric epic was instituted as a regular part of the Great Panathenaea festival at Athens.[28] Gregory Nagy has laid particular emphasis on a cultic and festival context for Homeric performance, as part of his argument that cult and the apparatus of cult are integral to the progressive pan-Hellenization of the two major epics.[29] Not many poems fit that mould, of course.

A few do, however. Musical contests were a fixture of many Greek religious festivals; the question is which other hexameter poems were fixtures. One Attic vase shows a rhapsode performing the line 'Even so once in Tiryns...'.[30] This line, attested nowhere else, could be the opening of an epic about Bellerophon, who went to Tiryns; it might perhaps be a line from the Homeric *Thebaid*, since the expedition against Thebes set out from nearby Argos. Whatever it is, a non-Homeric hexameter in the mouth of a rhapsode performing in Athens implies that the poetry performed at the Panathenaea was originally 'Homeric' poetry understood broadly, not just the *Iliad* and *Odyssey*. The *Hymn to Demeter* almost certainly had some role in the Eleusinian cult of Demeter and Kore: the hospitality scene where Demeter is welcomed into the house of Keleos (98–230) is an enactment of the religious rite of *Theoxenia*, where a divinity is welcomed into a house and has a place set for a feast; and some elements of the *Hymn* provide 'just so' stories for elements of Eleusinian cult, notably the *kykeōn* or initiatory potion (206–11), the mock battle or *ballētys* (263–7), and Demeter's teachings about the afterlife that awaits initiates (473–84). The *Hymn to Apollo* represents itself as being performed at the Delia festival (151–76), and a plausible case has been made that

---

[28] See n. 7 above.

[29] Nagy 1996: 39–43, 2009: 9–28.

[30] BM E 270, Attic, Cleophrades Painter, *c.*490–480 (='Homer' unplaced fr. 1 West). It is conceivable that the 'rhapsode' might be singing, accompanied by an *aulistēs* on the other side of the vase; but, taken together, his staff and the hexameter imply rhapsodic performance.

the combined Pythia–Delia of 523 BCE, celebrated on Delos by Polycrates, was the occasion when Cynaethus first performed a combined Delian–Pythian hymn to Apollo.[31] Thucydides shows that musical contests at Delos had ceased by his time (3.104.5).

Agonistic performance is a closely related form. This refers to a more direct, personal style of competition. We could compare it to medieval 'flyting', but a better way of capturing its immediacy is to think of modern American freestyle rap battles, like those depicted in the hit film *8 Mile* (2002). Agonistic poetry was not only a matter of being judged best in a line-up of performances, like those at the Great Panathenaea and the ones alluded to in some poems;[32] it could also be an aggressive face-to-face contest. In the *Contest of Homer and Hesiod*, the two poets compete to display their virtuosity in answering each other's riddles, giving moral aphorisms, and completing seemingly incompletable lines, as in these exchanges (*Contest* 9):

ὡς οἳ μὲν δαίνυντο πανήμεροι, οὐδὲν ἔχοντες
— οἴκοθεν, ἀλλὰ παρεῖχεν ἄναξ ἀνδρῶν Ἀγαμέμνων.

δεῖπνον δειπνήσαντες ἐνὶ σποδῶι αἰθαλοέσσηι
— σύλλεγον ὀστέα λευκὰ Διὸς κατατεθνειῶτος
— παιδὸς ὑπερθύμου Σαρπηδόνος ἀντιθέοιο.

(Hesiod:) *So they feasted throughout the day with no food—*
(Homer:) *Of their own; it was provided by Agamemnon, lord of men.*

(Hesiod:) *After making their feast among the sooty ashes—*
(Homer:) *They collected the white bones of the dead one, Zeus'—*
(Hesiod:) *Proud son, the godlike Sarpedon.*

This material is attested relatively late, but it seems to be representative. One source has Lesches, the poet of the *Little Iliad*, as the judge of the contest; one mentions another poetic duel, between Lesches and Arctinus; a third mentions duels, or at least poetic attacks, made by Syagrus upon Homer, and Cercops upon Hesiod.[33] Two early sources give vivid depictions of an agonistic poet choking on stage (an immediate loss in modern battle raps). In one exchange between two legendary seers in the Hesiodic *Melampodia*, Mopsus answers a riddle so well that

---

[31] Burkert 1979; M. L. West 1999: 376–82.
[32] *WD* 654–7; *Hymn. Hom. Ap.* 165–73; *Hymn* 6.19–20.
[33] Plut. *Conv. sept. sap.* 154a (Hes. test. 38); Phaenias *FGrH* 1012 F 10; Diog. Laert. 2.46.

'the sleep of death shrouded Calchas' (fr. 214). And a poetic duel between Thamyris and the Muses ends when the Muses 'in anger made him maimed, and took away his wonderful voice and made him forget his *kithara*-craft' (*Il.* 2.599–600). This last, with the reference to anger, sounds very like a battle where the participants 'diss' one another, competing in wit and semi-improvised insults: the 'maiming' is not divine vengeance for Thamyris' audacity but Thamyris choking because he has been successfully dissed.[34]

More peaceful is the idea of the court poet. Phemius and Demodocus in the *Odyssey*, and Apollo and the Muses in the *Iliad*, perform in the halls of great lords: the houses of Odysseus, Alcinous, and Zeus, respectively.[35] There they entertain the leisured nobles and their guests while they feast and dance. These poets are revered public figures and an integral part of aristocratic society: Phemius keeps company with the herald Medon, and Odysseus spares him in the slaughter of the suitors;[36] Demodocus is greatly honoured in Alcinous' hall. We should be sceptical of these images, and of the responses they get from their audiences, since they are authorial self-insertions: they are not-so-subtle hints at how real poets ought to be treated. The self-insertion is clearest in the case of Demodocus, who, like the Homer portrayed in the mythical biographies, is blind.[37] And the hints had some success: certainly tyrants such as Polycrates, Hipparchus, and Hieron gave great favour to Anacreon, Simonides, Pindar, and others. But there is no evidence of any historical hexameter poet enjoying a comparable status.[38]

It is best to interpret these Homeric scenes as self-aggrandising versions of sympotic performance. The symposium was an integral part of early and classical Greek aristocratic life. It combined communal eating, drinking, games, poetry, and sex. It bound together male social groups culturally and politically, and provided a forum for personal

---

[34] Also comparable in hexameter are the face-offs in Theoc. *Id.* 5, 6, ps.-Theoc. *Id.* 8, 9, and the pairs of songs in Theoc. *Id.* 7, 10. Pretagostini 2006: 57–61, following Serrao, believes we can be confident in a historical reality behind Theocritus' singing contests (though that would not imply any link to earlier agonistic contexts); Gutzwiller 2006: 17–18 sees instead a literary model, Euripides' lost *Antiope*.

[35] Phemius: *Od.* 1.150–5, 1.325–52, 17.358–9, 23.130–6, 23.143–7. Demodocus: *Od.* 8.62–92, 8.254–389, 8.470–522. Apollo: *Il.* 1.601–4, 24.62–3; *Shield* 201–3.

[36] *Od.* 16.252, 22.330–80.

[37] *Od.* 8.62–4; see also Introduction, pp. vii–viii.

[38] Xenophanes may possibly have been a guest of one of the Sicilian tyrants: Diogenes Laertius states that he visited Sicily (Xenoph. fr. A 1§18), and his lifetime overlapped with Gelon's reign.

and social education as well as entertainment. Poetry was an important feature. Clay is sufficiently struck by certain passages in the *Hymns* to suggest that hymns, theogony, and heroic narrative may originally have been performed in a sympotic context.[39] Irwin points out that the 'tribe(s) of women' named as the subject of the *Catalogue* (fr. 1.1) are a theme of sympotic poetry, and interprets the poem as posing a question about who the 'best' women in the present would be. More fundamentally, she argues that the *Catalogue*'s ethos of sexual activity and its conception of social stratification – some women and men are the 'best' – mesh well with a sympotic ethos: 'As early as line 4, the poet undresses his female subjects' (*mitras allysanto*, 'they loosened their girdles'), and in line 6 he proceeds to talk about feasts and who gets to sit with whom.[40] And Murray sees the *Odyssey* (but not the *Iliad*) as pervasively flavoured by a sympotic setting.[41]

The *Hymn to Hermes* only reinforces the impression of the symposium as a central theme.[42] Here is the first-ever performance of hexameter poetry (*Hymn. Hom. Herm.* 54–61):

θεὸς δ' ὑπὸ καλὸν ἄειδεν

ἐξ αὐτοσχεδίης πειρώμενος, ἠύτε κοῦροι
ἡβηταὶ θαλίηισι παραιβόλα κερτομέουσιν,
ἀμφὶ Δία Κρονίδην καὶ Μαιάδα καλλιπέδιλον,
ὡς πάρος ὡρίζεσκον ἑταιρείηι φιλότητι,
ἥν τ' αὐτοῦ γενεὴν ὀνομακλυτὸν ἐξονομάζων·
ἀμφιπόλους τε γέραιρε καὶ ἀγλαὰ δώματα νύμφης
καὶ τρίποδας κατὰ οἶκον ἐπηετανούς τε λέβητας.

[Hermes] sang beautifully to [the lyre], impromptu, experimentally, as young men at dinners (*thaliai*) make ribald interjections: (he sang) about Zeus son of Kronos and fairshod Maia, how they used to talk love in companionable intimacy, and declaring his own renowned lineage. He also celebrated the servants of [Maia], and her splendid home, the tripods disposed about it and the unending cauldrons.

Hermes' first song evokes men at a symposium, and also imitates standard hexameter forms, complete with a hymnic prelude to Zeus, a praise poem, and a genealogy. His second song (418–33) is even clearer:

---

[39] Clay 1989: 7.

[40] Irwin 2005a: 40–9, citing Semonides fr. 2 and Phocylides fr. 2 on 'tribes of women'.

[41] Murray 2008 (note the helpful survey of views on Homeric performance at 161–4).

[42] However, see Johnston 2003 on possible links between the *Hymn* and the Hermaia festival, and between Hermes' cattle raid and initiation songs: 'Public recitation of myth, then, almost functions as a ritual itself, as listeners negotiate the tensions that the myth expresses' (170).

there, a hymnic prelude to Memory is followed by a theogony that organizes the gods into social strata, honouring them 'according to seniority
and affiliation', exactly the kind of stratification that we associate with
the aristocratic symposium. Apollo, impressed, compares the invention
of the lyre to the idea of passing things to the right at feasts (454). In
turn Hermes gives him the lyre as a present and portrays it as a *hetaira*
at a symposium: he instructs Apollo to '[t]ake her confidently to the
banquet (*dais thaleia*) and the lovely dance and the bumptious revel
(*kōmos*)', and advises that 'If one questions her with skill and expertise,
she speaks all kinds of lessons to charm the fancy' (482–8).

# V FRAGMENTS

We have lost much more early hexameter poetry than we have intact. We possess a certain amount of information about the lost poems, and even quotations from them, but only in a minority of cases: for the most part, we do not possess any fragments of their text. In several cases where a poem is attested by only a single source, we cannot even be certain that it really existed.

Even when a poem is lost, if it can be partially reconstructed by compiling pieces of fragmentary evidence from disparate sources, we may end up with enough of a basis for thinking about it as a poem. There are special problems, however. Often we have no way of knowing where and how a given fragment fits into the poem; even if we do, there is no guarantee that the fragment is representative of the poem as a whole. The fewer and sparser the fragments, the more hazardous it is to guess at what the poem was really like.

So it regularly happens that fragments convey little information in their own right. However, the surviving fragments of some hexameter poems are full enough for us to make intelligent guesses about how the poems worked, and even how they influenced other writers. This chapter offers some suggestions on how to approach these partially salvageable poems: the *Catalogue of Women* and the epics in the Epic Cycle. Together, their fragments amount to well over 1,500 lines. The surviving fragments of the *Catalogue* alone are much more substantial than, say, Hesiod's *Works and Days*, even though the latter has survived intact.

## 1. Introduction to fragments

When we open an edition of a fragmentary poem, we will find three basic types of fragments: (a) testimonia, (b) quotations, and (c) papyrus fragments.[1] A very few editions will also include (d) 'vestigial fragments', where there is inadequate evidence, or only indirect evidence, to tie a fragment to the poem with certainty.

---

[1] For an overview of best practice in critical editions of fragmentary poems, see M. L. West 1973b: 95–7.

(a) **Testimonia** are pieces of information about the poem gleaned from surviving ancient authors. For example, if Pausanias' *Periegesis* (*Guide to Greece*) happens to report something about the *Cypria* in passing, that becomes a testimonium to the *Cypria*.

(b) **Quotations** occur when surviving ancient authors give us the exact wording of the lost poem. There are many reasons why an author might quote a few lines; for example, an ancient scholar writing a commentary on a surviving text may quote passages for parallels or for contrasts. One particularly rich source of quotations is Athenaeus' *Deipnosophistae* (*Scholars at Dinner*), which portrays a long conversation between dinner guests who often quote old poems to each other.

(c) **Papyrus fragments** are the most direct of all, since they are actual ancient editions of the lost poems; but they are also the most tantalizing, since they tend to be very badly damaged. A few papyrus fragments of the *Catalogue of Women* contain more than a hundred lines each, but much of the text is missing because the papyrus is eroded or torn. Very many papyrus fragments consist of only a few letters. However, even when a papyrus is badly damaged, it can often be supplemented in various ways. If it overlaps with a quotation in a surviving ancient author, gaps can be filled in with certainty. Otherwise, modern editors have some deduction work to do; as this type of supplement is open to disagreement, different editions will often print different supplements.

It is important to recognize straightaway that, while the *Catalogue of Women* is very richly represented in papyrus fragments, few other hexameter poems are – at least, so far as we can currently tell. We have pieces of almost as many separate papyrus copies of the *Catalogue* as of the *Theogony* and *Works and Days* put together, showing that the poem was extremely popular in Roman-era Egypt.[2] There are also many hexameter papyrus fragments that have not been reliably identified. In contrast, we do not have a single papyrus of any Cyclic epic.[3] That does not necessarily mean that Roman-era readers had stopped

---

[2] See p. 14 n. 41.

[3] A few papyri have been found that contain new testimonia and quotations of Cyclic epics: *Aethiopis* fr. 2 (see also fr. 1 with M. L. West's note, 2003a: 115 n. 21; for detailed discussion see M. L. West 2001: 283–5); *New Jacoby* 18 F 1–2, a mythographic text (F 1=*Little Il.* arg. 2 Bernabé); two references in Philodemus' works (*Alcmaeonis* fr. 7, *Cypria* fr. 2); and, recently discovered, p.Oxy. 5094, a reference to the *Cypria* in connection with the grammarian Demetrius of Scepsis and with one Dymas (probably Hecuba's father).

reading the Cyclic epics altogether, but it does indicate a very great dis-
parity in popularity.[4]

(d) **Indirect fragments** and **vestigial fragments**. I use these terms
here to refer to cases where a text preserves information that may be
derived from a given lost text, but where there is no direct evidence
for attribution. Indirect fragments are ones where there is a close
enough match with a well-attributed fragment that a reliable link is
forged. Even then there can still be dangers, but these are usually fairly
secure. Indirect fragments are usually testimonia (direct quotations
tend to have better attributions in ancient authors); but a large propor-
tion of the papyrus fragments of the *Catalogue of Women* also relies on
indirect links.

In the case of vestigial fragments, no external evidence survives to
complete the link, meaning that there is no definite evidence for an
attribution. As the name suggests, vestigial fragments do not normally
appear in critical editions: careful editors tend to include fragments
only when there is good evidence for the attribution. However, there
can be exceptions, depending on a variety of factors. We shall turn to
the problem of vestigial fragments in the last part of this chapter.

A well-constructed edition of a fragmentary text will present the following information.

(a) There will usually be two sections headed **Testimonia** and
**Fragments**. In this case, 'Testimonia' means reports about the
poem's author and about the poem as a whole; this information is
the main basis for our conclusions about authorship, performance history, date, and so on. There will usually be testimonia in the
'Fragments' section too, but those will relate to specific episodes within
the poem.

(b) Each testimonium and fragment will be headed with a **number**
by which to cite it. Readers and scholars may cite items in the
'Fragments' section as fr. 1, fr. 2 (or F 1, F 2), etc.; and the
'Testimonia' section as test. 1 (or T 1), etc. An exception is the fragments of Xenophanes, Parmenides, and Empedocles: for them, the
standard Diels–Kranz numbering uses A 1, A 2, etc. for testimonia,
and B 1, B 2, etc. for fragments. The arrangement and numbering of
fragments is the editor's responsibility and changes with each new

---

[4] See also pp. 25–6 on the loss of the Cycle. The papyrus that contains *Little Il*. fr. dub. 32 Bernabé
is probably too late to be Cyclic.

edition, either because of new discoveries about the poem's structure or because of scholarly disagreement.

The *Catalogue of Women* and the Epic Cycle both exist in several different editions, each with a different numbering, and this naturally causes confusion. So editions will normally contain an index – the *comparatio numerorum* – that cross-references the fragment numbers in the present edition to those of older editions. If confusion is possible, one should cite the name of the editor for maximum clarity: thus '*Cat.* fr. 204 M–W' is shorthand for the *Catalogue of Women*, fragment 204 in the edition by Merkelbach and West. Sometimes it is desirable to cite multiple editions: for example '*Cat.* fr. 204 M–W = 155 M', where M refers to the Loeb edition edited by Most.

(c) The fragment's **source** will appear next to the fragment number. In the cases of testimonia and quotations, this will be a surviving ancient text; in the case of papyrus fragments, it will be a papyrus catalogue number. Papyrus collections are usually designated by the place where they are currently held, or by the archaeological site where they were found: 'p.Lond.' refers to papyri held in London, while 'p.Oxy.' refers to papyri found at Oxyrhynchus in Egypt.

(d) The **context** for the fragment will normally appear in small type, especially if the fragment is a quotation. This is done to give the reader an idea of the ancient writer's knowledge of the passage, and intent in quoting it. Papyrus fragments, by their nature, have no context, so there will be no small type. Testimonia are effectively *all* context and *no* text, so they may be printed entirely in small type.

(e) Finally, the surviving **text** from the poem (if any) will be given in full-size type. In papyrus fragments, editors try to supplement gaps in the papyrus where it is possible to do so reliably; such text should be printed in square brackets, both in the Greek text and in the translation. There are other elaborate conventions that editors follow in the Greek text for papyri, but we do not need to go into those here.[5]

## 2. Examples of fragments

To put all of this in some context, let us look at a couple of examples. First, a fragment from West's Loeb edition of epic fragments. The following comes from the *Little Iliad* (West 2003a: 128–9):

---

[5] See M. L. West 1973b: 77–98 for a detailed guide to the standard conventions.

**5 Schol. (T)** *Il.* 16.142, 'ἀλλά μιν οἶος ἐπίστατο πῆλαι Ἀχιλλεύς'

οἱ δὲ πλάττονται λέγοντες ὡς Πηλεὺς μὲν παρὰ Χείρωνος ἔμαθε τὴν χρῆσιν αὐτῆς, Ἀχιλλεὺς δὲ παρὰ Πηλέως, ὁ δὲ οὐδένα ἐδίδαξεν. καὶ ὁ τῆς Μικρᾶς Ἰλιάδος ποιητής·

> ἀμφὶ δὲ πόρκης
> χρύσεος ἀστράπτει, καὶ ἐπ' αὐτῶι δίκροος αἰχμή.

**5 Scholiast on the *Iliad*, 'only Achilles knew how to wield it [Achilles' spear]'**

Some tell the fictitious tale that Peleus learned the use of it from Chiron, and Achilles from Peleus, and that he taught nobody else. The poet of the *Little Iliad* says:

> *About it a collar*
> *of gold flashes, and on it a forked blade.*

As the heading indicates, this is *Little Iliad* fr. 5 in West's numbering; and the fragment comes from scholia – ancient glosses and commentaries – on the *Iliad*. The parallel Greek text gives detailed information on its source: the fragment is from the T collection of scholia, and the gloss relates to *Il.* 16.142, 'only Achilles knew how to wield it'. Below the heading is the context, in smaller print, where the ancient scholiast explains the story of how Achilles learned to use the spear; finally, the scholiast quotes a line and a half from the *Little Iliad*.

From this we gain the following information:

(a) The fragment is a *quotation*.

(b) From the context we can infer that Achilles' spear appeared in the *Little Iliad*; and that the lines quoted refer to the spear.

(c) Both the context and the quoted lines give some information about the spear as depicted by the *Little Iliad* poet.

(d) As to the lines' *context in the original epic*: there we enter the realm of deduction and conjecture. In an ideal world, we would consult a modern commentary to see what the editor has to say about the fragment. But modern scholars have not written many commentaries on fragmentary texts – there is not a huge market for them – and, where commentaries do exist, they are very often in languages other than English. In the following section we shall look at some tactics that a diligent reader might follow.

For a second example, we turn to a fragment from Most's edition of Hesiodica. The following comes from the *Catalogue of Women* (Most 2007: 110–11):

47 [73 MW; *2 H] P. Lond. 486c, P. Oxy. 2488B

ἢ' οἵη Σχ[οινῆος ἀγακλε]ιτοῖο ἄνακτος
παῖς εἰκυῖα θεῆι]σι ποδώκης δῖ' Ἀταλάν[τη
        Χαρί]των ἀμαρύγματ' ἔχο[υσα
πάντων ἀνθρώπων ἀ]παναίνετο φῦλον ὁμιλ[εῖν
ἀνδρῶν ἐλπομένη φεύγ]ειν γάμον ἀλφηστάων[.
                ]τανισφύ[ρ]ου εἵνεκα κού[ρης
        ] αμ[         ]γον εννε[
                ] [ ]ρδ[


47 London papyrus


Or like her: [the very glorious] lord [Schoeneus'
daughter, like the goddesses,] swift-footed godly Atalanta
        ] possessing the Graces' radiance
she refused to associate with the tribe [of all human beings
hoping to escape] marriage [with men] who live on bread
        ] for the sake of the long-ankled maiden
                ][
                ] [

So we may see that this is *Cat.* fr. 47 in Most's numbering. It comes from two papyri, one held in London, the other found at Oxyrhynchus. The translation mentions only the London papyrus: the Oxyrhynchus papyrus adds little new text, but matters for other reasons, as we shall see below. In the Greek text, Most cross-references the fragment to fr. 73 in the critical edition by M(erkelbach) and W(est) and fr. *2 in H(irschberger)'s critical edition.

After the heading we plunge directly into the text: papyrus fragments do not come with any context. To compensate for this, Most has provided a convenient heading prior to the fragment (not reproduced above), which introduces the present group of fragments: *Atalanta, Daughter of Schoeneus, Athamas' Other Son by Themisto (Book 2, Lines 1ff.)*.

Within the text we see several square brackets: some encircle phrases, others mark off blank areas. These represent the edges of the papyrus scrap. Where the text has been supplemented, it is not normally

mere guesswork: missing text can often be deduced from our knowledge of the stories and characters involved (hence the supplement of
'Schoeneus' in the first line); by grammatical necessity; or by repeated
formulaic phrases (in the Greek text, 'possessing the Graces' radiance'
is missing parts of 'Graces' and 'possessing', but the formula is a common one and there is no doubt about the wording). But different editors are more or less adventurous about supplementing the text. In
comparison with other editions of the *Catalogue*, Most is relatively daring (while still keeping his feet planted firmly on the ground), on the
principle that an expert opinion is better than none at all.

So we may infer the following:

(a) The fragment is a *papyrus fragment* from an ancient edition of the
poem.

(b) Most's headings, and the reference to Atalanta in line 2, tell us
that this is part of the story of Atalanta.

(c) We may infer some points about the *Catalogue*'s Atalanta narrative, if we look at the text in conjunction with the subsequent fragments
and the story as known from other sources. This fragment tells us about
Atalanta shunning human company and hoping to escape marriage –
rather like Euripides' Hippolytus. This in turn sets the scene for the
athletic competitions mentioned in other accounts: Atalanta's hopeful
suitors fail to defeat her in a race and so are executed, until
Hippomenes comes along and uses a trick to defeat her and marry her.[6]

Going beyond this point requires more in-depth research. In this
case, comparison of critical editions will show that Merkelbach and
West, Hirschberger, and Most all print different texts for this fragment.
For the purposes of gaining an acquaintance with the poem such differences can often be ignored: close comparison is only necessary if one
wants to put weight on the fragment as evidence in an argument. But
these differences sometimes have an impact on how and where the editor places the fragment. Here, Most has accepted a conjectural connection between the end of fr. 46 and the start of fr. 47; that is his basis for
identifying this as the start of Book 2, and for his inclusion of the text
'Or like her...' at the start of the fragment (the other editions leave the
first half of line 1 blank).[7] Moreover, Most assigns the fragment to the
*Catalogue* partly because of its content (the story of Atalanta) and partly
because one of the two papyri – p.Oxy. 2488B – comes from the same

---

[6] See especially ps.-Apollod. *Bibl.* 3.9.2 (though there the winning suitor's name is Melanion).
[7] For the conjectural connection see Most 2007: 109, bottom; cf. M. L. West 1985: 67.

manuscript as p.Oxy. 2488A, which contains part of *Cat.* fr. 82; in this he follows Merkelbach and West. This is therefore an 'indirect fragment', according to the definition given above. Hirschberger, however, relegates the fragment to 'fragments of unknown poems' (ἀδήλων ἐπῶν): partly because some details lead her to doubt that p.Oxy. 2488A and 2488B are parts of the same text, and partly because of her beliefs about other fragments that deal with the Atalanta story.[8] The balance of probabilities favours Most, but new evidence could in principle prove Hirschberger right one day.

If these details seem tiresome, we should be the more thankful for these scholars' efforts to piece all this information together. The whole point of their editions is to make sure that other readers do not *need* to go into as much depth.

### 3. How to approach a fragmentary text

The second example above illustrates that a fragment taken in isolation is often very unclear. The best guide to understanding a fragment and its place in a poem is an acquaintance with the other fragments in the poem. This naturally means a great deal more labour, and it does not always work: sometimes the information is just too sparse to make anything of it. That is unfortunate but unavoidable. Knowledge does not come cheap. Sometimes no amount of research will help: the information may be lost forever. The following suggestions may make the process slightly easier for apprentice researchers.

(a) Although older editions are often freely available online, make sure to use a recent edition where possible. For the *Catalogue*, in particular, no-one should ever use the old Loeb edition of the Hesiodica by Evelyn-White (1914): so much new information has come to light in the last century that it is utterly obsolete in every way.

(b) If your edition contains an introduction and subheadings, these will give a good impression of how the editor imagines the fragmentary text, and will help explain the decisions he or she has made. An introduction may help explain why edition A includes such-and-such a fragment while edition B does not.

(c) Go through the fragments making rough notes on any structures and patterns that you can see. This is especially important where

---

[8] See Hirschberger 2004: 458–9; D'Alessio 2005: 213–16.

subheadings are not provided. For example: in West's edition of the
*Returns*, several of the fragments report on various mythological and
genealogical details that have nothing to do with the Greek heroes
returning from the Trojan War. Fr. 3 is about Tantalus, fr. 4 about
Clymene and her father, Minyas, fr. 5 about Maira and her father,
Proitos, and so on. At fr. 10 we start to see references to the story
of Agamemnon's homecoming; so the problematic sequence is frs.
3 to 9. The reader should make notes on this pattern and then examine
this group in the light of the other fragments to try to infer why the
editor has arranged the fragments in this way.

The answer is not long coming. Prior to this group, fr. 1 informs us that
the *Returns*, like the *Odyssey*, contained 'mention of Hades and the terrors
in it'; and fr. 2 mentions that 'the Cyclic poets' used the term *nekades* to
refer to 'the souls of the dead'. Careful note-taking on this material should
lead straight to the appropriate conclusion: the *Returns* contained an
Underworld episode, like the one in *Odyssey* 11, which incorporated a catalogue of the souls of legendary figures of the past, as witnessed by some
hero (we do not know who); frs. 3 to 9 must come from this catalogue.[9]

(d) In the specific cases of the Epic Cycle and the *Catalogue*, extra
tools are available to assist the reader in reconstructing the shape of
the poems. The idea is to draw up a masterplan on a separate sheet:
with this in hand, the reader will find it easy to annotate the plan
with indications of particularly interesting fragments.

In the Epic Cycle, Proclus' summaries should be the basis for drawing up a masterplan. With a list of episodes laid out down one column,
the reader will often find it possible to place fragments in their correct
spot. Take, for example, the *Little Iliad* fragment quoted earlier.
Proclus' summary makes it clear that Achilles ought to be dead before
the start of the *Little Iliad*; so the question should naturally follow, what
is the occasion for mentioning his spear? Further reading will show that
the answer lies in one of the following passages in Proclus.

The awarding of the armor takes place, and Odysseus gets it in accord with Athena's
wishes...

And Odysseus fetches Neoptolemus from Scyros and gives him his father's armor...

---

[9] See further Davies 2001: 80–1; Burgess 2001: 142–3; Marks 2010: 10. Davies 2001: 82–3
disputes the attribution of fr. 3 (=fr. 9 Davies) to the Underworld episode. Burgess thinks that
the omission of the episode in Proclus' summary may be a result of a Hellenistic edition that systematically cropped overlapping epics; we shall revisit this disputed theory in chapter VI.

Here we have two contexts in which the spear might easily be described: 'armour' is a rendition of *hopla* ('arms', including weapons). It is *possible* that the lines appeared in some other context, but these two episodes are such a good fit that the reader can be quite confident in this conclusion. West's ordering of the fragments indicates that he thinks that the spear description belongs most easily in the first episode; but an intelligent reader could perhaps find grounds for debating the point.

In the case of the *Catalogue*, Most's helpful section headings can serve as the basis for the episodes that the reader will list down one column of a separate sheet. The resulting list would look like this:

Book 1
Proem (Book 1, lines 1ff.) – fr. 1
The descendants of Deucalion – fr. 2 to fr. 10.24
    Deucalion's children: Pandora, etc. – fr. 2
    Thyia's sons – fr. 7
    Magnes' sons – fr. 8
    Hellen's sons: Dorus, Xuthus, Aeolus – fr. 9 to fr. 10.24
The descendants of Aeolus – fr. 10.25 to fr. 71
    Aeolus' children – fr. 10.25–34
    Perimede's children – fr. 10.35–57
(etc.)

It would, of course, take several sheets to include *all* of Most's subheadings. As an alternative, see the much less exhaustive list in Chapter I, which highlights some of the most interesting episodes.

### 4. Vestigial fragments

Early hexameter poetry, especially the *Catalogue* and the Epic Cycle, is deeply preoccupied with legendary narratives; but much of what we know about these legends comes from later sources, and often without source attributions. Later reports of legends undoubtedly include information that is derived in one way or another from the lost poems, but we have no way to tell when they are doing so. Commentaries could discuss this material – where the commentaries exist. As things stand, this invisible testimony is doomed to hover outside the margins of our editions as vestigial fragments.

Editors of fragments are on the whole a cautious bunch, and require reasonably high standards of evidence for attribution. Best of all is an explicit attribution; next best is an 'indirect' fragment, where there is sufficient overlap with a 'solid' fragment to conclude that it is more than a vestige. And there is no doubt that this is the correct course to follow. The other way lies pure speculative madness. However, even the best editors are willing to make exceptions sometimes. M. L. West's Loeb edition of the *Homeric Hymns* assigns substantial papyrus fragments to the *Hymn to Dionysus* (*Hymn* 1) that do not appear in older editions, even though there is no solid evidence to connect them to the *Hymn*.[10] And Alberto Bernabé's edition of the Orphic fragments classifies each fragment as T (testimonia), F (fragments of text), or V (vestigial fragments).

The issues are especially pronounced with legendary material in a group of mythographic texts – that is to say, compendia of myth – which mostly date from the first century BCE to the second century CE.[11] (There were other mythographers writing outside this time frame, of course.) One such text, the *Library* of pseudo-Apollodorus, is especially important: it is our chief guide to the structure of the genealogies in the *Catalogue of Women*, and its account of the Trojan War is so close to Proclus' summaries that West, in his edition, splices the two together as a single text.[12]

So pseudo-Apollodorus can be accepted as legitimate testimony, at least sometimes, even though explicit evidence is missing. But what about the *Fabulae* of pseudo-Hyginus? In the *Fabulae* some Trojan War episodes are very similar to what we find in Proclus; others are quite different.[13] Then there are Conon (Augustan-era) and Ptolemy the Quail ('Ptolemaios Chennos', first century CE), both of whom are more eclectic and who survive only as summaries in Photius' *Myriobiblon*;[14] Philostratus' *Heroicus* (third century); several late lexicographers and encyclopaedias that replicate some of the same material; and, most mysterious of all, the *Ephemeris* of Dictys of Crete (late first or early second century), a semi-novelistic prose account of the

---

[10] M. L. West 2003b: 26–31. Faulkner 2011b: 10 outlines reasons for doubting the early dating of the papyrus text.

[11] See Cameron 2004 for a general guide to Roman-era mythography.

[12] West has his opponents in this: see Davies 1986: 100.

[13] *Fab.* 90–127. See Smith and Trzaskoma 2007: xlii–xliv on pseudo-Hyginus' authorship and date (both are unknown).

[14] Conon: *New Jacoby* 26 (Phot. *Myr.* cod. 186, 130.ii.24–142.ii.14). Ptolemy the Quail: Phot. *Myr.* cod. 190, 146.i.40–153.ii.29.

Trojan War that has links to several of the authors already named but departs from the tradition in other respects.[15]

Let us take an example of an indirect fragment as an illustration. It seems that *Little Iliad* fr. 11 was the basis for a proverbial phrase, 'Diomedian compulsion'. Pausanias' *Collected Attic Words* reports the story as follows:

> Others say that Diomedes and Odysseus were on their way back from Troy at night after stealing the Palladion, and Odysseus, who was behind Diomedes, intended to kill him; but in the moonlight Diomedes saw the shadow of his sword, turned round, overpowered Odysseus, tied him up, and forced him to go ahead by beating his back with his sword.

Pausanias does not indicate his source. The mythographer Conon tells a slightly different version of the story, adding a few details, and with one important difference: it is Odysseus who beats Diomedes on their way back to the ships, not *vice versa*.[16] Again there is no attribution. It is only Hesychius' *Lexicon* that provides a direct link:

> 'Diomedian compulsion': a proverbial expression....The author of the *Little Iliad* connects it with the theft of the Palladion.

But Hesychius' report is also the most sketchy. Which is closer to the Cyclic epic, Pausanias' account or Conon's? Other late sources side with Pausanias; and our summary of Conon may be in error through missing a pronoun. So, for now at least, Pausanias is the winner. Even so, caution is needed: if we look at the full text of Pausanias we see that he also links the proverb to a totally unrelated story, about the Thracian Diomedes compelling guests to sleep with his daughters.

Let us now consider a true vestigial fragment, a story that has no substantiated link to an early poem. In Book 6 of Ptolemy the Quail's *New History*, as summarized by Photius, we find the following intriguing snippet:[17]

> [Ptolemy writes] that when Priam came to Achilles to supplicate him and beg for the bones of Hector, Andromache and her sons came along with him.

---

[15] Dictys is best known through the 'Latin Dictys', translated from the lost Greek original by L. Septimius in the third or fourth century CE; the standard edition is Eisenhut 1973. However, several other independent witnesses are also available. The original was written sometime between 66 CE and *c.*150 CE (Gainsford 2012b: 59–60).

[16] Conon, *New Jacoby* 26 F 1 §34 (Phot. *Myr.* cod. 186, 136.ii.36–137.i.26). M. L. West 2003a: 132–3 n. 40 gives a summary (including explanatory comments not in Photius' text).

[17] Phot. *Myr.* cod. 190, 151.ii.57–152.i.1.

This is obviously non-Homeric: in the *Iliad*, Priam visits Achilles' tent unaccompanied, making his daring all the more astonishing to Achilles and his men, and Andromache and Hector have only the one son, Astyanax.[18] Has Ptolemy made it up? If not, where does it come from?

One candidate is Aeschylus' lost *Lytra* or *Ransom of Hector*. Unfortunately, we know almost nothing about that play. If it belongs to the period when Attic tragedy featured only two actors it is unlikely to be Ptolemy's source, since two speaking parts are already accounted for by Priam and Hermes/Achilles. A more likely possibility is the Cyclic *Aethiopis*. Proclus' summary of the *Aethiopis* opens after the end of the *Iliad*, with the arrival of Penthesileia; but there is good evidence that the Cyclic epic actually overlapped with the *Iliad* and included the ransom and funeral. Some Roman-era 'Homer cups' depict a triptych of scenes (implying that they belong to a single narrative) showing (a) the ransom, (b) Priam and Penthesileia at Hector's grave, and (c) Achilles and Penthesileia in battle.[19] Weitzmann has independently interpreted a second-century-CE sarcophagus lid from the Villa Borghese as evidence that the *Aethiopis* included Hector's funeral.[20] And *Aethiopis* fr. 1 (three lines linking Hector's funeral to Penthesileia's arrival) appears to be a quotation from within the *Aethiopis*; it is certainly not the *start* of the poem, so again an overlap is indicated.[21]

Things get more complicated when we compare another account of the ransom, found in Philostratus' *Heroicus*:[22]

[Homer] says that Achilles died at the hands of Paris and Apollo; he seems to have known the business at the Thymbraean [temple]...As for the sacrifice of Polyxena on his grave, and everything you hear from the poets about his love, it was like this. Achilles fell in love with Polyxena and was negotiating for her marriage to him, on condition that the Achaians withdraw from Ilion. And Polyxena loved Achilles too, and they saw each other at the ransom of Hector; for when Priam came to Achilles, he made his daughter lead him by the hand...

This is a remarkable passage. The story of the human sacrifice of Polyxena at Achilles' grave goes back to the Cyclic *Iliou persis*, and

---

[18] *Il.* 24.358–676, 6.399–403, 6.466–83, 24.723–39.

[19] *Aethiopis* test. 11 Bernabé (omitted by Davies 1988 and M. L. West 2003a, presumably because an explicit attribution is lacking). Kopff 1983 forcefully argues that the triptych reflects the Amazonian part of the epic faithfully; see Burgess 2001: 140–1 for further discussion of the cups' validity as evidence.

[20] Weitzmann 1959: 42–7.

[21] See pp. 120–2.

[22] Philostr. *Her.* 51.1–4.

was repeated often. But the earliest datable source to refer to a *romance* as such is Seneca the Younger's *Troades*, and even there it is not actually enacted but a posthumous union intended by Achilles' ghost, contradicting the more traditional story of Achilles marrying Medea in the afterlife.[23]

Pseudo-Hyginus includes the Polyxena romance too. However, we do not know the date of his *Fabulae*; worse, his account of Achilles' death is closer to an episode in the *Iliad* than to anything we know of the *Aethiopis*.[24] Finally, there is the Latin version of Dictys of Crete, which portrays the ransom with both Andromache *and* Polyxena alongside Priam; and Andromache brings her *two* sons, Astyanax and Laodamas.[25] Dictys therefore lies at the centre of this problem.

It is not certain what has happened here. Philostratus might have adapted the whole thing from Dictys; but Philostratus cites his source as 'poets' (Dictys was prose). In view of that, it is conceivable that Polyxena's role has its origins in Sophocles' lost *Polyxena*, or something of the kind. My own reading of the situation is that Philostratus refers to 'poets' as sources for the romance but not for the ransom. Polyxena's involvement in the ransom would then originate with Dictys. And, indeed, Philostratus matches Dictys in a few other respects: not least, the setting of Achilles' death at the temple of Thymbrian Apollo, rather than at the gates of Troy. Pseudo-Hyginus, too, has connections to Dictys: both *Fab.* 110 (the romance with Polyxena) and the following *Fab.* 111 (Hecuba's transformation into a dog) are closer to Dictys than to any other surviving account.[26] Note that this interpretation would make pseudo-Hyginus later than Dictys, which is not the conventional view.

But we lack direct evidence, so the question over Andromache is not an open-and-shut case. Her role in the ransom, and the presence of her

---

[23] Sen. *Tro.* 938–44. For Medea see Ibycus fr. 291, Simonides fr. 558 *PMG*.

[24] Romance: *Fab.* 110; death of Achilles: *Fab.* 107. In the latter there is no mention of Memnon; Apollo assumes the guise of Paris and kills Achilles, echoing his assumption of Agenor's identity to deceive Achilles in *Il.* 21.595–22.24.

[25] Latin Dictys 3.20–7; cf. Malalas 5.24–5 Thurn, Cedrenus 224.4–225.3 (each of these texts is derived, at least semi-independently, from the lost Greek Dictys).

[26] Hecuba's transformation in the Chersonese, an aetiology for the placename *Kynossema* ('dog's grave'), appears as early as Eur. *Hec.* 1265–74; cf. Thuc. 8.104.5. But only in pseudo-Hyginus and Dictys is this aetiology combined with the story of her being awarded as captive to Odysseus: see ps.-Hyg. *Fab.* 111; Dictys, witnessed in p.Oxy. 4944 lines 9–21, Cedrenus 232.11–16, *Suda* κ.2722, and the '*Odyssey* hypothesis' (Dindorf 1855: 4, lines 4–9). The parallel is not apparent in the Latin Dictys (5.15) because of a mistranslation: see Gainsford 2012b: 78. In ps.-Apollod. epit. 5.24 it is Helenus, not Odysseus, who takes Hecuba to the Chersonese.

two children, are attested in Ptolemy the Quail and in Dictys, and nowhere else – though the Borghese sarcophagus, mentioned above, may hint at Andromache's involvement.[27] It is distinctly possible that Dictys reflects the *Aethiopis* reasonably closely in these respects; indeed, it would follow that the opening episodes of the *Aethiopis* – Hector's death, ransom, and funeral – are likely to have gone along much the same lines as Dictys' account, which is dominated by non-Homeric elements in each of these episodes.[28] But not with respect to Polyxena: the Achilles–Polyxena romance is best explained as something new, a novelistic trope that did not exist prior to Dictys.

The relationships between all of these sources, mythographic and otherwise, have been explored for some time, but nowadays they are somewhat under-studied. Erich Bethe argued that a single mythographic handbook, dating to the first century BCE, was responsible for the legendary material in the historian Diodorus of Sicily, as well as in Proclus, pseudo-Apollodorus, and pseudo-Hyginus.[29] Albert Hartmann, who explored other mythographic sources relating to Odysseus' death, claimed to have rediscovered a Hellenistic mythographic text – not necessarily Bethe's handbook – by collating further miscellaneous texts: Hartmann's texts follow a distinctive pattern of referring, in the same sequence, to (a) the Telegonus story; (b) a prophecy from Aeschylus' lost *Psychagogoi*; and (c) an Italian folktale where a witch transforms Odysseus into a horse and keeps him until he dies in old age.[30]

Such concoctions are delightful in their own right, but this kind of *Quellenkritik* ('source analysis') is now, regrettably, considered old-fashioned. More recently Davies, following Wagner and Severyns, has fiercely argued against Bethe's thesis. However, he overshoots his aim: his objection is really to the fact that Bethe thought Proclus

---

[27] Weitzmann 1959: 45: following Penthesileia's arrival is a scene of Andromache holding Hector's ashes and being consoled by Paris. The identification of the seated female figure as Andromache is not perfectly certain, and it could in principle be Hecuba (thus Moreno and Stefani 2000: 85); but Andromache is far more likely.

[28] Latin Dictys 3.15–4.2. It is also possible that the *Iliad* is competing against an older version of the ransom with Andromache present: the *Iliad* is oddly emphatic about Priam's aloneness, as De Jong observes (2012: 168).

[29] Bethe 1887: 80–99; the idea appears repeatedly in Bethe's later work.

[30] Hartmann 1917: 37–8. The texts are schol. V on *Od.* 11.134, Sext. Emp. *Math.* 1.267, and Servius auct. on *Aen.* 2.44. The Italian setting of the folktale emerges in a further appearance in Ptolemy the Quail, at Phot. *Myr.* cod. 190, 150.i.12–19 (which also links the story to an ancient textual-critical debate over *Od.* 11.134). Hartmann 1917: 1–43 serves as an excellent introduction to these texts in the context of mythography generally.

interfered with his source, whatever that source may have been, and Davies makes a good case that Bethe was wrong about this. However, that has no bearing on the question of whether Proclus was working from a Hellenistic mythographer, as Bethe thought, or directly from the Epic Cycle, as Davies thinks.[31] Most recently, Alan Cameron has examined the sources for various mythographic or mythographic-style texts; while he accepts that a chain of influences and cross-influences may exist, he is basically agnostic about its recoverability.[32]

We must not be too cynical about the efforts of Bethe and Hartmann. Their work was flavoured with an enthusiasm inspired by the successes of the physical sciences in the late nineteenth century, which gave humanists the sense that they could use scientific method-ologies to recover almost anything about the ancient world that they wanted. That is certainly over-optimistic, but cynicism is not the cor-rect response. We can simply be more realistic. There is no doubt that Bethe's and Hartmann's *Quellenkritik* was onto something. The question is what that something was, and what an improved form of their methodology would look like.

---

[31] Davies 1986: 104–9, 2001: 7; see also Wagner 1892; Severyns 1938–63 vol. 3. Burgess 2001: 25–30 summarizes the debate.
[32] Cameron 2004, especially 33–51.

# VI RELATIONSHIPS BETWEEN POEMS

The first part of this final chapter outlines some modern scholarship on the ways in which ancient poems and poetic traditions developed around one another and interacted with each other. The second part of the chapter is more to do with ancient textual transmission and presents a catalogue of evidence for ancient editorial manipulation of the boundaries between poems, here described as 'cropping' and 'splicing'.

## 1. Modern scholarship: neoanalysis and other 'systemic' interpretations

Modern scholarship on 'epic interactions' has to tread a fine line between pure literary exegesis and strong claims about historical actualities. Of these, exegesis is relatively theoretical, and is to some extent the creation of modern literary critics; claims about actualities relate more to source criticism and to testable models of the development of Archaic poetry.

Neoanalysis, the study of the Homeric epics' adaptation of non-Homeric material, tends towards the latter. (Here 'non-Homeric' means especially Cyclic legend and poetry.) The scholarship is extensive, so for more in-depth coverage the reader should refer to one of the core works of neoanalytic scholarship; many of these are in German but several serviceable surveys in English exist.[1]

The classic paradigm of the neoanalytic approach is the 'Memnon theory', according to which the Iliadic story of Achilles, Patroclus, and Hector draws on the story of Achilles, Antilochus, and Memnon that we find attested for the *Aethiopis.[2] The asterisk on *Aethiopis indicates a conjectural pre-Homeric form of the *Aethiopis* legend, so as to avoid equating Arctinus' *Aethiopis* with the legend, and to avoid the unnecessary assumption that it was specifically Arctinus' poem that the *Iliad* used as a model.

---

[1] Core works: Pestalozzi 1945 (the Memnon theory); Kakridis 1949 (methodology); Kullmann 1960 (*Iliad*); Danek 1998 (*Odyssey*). English-language surveys: Clark 1986; Dowden 1996; Willcock 1997; Edwards in Finkelberg 2011b: ii.566–7. See also two collections of essays: Montanari, Rengakos, and Tsagalis 2012; Fantuzzi and Tsagalis 2015a.

[2] Schadewaldt 1965: 155–202 is the most influential treatment; in English see Burgess 2009: 72–92, with bibliography.

Table 1. Adaptation of the *Aethiopis* in some major plot-lines of the *Iliad*

| *Aethiopis*, 'Memnonis' | *Iliad*, 'Patroclus sequence' | *Iliad*, 'Achilles sequence' |
|---|---|---|
| Thetis prophesies that Achilles will die after killing Memnon | — | Thetis prophesies that Achilles will die after killing Hector |
| Memnon kills Antilochus | — | Hector kills Patroclus |
| Achilles kills Memnon | Patroclus kills Sarpedon | Achilles kills Hector |
| Divine scales used to represent the duel's outcome | — | Divine scales used to represent the duel's outcome |
| Achilles attacks gates of Troy | Patroclus attacks gates of Troy | Achilles considers attacking gates of Troy, *Il.* 22.378–84 |
| Achilles killed by Paris and Apollo | Patroclus killed by Hector, Euphorbus, and Apollo | — |
| Battle over Achilles' corpse; Aias and Odysseus recover the body | Battle over Patroclus' corpse; Menelaus and others recover the body | — |
| Funeral and games for Achilles | Funeral and games for Patroclus | — |
| Thetis, Nereids, and Muses lament the dead Achilles | Thetis and Nereids lament (living) Achilles, *Il.* 18.35–69 | — |

Table 1 shows some of the main parallels. It follows Burgess in distinguishing two distinct sequences of motifs in the Iliadic story: in each sequence, characters act out parts of a single story pattern.[3] Since the point of this story pattern is that Achilles dies at the end, it appears that the *Aethiopis* version is primary: Achilles can only die once, so in the *Iliad* several elements relating to his death are transferred to Patroclus, creating a 'Patroclus sequence'. The parallels are not exact, of course, and the theory has weathered criticism from many different angles.

Recent studies have defined neoanalysis as the study of 'motif-transference' from pre-Homeric epic to Homer.[4] In its most orthodox

---

[3] Burgess 2009: 93–7.
[4] Kullmann 1984: 309; Burgess 2006: 149, 2009: 59; Currie 2006: 4–5; Tsagalis 2011: 218.

form, neoanalysis is based around specific texts and specific poems, and aims to analyse the chain of dependencies between them. In this sense it is a successor to the older, analytic school of Homeric scholarship: analysis aimed to establish which variant of a repeated element *within Homer* was the original and which the copy; neoanalysis works with whole poems and tries 'to establish which poem was the donor and which the recipient' of a given story element.[5] However, few now doubt that Homeric epic drew on *precursors* of the Cyclic epics, whether written or purely oral, and not on the specific poems known to Hellenistic scholars. In other words, to use the terminology outlined in Chapter III, modern neoanalysis is the study of motif-borrowing between strands of oral epos legend. Still looser forms of neoanalysis also allow for the possibility of non-poetic legend as source material; however, it then becomes hard to tell the difference between neoanalysis and the study of traditional tropes in the most general sense.

Neoanalysis traditionally focuses on the *Iliad*, where Kullmann's opus *Die Quellen der Ilias* (*The Sources of the Iliad*, 1960) analyses numerous episodes as Cyclic borrowings: the omen of the sparrows at Aulis (*Il.* 2.301–30), foreshadowings of Astyanax's death in the sack of Troy (24.727–38), and so on. But the *Odyssey* provides plenty of grist for the mill too. There, Danek's *Epos und Zitat* (*Epic and Citation*, 1998) has had an especially great impact on the study of Odysseus' wanderings (*Od.* 9–12). Danek sees traces of an *\*Argonautica* in some of the fantastic elements (Circe, the Laestrygonians, etc.), existing alongside an older *\*Odyssey*.[6] The *\*Argonautica* provided the monsters and magic; the older *\*Odyssey* offered the more mundane aspects of the homecoming. Some further Cyclic elements include the stories that Nestor, Menelaus, and others tell about events at Troy; the returns of Menelaus and Agamemnon (*Od.* 3.262–312, 4.351–586, 11.405–34); and many more. But Danek often considers the evidence for borrowing too thin to conclude that a specific poem was the source material. In many cases he judges (rightly) that it is extravagant to postulate specific texts as sources; oral epos legend and non-poetic legend are more likely candidates.[7] Most interesting are occasions when the *Odyssey* outlines possible alternatives for how the story will develop, only for one alternative to be rejected

[5] Currie 2006: 4.
[6] See also (more speculative) M. L. West 2005.
[7] See similarly pp. 57–63 above.

and suppressed. Danek sees these not as allusions to other poems but as traces of alternate versions of the *Odyssey* itself: an *\*Odyssey* where Telemachus visits Crete, an *\*Odyssey* where Odysseus is reunited with Laertes at an early stage, and so on. The *Odyssey* is not just played against a Cyclic backdrop: there is a whole landscape of potential *\*Odysseys* in the background.

There are various bastions of resistance to neoanalysis. One form of resistance is to distance Homer from the Cyclic epics. An influential study by Griffin argues that, unlike the Cyclic poems, Homeric epic conscientiously avoids fantastic elements and morally base elements.[8] However, even if this is right, it does not impugn neoanalysis as a purely analytic tool (as Griffin himself points out).

A second avenue of resistance is to reverse the relationship: the Cyclic epics plunder Homer, not the other way round. According to this view, the Cyclic epics were composed with an agenda of filling in the gaps around Homer. To this end, each epic took isolated Homeric references to minor events and built larger poetic edifices out of these titbits.[9] In cases such as the Memnon theory where the parallels are very extensive, this is simply the wrong objection (the Cyclic poets are supposed to have focused on *minor* points). But the argument still pops up every now and then: for example, in scholarly discussions of Eugammon's *Telegony*.

Eugammon himself is certainly post-Homeric – he can have lived no earlier than 631 BCE, when his home city of Cyrene was founded – and it is sometimes inferred that his story of Telegonus' wondrous spear, made from a poisonous ray's sting, is derived from a distorted interpretation of Teiresias' prophecy of Odysseus' death 'from the sea' (*Od.* 11.134). But as we saw in Chapter III and in Danek's analysis, to postulate that a given story belongs to a specific poem and had no previous existence is nearly always the extravagant alternative, not the parsimonious one. It is also an argument from silence: new evidence can disprove it. And, as it happens, robust evidence for a pre-Homeric *\*Telegony* legend does exist. The basic story of Odysseus' confrontation with Telegonus is a variant of a very old Indo-European folktale, the 'mortal combat of the father and son' (also known as the 'Sohrāb and Rostam' type), which

---

[8] Griffin 1977.

[9] This was Welcker's view of the Cycle; see Kullmann 1960: 18–19, who calls the process *Herausspinnung* ('spinning off'). The same argument still appears in West's characterization of the 'cyclic approach' (M. L. West 2013: 18–20; similarly 57, 132, 167, 245, 289–90).

has several extremely close parallels in Indian, Persian, Irish, German, and Russian epic and folktales.[10] There is no doubt that it is very old and very traditional. A sceptic – someone who dislikes the idea that the Telegonus legend informed the Homeric *Odyssey* – might take refuge in claiming that, even if the story-type is old, still Telegonus himself was Eugammon's invention; or, if Telegonus should be proven to be old, still his magic spear is late. These cannot be ruled out (in fact, the last suggestion may be true: the one surviving image of Telegonus shows him armed with a bow, not a spear[11]). But they are still arguments from silence. The notion that the Cyclic poets created their material by reworking hints given in Homer may well be true in some cases, but is indefensible as a default presumption.

But a third objection to neoanalysis, and by far the most serious one, is that it is catastrophically vulnerable to confirmation bias. Any story is a complex set of data; when you look for parallels and patterns in two complex datasets, you will invariably find them. It is therefore dangerously easy for neoanalysis to rely on arguments from similarity and coherence. For example: one criterion that has been used to detect neoanalytic borrowings is 'fissures in a narrative' – that is, inconsistencies or apparent failures of logic.[12] Eurycleia's recognition of Odysseus in *Odyssey* 19 has no lasting impact on the epic's plot; this supposed 'fissure', therefore, could possibly be a result of 'motif transference' from an older poem – in this case, an older \**Odyssey*.[13] But a possibility in principle is a far cry from evidence.

The underlying epistemological question is whether a given parallel is a case of systematic adaptation of a prior narrative or merely a trope, a conventional stock element or an echo with no broader significance.[14] The table above omits one \**Aethiopis* episode which is

---

[10] See M. L. West 2007: 440–2; Gainsford 2012a: 267–72.

[11] *LIMC* 'Kirke' 54 (Budapest Museum of Fine Arts 50.101; Acrae, Sicily, *c*.400 BCE) shows Circe giving a bow to Telegonus (named); no spear is visible in the fragment. Telegonus' counterparts in the Indian variants use bows. M. L. West 2013: 307–15 conjectures that the tip of Telegonus' spear, a ray's poisonous sting, came from an alternate story of Odysseus' death, supposedly reported in a fragmentary oracle in Aesch. *Psychagogoi* fr. 275 Radt. This cannot be right: on the symbolic character of oracles, especially their animal imagery, see pp. 28–31; and the argument requires an assumption that Odysseus was invulnerable, something for which no evidence exists.

[12] Tsagalis 2011: 220–1.

[13] Danek 1998: 379–82; Currie 2006: 16–20.

[14] On this distinction see also Kullmann 1984: 311–16 (neoanalytic adaptations are somehow distinct from oral traditional tropes); Finkelberg 2011a (neoanalytic adaptations are special because Homer is special).

especially liable to this criticism. In *Iliad* 8.80–115 Nestor, trapped with a disabled chariot and threatened by Hector, is rescued by Diomedes. Ostensibly this episode draws on a moment in the *\*Aethiopis* where Antilochus rescues Nestor from Memnon (leading to Antilochus' death at Memnon's hands).[15] But, in the *Iliad,* the parts of the poem where adaptation is beyond doubt – the 'Achilles sequence' and the 'Patroclus sequence' in the table above – have no connection to the Nestor episode in Book 8. That episode is isolated from other parts of the *\*Aethiopis* narrative: it might as well be a stock scene. By contrast, the Achilles and Patroclus sequences feature extensive borrowings and both sequences revolve around a tightly focused cluster of three characters (Achilles, Patroclus, and Hector): these clearly represent systematic exploitation of older material.

Some recent studies have been taking these methodological problems very seriously, and have pondered the standard of evidence required for demonstrating a neoanalytic link between poems, as opposed to a vaguer kind of echo.[16] But the Memnon theory remains a *rara avis*: other cases where echoes can be corroborated are few indeed. So it is hard to see prospects for a reliable, universally applicable, methodology whereby neoanalysis can attain any degree of certainty about adaptations, other than in exceptionally well-established cases.

Let us turn from neoanalysis to a more purely literary kind of criticism on the interplay between poems. As with neoanalysis, the scholarship often takes Homer as its departure point.

Many critics, led especially by Nagy's book *The Best of the Achaeans*, see the *Iliad* and *Odyssey* as complementary: the Homeric epics developed around one another, responding to each other and resonating in unique ways. Together they form a complete system, in terms of their mutual evaluation of one another and their celebration of two complementary ideals of heroism: *Iliad* vs. *Odyssey; kleos* ('fame') vs. *nostos* ('homecoming'); Achilles vs. Odysseus; *biē* ('might') vs. *mētis* ('artifice').[17]

This vision makes Homer a walled garden. His poetry ends up being 'special' in ways not shared by Hesiod, the Cycle, or any other

---

[15] The main extant source for the *\*Aethiopis* episode is Pind. *Pyth.* 6.28–42, with scholia. See Kelly 2006: 3–12 (with extensive bibliography); Burgess 2009: 74–5.

[16] See especially Currie 2006; Tsagalis 2011.

[17] Nagy 1979, esp. 45–9.

hexameter poems.[18] That is all very well for a type of criticism designed to celebrate the Homeric epics' pre-eminence after the fact. But if this form of criticism also makes claims about the historical development of hexameter poetry, in terms of cause and effect, then its dependence on teleology becomes a problem.

The problem is that it pre-emptively excludes all hexameter poetry other than the *Iliad* and *Odyssey* from consideration.[19] There is no doubt that the Homeric epics stand out from the crowd: they are uniquely long, uniquely elevated, uniquely excellent. No-one seriously believes that the *Aethiopis* was as pre-eminent as the *Iliad*. But a walled garden? The idea that Arctinus was somehow forbidden from drawing on the epic tradition in the same ways that Homer did is surely wishful thinking. The reverse is also true: as neoanalysis shows, the *Iliad* plays far more heavily on an \**Aethiopis* tradition than it does on the *Odyssey*; and the *Odyssey* depends much more on an \**Oresteia* tradition than it does on the *Iliad*.[20]

Finkelberg tries to shore up the garden wall by distinguishing different kinds of intertextual play. For her, the Homeric epics possess reciprocity: they do not presuppose each other specifically but only a common inherited tradition, so their interplay is relatively subtle. Where one poem plays specifically on another, by contrast, the relationship is asymmetrical and much more obvious: the *Iliad* plays on an \**Aethiopis*, but Arctinus' *Aethiopis* did not play on the *Iliad* (so far as we know).

This allows the *Iliad* and the *Odyssey* not only to distance themselves from the Cycle poems but also to turn these poems into raw material, as it were, for creating something completely new. ...Homer uses his tradition in a highly idiosyncratic way.[21]

Even this form of the 'walled garden' approach has problems, though. If the *Iliad* is playing specifically on an \**Aethiopis*, then it is playing on a form of the \**Aethiopis* that is in some sense canonical. That is: we have to presuppose more solidity in this hypothetical \**Aethiopis* than in the Homeric *Odyssey*! So this interpretation involves a strong historical

---

[18] Griffin 1977 is a seminal statement of this view.

[19] E.g. Austin 1991: 233–4: 'Mycenaean history crystallized into two separate epics evolving concurrently and synergistically, celebrating two kinds of hero'. Epics on Heracles, Oedipus, or Jason may as well not have existed.

[20] See above, and see also Slatkin 1991: 21–49 (\**Aethiopis*); Olson 1995: 24–42 (\**Oresteia*).

[21] Finkelberg 2011a: 200.

claim: that prior to the *Iliad* the *\*Aethiopis* had reached a canonical form, while the *Odyssey* was still fluid.

Opposing the 'walled garden' approach is a trend of interpreting all hexameter as a coherent whole, with systemic organization on a large scale. Thalmann sees hexameter as unified by a single world-view, defined by symmetry and antitheses, and geared towards making the cosmos intelligible rather than a mere jumble of events.[22] Slatkin develops this view by interpreting each sub-genre of hexameter as 'a classification of cultural phenomena': heroic poetry is complementary to wisdom literature, Homer to Hesiod, but they all 'exist within, and serve to complete, a conception about the way the world is ordered'.[23] For Ford, epic is a chronological continuum stretching from Hesiod's Chaos all the way to Eugammon's Telegonus without a break: poems anticipate or reflect other parts of the continuum, creating resonances and an overall unity.[24]

The most complete statement of this 'systemic' reading is Clay's influential interpretations of the Homeric *Hymns* and the Hesiodic poems. For Clay, not only is the *Odyssey* a response to the *Iliad*, but the *Works and Days* is a response to the *Theogony*; the *Catalogue* forms a triptych with them both;[25] the *Hymns*, too, pursue a well-defined agenda that links the divine realm to the mortal world. Hexameter is thus a much larger system than just Homer, but it is still a system. So the *Hymns* describe mythological moments: stories that change the cosmos, and authorize individual gods' roles and the relationship between gods and mortals. The *Theogony* and *Works and Days* 'form a unified whole embracing the divine and human cosmos' respectively. And heroic epic describes a time when the mortal and divine spheres were more closely linked than in the present.[26] As Clay writes: 'one might argue that the Homeric Hymns were created *in order* to fill the perceived gap between Hesiod and Homer and thus to provide accounts of the major events in the evolution of Olympus'.[27]

This picture of hexameter as a larger unity has a certain appeal – but only until one inquires about the origin of the system. Who devised and enforced this division of labour? Where does it leave the dozens of other

---

[22] Thalmann 1984: 1–6.
[23] Slatkin 1991: 260.
[24] Ford 1992: 45.
[25] Similarly Ormand 2014: 6–9. Graziosi and Haubold 2005: 36–8 argue instead that the poems were *read* as a triptych in antiquity.
[26] Clay 1989; 2003, esp. 166.
[27] Clay 1989: 268 (Clay's emphasis).

hexameter poems that are attested: the Thebaids, the Heracleas, the Descents to Hades? Clay's tightly knit top-down organization can hardly have been a code of unbreakable rules followed unquestioningly by the Cyclic poets, Eumelus, Musaeus, and others.

A more careful approach is to think about the poems' complementary character in terms of later reception, rather than in terms of their historical composition. This is the tactic followed by Graziosi and Haubold.[28] One reason is simply that our selection of extant texts is pre-determined and out of our control. For us, the extant poems constitute a 'found' canon, with literally no existence other than as a coherent system, and this illusory coherence has guided a lot of modern interpretation. But in antiquity, too, by the fifth and fourth centuries BCE the Hesiodic and Homeric poems were already *read* as complementary. Plato and Aristotle saw Hesiod and Homer as systemic canons, in much the same way that Ford and Clay do.

And comparable principles may have operated in other corpuses too. It would be unsurprising if new evidence emerged one day that showed similar kinds of relationships between the Derveni *Theogony* and the Orphic *Hymns*, for example; or between the Epimenidean *Theogony*, the *Birth of the Kouretes and Korybantes*, and the *Genealogies*. If ancient readers perceived these poems as complementary and resonating with one another, as they did the Homeric and Hesiodic canons, it could help explain how the Orphic and Epimenidean poems gravitated into their own groups and created their own canons.

## 2. Ancient transmission: cropping and splicing

In the centuries after their composition, some poems were combined or edited by either 'splicing' or 'cropping'. Here 'splicing' refers to the editorial practice of joining two originally separate poems and publishing them together as a single continuous text. 'Cropping' describes situations where poems were abbreviated after composition, either to avoid overlaps with other poems or to publish an extract as a separate poem.[29] The remainder of this chapter is a catalogue of the evidence for 'cropping' and 'splicing' at the boundaries between poems.[30]

---

[28] Graziosi and Haubold 2005, esp. 21–34.

[29] 'Cropping' was coined by Burgess 2001, 'splicing' by the present author.

[30] For previous partial surveys see Burgess 2001: 135–43 (Epic Cycle); Cingano 2009: 109–30 (Hesiodic corpus).

Individual cases of editing cannot in general be dated. In one case, the *Hymn to Apollo*, if the poem we have is a result of splicing, it is most likely that it dates to the Archaic period.[31] If Burgess' 'cropping hypothesis' about the Epic Cycle is correct, that should probably be dated to the fourth century, on the supposition that compilation of the Cycle post-dates the literary sense of 'cyclic'.[32] No substantial splicing or cropping would have taken place after the Hellenistic period.

### (a) The Hesiodic Theogony and Catalogue(s) of Women

*Th.* 1021–2 = *Cat.* fr. 1.1–2. In one ancient papyrus and two medieval copies the *Theogony* ends at line 1020; 1021–2 appear in some manuscripts added in a second hand; in only one are they an integral part of the text.[33] This indicates that at some point the *Theogony* and *Catalogue* were spliced together in some, but not all, editions.

West argues that the splice extends much further into the *Theogony*.[34] The authenticity of the last section of the poem, from line 901 (or 930 or 965) onwards, has often been doubted.[35] Since this section is largely devoted to a 'little catalogue' of goddesses who had sex with mortal men (965–1020) – an inversion of the *Catalogue*'s theme of women who had sex with male gods – the whole thing could be a large splice designed to join a shorter proto-*Theogony* to the *Catalogue*. West's suggestion that 1021–2 was intended to point readers to a subsequent scroll on the shelf is also possible; that would be a milder form of splicing (the doing of a librarian rather than an editor).[36]

*Cat.* fr. 2 poses a related problem. The source of the fragment, John Lydus, discusses Latinus and Graecus as eponymous ancestors of the Latins and Greeks. Lydus elliptically mentions 'brothers'; then, naming Hesiod's 'catalogues' as his source, quotes *Theog.* 1013 ('Agrius and Latinus' [=*Cat.* fr. 2.1]) and *Cat.* fr. 2.2 (on Hellen's children). The

---

[31] Either because the hymn was compiled for the 523/522 Pythia–Delia (Janko 1982: 112–15; Chappell 2011: 72–3) or because one part of the hymn was designed with the other in mind (Chappell 2011: 62).

[32] See pp. 27–8.

[33] M. L. West 1966: 437.

[34] M. L. West 1966: 48–50, 1985: 126–7; Most 2006: xlix. However, West's insistence that *Cat.* fr. 1 was not the beginning of the original *Catalogue* is uncompelling. Muse invocations can certainly occur inside a poem but *Cat.* fr. 1 is an absolutely typical proem; see pp. 45–8.

[35] M. L. West 1966: 397–9, with bibliography; cf. Kelly 2007: 389–96, applying a new test from internal structural evidence, with inconclusive results.

[36] M. L. West 1966: 437.

reference to 'brothers' is puzzling, for fr. 2.2 makes it clear that Graecus is Pandora's son, and not related to Latinus or his mother, Circe. Various emendations and transpositions have been proposed,[37] but it is fairly clear that Lydus is quoting from two separate sources.

If the last section of the *Theogony*, the 'little catalogue', is indeed a splice between a proto-*Theogony* and the *Catalogue*, an ancient reader might well refer to both of them jointly as 'Hesiod's catalogues'. On this reading, then, Lydus combines *Theog.* 1013 and *Cat.* fr. 2.2 because they do indeed both come from 'Hesiod's catalogues', plural: one from the 'little catalogue' in the *Theogony*, the other from the *Catalogue of Women*.

### (b) The Catalogue of Women *and the* Shield

*Shield* 1–56 = *Cat.* fr. 138.8–63, the story of Heracles' birth. *Shield* argument *a* (=*Cat.* fr. 139 = Hes. test. 52) informs us that the passage comes from *Cat.* Book 4; its testimony is confirmed by two overlapping papyri containing *Cat.* fr. 138.1–7 and *Shield* 1–18.[38] The simplest inference is that the *Shield* poet himself took the passage from the *Catalogue* and used it for the opening of his poem.[39]

West and Most, by contrast, argue that the passage was interpolated into the *Shield* after both poems were composed.[40] They do so for contradictory reasons: West, because the passage is too similar to *Shield* 78–88, where Heracles refers to the birth story again (but without repetition); Most, because the passage is too dissimilar to the rest of the poem (but this is not a poem known for its structural or thematic perfection). Neither position is very compelling.

### (c) The Catalogue of Women *and the* Cypria

We do not have the end of the *Catalogue*, but in the last major fragment, fr. 155.94–180, the marriage of Helen is followed by Zeus planning a

---

[37] Hirschberger 2004: 172 summarizes a range of views; Dräger 1997: 27–42 is the most detailed discussion.

[38] Hirschberger 2004: 362.

[39] Wilamowitz-Moellendorff 1905: 122; Russo 1965: 33 n. 34; Janko 1986: 39 (comparing *Hymn. Hom. Ap.*); Effe 1988: 161. Few now believe that the same poet composed both poems. Among those who do, their further views diverge greatly: for Van der Valk 1953: 277–9, the poet recycled his own material when composing the *Shield*; for Martin 2005: 173–5, all 480 lines of the *Shield* come from *Cat.* Book 4.

[40] M. L. West 1966: 49–50 n. 5, 1985: 136; Most 2006: lviii–lix.

major war to destroy the races of mortals and demigods (99 ἀϊστῶσαι...ὀλέσθαι).[41] This plan has often been linked to a fragment of the *Cypria* describing Zeus's plan for the Trojan War (*Cypria* fr. 1.4–7):[42]

κουφίσαι ἀνθρώπων παμβώτορα σύνθετο γαῖαν,
ῥιπίσσας πολέμου μεγάλην ἔριν Ἰλιακοῖο,
ὄφρα κενώσειεν θανάτωι βάρος. οἱ δ᾽ ἐνὶ Τροίηι
ἥρωες κτείνοντο, Διὸς δ᾽ ἐτελείετο βουλή.

...[Zeus] resolved to relieve the all-nurturing earth of mankind's weight by fanning the great conflict of the Trojan War, to void the burden through death. So the warriors at Troy kept being killed, and Zeus' plan was being fulfilled.

It would seem that a similar *Dios boulē* ('Zeus's plan') lies behind the passage near the end of the *Catalogue*. The *Catalogue* follows up its *Dios boulē* passage with a digression, whose relevance is uncertain, about the passing of seasons and a snake's life cycle (124–44 and probably as far as 147).[43]

There is no indication that the end of the *Catalogue* and the start of the *Cypria* were ever actually spliced together. However, on a mythological level (rather than textual), Clay has insisted that *Cat.* fr. 155 is designed to embed the Trojan War in a 'a continuum with the cosmogonic background and the dynamics of the succession myth' – a continuum that stretches from the *Theogony* to the fall of Troy and the returns.[44]

From *Cat.* fr. 155.95 onwards there are several abrupt shifts in topic and in tone. The less than organic character of the passage may result from an attempt to forge a link between 'Hesiodic' and 'Homeric' forms, between the *Catalogue* and heroic epic, by combining echoes of both types of poetry. **Hesiodic echoes:** the end of the heroes

---

[41] On this passage see Koenen 1994: 26–34; Clay 2003: 168–74; González 2010; Ormand 2014: 202–16.

[42] Thus Koenen 1994: 26–9; Clay 2003: 168–72; Finkelberg 2004: 11–15; Cingano 2005: 118–19 (with further bibliography); González 2010: 395. Clay argues that the *Catalogue*'s reference to γένος...πολλόν ('plentiful race' of mortals, *Cat.* fr. 155.98–9; Most: 'most of the race') also echoes the *Cypria*'s μυρία φῦλα ('countless races', *Cypr.* fr. 1.1). Finkelberg adduces further parallel passages.

[43] The passage resists interpretation. Clay 2003: 173–4 suggests that the passage describes a storm at Aulis, followed by the omen of the birds and the snake (cf. *Il.* 2.301–30; *Cypr.* arg. 6). However, the frequentative verbs at 124–8 would be incomprehensible in a passage describing a one-off event. See also above, p. 13.

[44] Clay 2003: 171.

(*Cat.* fr.155.96–*c.*106) evokes the Hesiodic Myth of the Races (*WD* 156–73);[45] and the passage where trees bow before Boreas, and a snake gives birth and retires underground in winter ('the hairless one'; *Cat.* fr. 155.124–43), closely echoes the Hesiodic description of Boreas bending trees and an octopus gnawing its foot in hidden places ('the boneless one'; *WD* 504–28). **Homeric echoes:** the catalogue of Helen's suitors (*Cat.* frs. 154, 155.1–75, 156) resonates with the catalogues in the *Cypria* and the *Iliad*; and lines 118–19 (καὶ π]ολλὰς Ἀΐδηι κεφαλὰς ἀπὸ χαλκὸν ἰάψ[ει]ν / ἀν]δρῶν ἡρώων, 'and] the bronze was going to send to Hades many heads of heroic men') evoke *Il.* 1.3–4 (πολλὰς δ' ἰφθίμους ψυχὰς Ἄϊδι προΐαψεν / ἡρώων, '[Achilles' wrath] sent to Hades many strong souls of heroes').

### (d) The Works and Days *and the* Bird Omens *(or* Ornithomancy*)*

The *Works and Days* ends (826–8):

> ... εὐδαίμων τε καὶ ὄλβιος ὃς τάδε πάντα
> εἰδὼς ἐργάζηται ἀναίτιος ἀθανάτοισιν,
> ὄρνιθας κρίνων καὶ ὑπερβασίας ἀλεείνων.

Happy and blessed is he who knows all these things and does his work without giving offense to the immortals, distinguishing the birds and avoiding trespasses.

A scholion on line 828 (=Hes. test. 80) reports: 'At this point some people add the *Bird Omens*, which Apollonius Rhodius...marks as spurious.' Apollonius' testimony, then, would make this a case of splicing.[46]

Some argue instead that *WD* 828 'distinguishing the birds' is programmatic for a subsequent episode, the *Bird Omens*, which has been cropped.[47] The question hinges on a phrase in Pausanias' overview of the Hesiodic corpus:

Βοιωτῶν δὲ οἱ περὶ τὸν Ἑλικῶνα οἰκοῦντες παρειλημμένα δόξῃ λέγουσιν ὡς ἄλλο Ἡσίοδος ποιήσειεν οὐδὲν ἢ τὰ Ἔργα...ἔστι δὲ καὶ ἕτερα κεχωρισμένη τῆς προτέρας, ὡς πολύν τινα ἐπῶν ὁ Ἡσίοδος ἀριθμὸν ποιήσειεν, ἐς γυναῖκάς τε ᾀδόμενα καὶ ἃς μεγάλας

---

[45] Thus Cingano 2005: 119.
[46] Thus Cassanmagnago 2009: 969–70 n. 192; Kelly 2007: 387–9 corroborates this view with internal structural evidence.
[47] M. L. West 1978: 364–5; Most 2006: 189 (implicitly, by translation); Cingano 2009: 103–4.

ἐπονομάζουσιν Ἠοίας,…καὶ ὅσα ἐπὶ Ἔργοις τε καὶ Ἡμέραις.

The Boeotians who live around Helicon say that of the poems commonly ascribed to him Hesiod composed nothing but the *Works*.…But there is another opinion, different from the first one, according to which Hesiod composed a very great number of hexameter poems: the poem about women; and what they call the *Great Ehoiai*;…and everything ἐπί the *Works and Days*.[48]

The cropping interpretation takes ἐπί in the scholastic sense of 'after': thus 'everything after *WD* 828', referring to the *Bird Omens*.

However, the non-specialist meaning 'in addition to, besides' is a much better fit for Pausanias' non-academic register, and also for his flow of logic: he is specifically discussing whether Hesiod wrote anything other than the *Works and Days*. Therefore 'everything ἐπί the *Works and Days*' means simply the entire Hesiodic corpus. The passage has no implications for the *Bird Omens*.

This more conservative interpretation of ἐπί removes the challenge to Apollonius' testimony. The *Bird Omens* and *Works and Days*, in that case, were composed independently, and one was later spliced onto the other.

### (e) The Hymn(s) to Apollo

Of all cases of splicing and cropping, this is the most problematic. As we saw in chapter I, it is often supposed that this *Hymn* was compiled from a 'hymn to Delian Apollo' (1–178) and a 'hymn to Pythian Apollo' (179ff.). The former ends with a fairly standard 'farewell':

αὐτὰρ ἐγὼν οὐ λήξω ἑκηβόλον Ἀπόλλωνα
ὑμνέων ἀργυρότοξον ὃν ἠΰκομος τέκε Λητώ.

And myself, I shall not cease from hymning the far-shooter Apollo of the silver bow, whom lovely-haired Leto bore.

The niceties of formal hymnic structure suggest that the subsequent passage is the start of a new hymn: a bridge passage beginning at 179 ('O Lord, Lycia too is yours, and lovely Lydia…') leads into the 'Pythian' hymn, with a new attributive section, and by 207 ('How shall I hymn you, fit subject as you are in every respect?') we are clearly

[48] Paus. 9.31.4–5 (Hes. test. 42).

at the start of a new hymnic narrative.[49] The question is whether this structural shift is also a case of splicing. Richardson's recent commentary has complicated the question further, arguing for a single hymn with a three-part structure.[50] There is little prospect of resolving the matter to everyone's satisfaction.

### (f) *The* Thebaid *and the* Epigoni

We have only the barest hint of a splice between these two lost poems. The first line of the *Epigoni* is preserved as follows (fr. 1):

Νῦν αὖθ' ὁπλοτέρων ἀνδρῶν ἀρχώμεθα, Μοῦσαι.

*But now, Muses, let us begin on the younger men.*

The word 'younger' looks like it must mean: *in comparison to* the heroes of the previous Theban war, the Seven against Thebes. If it refers to a poem on that subject (which is by no means certain), the line could be either a splice that postdates both poems or, alternatively, a sign that the *Epigoni* was composed as a sequel to the *Thebaid*;[51] Alcidamas and Herodotus regarded both poems as Homeric (*Epigoni* test. 1, 5).

### (g) *The Epic Cycle*

Proclus' summaries of the Trojan epics form a single continuous narrative without overlaps. However, other evidence makes it clear that some poems originally covered more ground and overlapped with one another: for example, the *Little Iliad* contained episodes that are also attested for the *Aethiopis* and the *Sack of Ilion*. There are at least three ways of interpreting these discrepancies.

(1) Bethe believed that the *Cypria, Aethiopis, Little Iliad*, and *Sack of Ilion* were originally a single poem;[52] this thesis could explain confusion in the attribution of individual fragments. However, it requires ignoring almost all the attribution evidence that we *do* have, and should not be taken seriously.

---

[49] Thus Janko 1981: 12, 16–17.
[50] N. Richardson 2010: 9–13. See also pp. 21–2 above.
[51] M. L. West 2003a: 9.
[52] Bethe 1929: 211–16.

(2) Davies argues that not just the epics but also Proclus' summaries originally extended further, and that the overlaps in the summaries were excised by a Byzantine epitomizer.[53] This thesis addresses a textual question in Proclus, albeit perhaps not conclusively.[54] But it does not account for places where there is evidence of interference with a poem's actual text: specifically, at the interfaces between the *Cypria* and *Iliad*, *Iliad* and *Aethiopis*, and *Odyssey* and *Telegony*.

(3) Burgess, following Monro, prefers a 'cropping hypothesis': an editorial process trimmed the poems themselves, excising overlaps and inconsistencies, and deleting episodes at the beginnings and ends so as to create a continuous streamlined 'cycle'.[55]

Burgess' cropping hypothesis has the most explanatory power. It is also the most drastic: it requires the premises that ancient editors were willing to do great violence to their texts (even if only in a special Cyclic edition), and that uncropped editions must have continued to exist alongside the cropped Cycle, or no evidence of discrepancies would survive. But we have good evidence of extreme violence in at least one case (the start of the *Aethiopis*); and persuasive evidence, to my mind, in another (the end of the *Odyssey*). Furthermore, the evidence outlined above for cropping and splicing in non-Cyclic poems adds to its plausibility in the case of the Cycle. As things stand, Burgess' cropping hypothesis is the one to beat.

*Cypria*

**Beginning.** Not generally disputed in terms of where the plot begins. See above on a thematic link to the end of the *Catalogue of Women*.

**End.** Proclus' summary has the poem end with the Greeks awarding Briseis and Chryseis to Agamemnon and Achilles; the death of Palamedes; Zeus's plan to remove Achilles from combat; and a catalogue of Trojan allies. This would appear to lead directly into the *Iliad*.

However, *Cypria* fr. 31 appears to refer to the death of Astyanax in the sack of Troy; fr. 34 Bernabé (om. West) explicitly refers to

---

[53] Davies 1986: 96 and 101–4, 2001: 2, 7, 58–9; similarly M. L. West 2013: 15–16.

[54] Viz. the sense of Proclus' phrasing ἐπιβάλλει τούτοις (*Cypr.* arg. 1). Davies 1986: 101–2 argues for an intransitive meaning, 'After this comes [the *Cypria*]', instead of the older interpretation '[Proclus] adds to this'. ἐπιβάλλει is certainly intransitive after the end of the *Cypria* summary (ἐπιβάλλει δὲ...Ἰλιὰς Ὁμήρου, 'after [this] comes Homer's *Iliad*').

[55] Monro 1883: 316–21, 1901: 342–6; Burgess 2001: 135–48.

Polyxena's death. *Tabula Iliaca* 3C Sadurska groups together three scenes, of which the first two belong in the *Cypria* and the third in the *Iliad*.[56] The argument that the *Cypria* originally extended beyond the end of Proclus' summary has been put most forcefully by Burgess, who contends that the *Cypria* originally covered the entire Trojan War; he sees this corroborated by a Hellenistic reference to Cyprias as the author of a poem named as *Iliaca*.[57]

## *Iliad*

**Beginning.** Not disputed in terms of plot. An alternate proem is recorded which Bethe thought served to provide a bridge between the *Cypria* and the *Iliad* (=Cyclic *Iliad* test. Bernabé; om. West), but there are competing interpretations.[58]

**End.** Not disputed in terms of plot content. A couplet is recorded that appears to replace the *Iliad*'s final line with two lines that link directly to the arrival of Penthesileia (*Aeth.* fr. 1); this could in principle be a splice but is better interpreted as an internal fragment from within the *Aethiopis* (see below).

## *Aethiopis*

**Beginning.** Proclus has the plot begin with Penthesileia's arrival at Troy. Fr. 1 consists of two lines that link Hector's funeral to Penthesileia's arrival (see also *Iliad*, end, above). It is obvious that the lines are not part of a proem: there is no sense of a beginning, no Muse invocation, and the lines refer to Hector's funeral as an event that has only just been narrated.[59] Hence, either the lines are an attempt to splice the *Aethiopis* onto the *Iliad*[60] or they are taken from within the *Aethiopis*.[61]

---

[56] See further Kopff 1983: 58 and n. 13; *contra* Horsfall 1979: 49 (but Horsfall does not consider the possibility of a longer *Cypria*).

[57] Burgess 1996, 2001: 135–40, 2002.

[58] Bethe 1929: 384. Others interpret the passage as a quotation from a hymnic prelude: Ford 1992: 27; M. L. West 2011a: 81.

[59] This point leads Davies 1988: 48, 2001: 58–9 (following Wilamowitz) to reject the fragment as altogether spurious; however, he does not consider the possibilities that it could be a splice or an internal quotation.

[60] Thus M. L. West 2001: 283–5; Scafoglio 2004: 307–8.

[61] Thus Burgess 2001: 140–2.

Pictorial evidence from the Hellenistic and Roman eras suggests that Proclus' summary is a cropped form of the original *Aethiopis*. Four third-century-BCE Homer cups, MB 23–26 Sinn (=*Aeth.* test. 11 Bernabé), show three scenes as though linked: Priam's ransom of Hector's corpse; Priam and Penthesileia at Hector's grave; and Achilleus and Penthesileia in battle. This would indicate that the ransom of Hector appeared in the original *Aethiopis*, as well as in the *Iliad*.[62] *Tabula Iliaca* 9D Sadurska contains the same grouping, along with several further scenes from the *Aethiopis*. Weitzmann has independently interpreted a second-century-CE sarcophagus lid from the Villa Borghese as further evidence that the *Aethiopis* included Hector's funeral.[63] Images from the late Archaic and classical eras provide no guidance, unfortunately.[64]

In chapter V we saw mythographic evidence from Ptolemy the Quail, Dictys of Crete, and Philostratus, which suggested a version of the story where Penthesileia's arrival was interleaved with Hector's death, ransom, and burial, and where Andromache was present at Hector's ransom.[65] The reconstructed story goes as follows: Penthesileia arrives outside Troy; Hector goes to greet her, but Achilles ambushes and kills him on the way; Priam and Andromache ransom Hector's body; Penthesileia enters Troy during the funeral and makes a compact with Priam at Hector's grave.[66] Sources such as Ptolemy the Quail and Dictys must be treated very cautiously, of course. But, though

---

[62] The thesis that the Homer cups attest to a version of Hector's ransom in the *Aethiopis* has been argued most forcefully by Kopff 1983. See also Horsfall 1979: 47–8, arguing that the illustrations on Homer cups derive from picture-books of the Cycle (without the poems' full text) which also provided the basis for the *Tabulae Iliacae*.

[63] Weitzmann 1959: 43–6.

[64] The ransom of Hector was popular in Attic vase-paintings *c.*520–480 BCE (Friis Johansen 1967: 127–38; Lowenstam 2008: 51–63), but vase-painters of the time had their own language of tropes and cannot be expected to represent any poetry meticulously, or even at all (Lowenstam 1992, 2008: 1–12; Snodgrass 1998, esp. 127–50). The most that can be said is that in those decades the Iliadic version of the ransom enjoyed more prestige than the *Aethiopis* version, as indicated by the fact that many vases show Hermes accompanying Priam. Some scenes show Priam accompanied by a woman or women: see especially *LIMC* 'Achilleus' 645 and 643 (Kassel Antik. T.674; Athens NM CC.889). Schwarz 2006 links these to Dictys, as I do above, but identifies the lead woman as Polyxena; I suggest Andromache instead (see Gainsford 2012b: 65 n. 34, arguing that Polyxena's role in Dictys is probably a Dictyean invention).

[65] See pp. 99–102.

[66] Dictys *apud* Septimius 3.20–27, Malalas 5.24, Cedrenus 224.4–225.2; Ptolemy *apud* Photius cod. 190, 151.ii.37–152.i.1. (Ptolemy at 151.i.29–32 reports a version of Achilles' death that is either incompatible with the *Aethiopis* or else extremely telescoped; but this does not indicate that he avoided material from the *Aethiopis*, since it has always been obvious that Ptolemy is a hodge-podge of different stories.)

Dictys by himself does not provide clear evidence, he does provide good corroboration for the pictorial evidence. The text of *Aethiopis* fr. 1 also sits well with this reconstruction.

When we take the mythographic reconstruction in conjunction with the pictorial evidence, it appears that the *Aethiopis* itself originally contained an account of Hector's death and funeral. These events may have framed Penthesileia's arrival at Troy along roughly the same lines as the Dictys narrative. If so, (1) *Aethiopis* fr. 1 was not originally the start of the poem, but part of its internal narrative; (2) these opening episodes of the *Aethiopis* were cropped so as to avoid overlap with the *Iliad*.

**End.** Proclus has the poem end with the quarrel over Achilles' arms. Two sources put subsequent events in the *Aethiopis* too: test. 8 Bernabé (om. West; pictorial, *Tabula Iliaca* 1A Sadurska), Aias' madness; fr. 6 West (sch. Pind. *Isth.* 4.58b), Aias' suicide.

## Little Iliad

**Beginning.** Proclus has the plot begin with the award of Achilleus' arms to Odysseus. However, test. 7 Bernabé (Arist. *Poet.* 1459a–b) reliably puts the judgment of the arms in the *Little Iliad*; fr. 2 depicts Greek spies eavesdropping on Trojan women debating whether Aias or Odysseus was braver, an incident that is the deciding factor in the judgment of the arms.[67] (*Tabula Iliaca* 7Ti Sadurska can be disregarded: it depicts several *Aethiopis* scenes in its border, and an inscription reads *Little Iliad*, but it is clear that the inscription refers only to the central panel.)

**End.** Proclus has the plot end with the wooden horse being taken into Troy and the Trojans celebrating their supposed victory. However, three witnesses put events from the sack of Troy in the *Little Iliad* as well: fr. 16.I Bernabé ('Homer cup' MB 27 Sinn) associates Priam's death with the *Little Iliad*; fr. 28 (sch. Ar. *Lys.* 155) describes Menelaus' encounter with Helen during the sack of Troy; and fr. 29 (Tzetzes, sch. Lycoph. *Alex.* 1268) quotes the poem's description of Neoptolemos' acts in the sack of Troy (including the killing of

---

[67] In addition, two fragments are attached to the *Little Iliad* that both look like opening lines: fr. 1 (=fr. 28 Bernabé) and fr. 1 Bernabé. While it is in principle possible that these may indicate two different poems by the same title (Bernabé's conclusion), it is most likely that we have a case of a double-barrelled invocation: see Scafoglio 2006 and above, pp. 45–8.

Astyanax, *contra Sack of Ilion* arg. 4, where Odysseus is the killer). This testimony implies that parts, at least, of the sack of Troy were narrated in the original *Little Iliad* and were cropped.

### Sack of Ilion

**Beginning.** Not disputed.
**End.** Not disputed.

### Returns

**Beginning.** Not disputed.
**End.** Not disputed. However, the *Returns* contained a catalogue of dead heroes (frs. 3–9, omitted by Proclus), apparently following a pattern similar to that of *Odyssey* 11. This may imply one of the following: (1) (least likely) the *Returns* overlapped with the *Odyssey*; (2) the *Odyssey* borrowed from an earlier *\*Returns*; (3) the *Returns* borrowed from the *Odyssey*; or (4) (most likely) independent duplication: that is, a visitation to the Underworld was a traditional set piece, one that we also see in the fragments of the *Minyas*.

Athenaeus refers to the *Returns* as the *Return of the Atreidai* (*Returns* frs. 3, 12). This could conceivably be a separate poem, but it is more likely that Agamemnon's and Menelaus' homecomings were excerpted and disseminated separately; or, more likely still, that that part of the *Returns* was known under an informal title, as is the case with various episodes in Homer.

### Odyssey

**Beginning.** Not disputed.
**End.** After the reunion of Odysseus and Penelope, the transmitted text ends with a second underworld scene; a reunion with Laertes; and an abortive confrontation with the Suitors' families. However, the *Odyssey* scholia report that the Alexandrian scholars Aristarchus and Aristophanes placed the 'end' of the *Odyssey* at 23.296. (Two Roman-era copies have the text continue beyond that point.[68])

---

[68] P.Oxy. 956, second/third century CE; p.Ryl. 53, third/fourth century (at fol. 91v).

These scholia are extraordinarily controversial.[69] One school of thought takes them to mean that all of *Odyssey* 23.297–24.548 (the 'Epilogue') is a post-Homeric interpolation, added in the late Archaic period. In the opposite camp, some dismiss the Alexandrians as simply too eager to delete; others treat their use of the word 'end' (*peras* or *telos*) as metaphorical, referring to the climax of the plot rather than the end of the text. A third point of view sees the Epilogue as somehow related to the Cyclic *Telegony*. Merkelbach, following Schwartz, argues that much of the Epilogue was copied from the *Telegony* (supposedly by the 'B poet', a hypothetical reviser of the original *Odyssey*); Huxley considers that the *Telegony* took *Odyssey* 23.296 as its starting point, leaving an overlap between the two epics.[70]

A still more elegant explanation is that the Cyclic *Odyssey*[71] was a cropped form of the original *Odyssey*, designed to lead continuously into the *Telegony*, and that the cropping took place at 23.296. When the Cycle was compiled into a single, streamlined narrative, the burial of the Suitors appeared in both epics (*Od.* 24.412–19, *Teleg.* arg. 1); therefore, one of the two had to be removed. The editor(s) chose to crop the *Odyssey* rather than the *Telegony*. It seems likely that the *Odyssey* fell victim because some ancient readers, like some modern critics, were dissatisfied with the closing scenes of the *Odyssey*.

This interpretation has the merit of taking literally the scholiasts' use of the word 'end'; it accommodates many of Merkelbach's observations; it explains why a shorter *Odyssey*, ending at 23.296, would break off with an unanswered μέν ('on the one hand', answered in the transmitted text by 23.297 αὐτάρ ('then'); in the Cyclic *Odyssey*, the response would presumably come in the subsequent *Telegony* passage); and it fully explains not only Aristarchus' and Aristophanes' interference but also their continued emendations to the *Odyssey* text after 23.296. It does not imply, however, that Aristarchus and Aristophanes were *responsible* for Cyclic cropping: it implies only that they were aware of the Cyclic form of the text.

---

[69] See especially Page 1955: 101–36; Erbse 1997; Moulton 1974; S. West 1989; Kullmann 1992: 291–304; Kelly 2007: 384–7.

[70] Merkelbach 1969: 142–55; Huxley 1960: 27–8. Huxley's suggestion is perhaps prefigured by Kazantzakis' *Odyssey* (1938), which opens immediately after the slaughter of the Suitors.

[71] The existence of a Cyclic *Odyssey* is attested by two scholia: test. 1, 2 Bernabé.

## Telegony

**Beginning.** Proclus has the plot begin with the burial of the Suitors. Alternative witnesses claim otherwise, but they also contradict one another:

(1) Pseudo-Apollodorus epit. 7.33–4 groups together the reunions of Odysseus, Penelope, and Laertes as one set of episodes, and creates a second group from Odysseus' sacrifices to Hades, Persephone, and Teiresias, and the *Telegony* narrative. These groupings are consistent with *Odyssey* 23–24 but inconsistent with Proclus' *Telegony* summary.

(2) Clement of Alexandria claims that Eugammon 'took the whole book about the Thesprotians from Musaeus'.[72] This could indicate either that the *Thesprotis* was a separate poem which covered much of the same ground as the first part of the *Telegony* or that 'Thesprotis' was an informal reference to a part of the *Telegony*.[73] Clement tells us in the same passage that Panyassis took his account of the sack of Oichalia from Creophylus: there we can be certain that he is referring to two entirely separate poems. So the first option looks more likely.

(3) Scholia on *Od.* 23.296 state that Aristophanes and Aristarchus made that line the end of the *Odyssey*. This suggests cropping of the Cyclic *Odyssey* (see *Odyssey*, end, above).

(4) Alternatively, *Od.* 23.297–24.548 could be a late splice between the *Odyssey* and the *Telegony* (an alternative to Merkelbach's thesis; see *Odyssey*, end, above).

**End.** Not disputed. However, an interpolated line in *Theogony* 1014 that refers to Telegonus suggests some cross-editing between the two poems. This could account for the confusing fact that *Theogony* 1015–16 has two further children of Odysseus and Circe, Agrius and

---

[72] Clem. Al. *Strom.* 6.25.1 (=*Teleg.* test.).

[73] If a *Thesprotis* existed as a separate poem, several conjectures exist for how it may have opened: (a) exactly as in Proclus' *Telegony* summary; (b) Odysseus departs Ithaca after renouncing Penelope for her infidelity with the Suitors (Peradotto 1990: 73–4 n. 13); (c) like (b), but after Penelope gives birth to the god Pan (Servius auct. *ad Aen.* 2.44); or (d) after a dispute between Odysseus and the Suitors' families, resulting in Odysseus being exiled to Aetolia (ps.-Apollod. epit. 7.40; cf. Plut. *Quaest. Graec.* 294c–d: similar but Odysseus emigrates to Italy). As to how the *Thesprotis* ended, the most likely scenario involves an aetiology for cults to Odysseus in Thesprotia and/or Aetolia, at towns founded by Odysseus or focused around his grave: see Arist. fr. 508 Rose; Nicander *FGrH* 271–2 F 7; Lycoph. *Alex.* 799–804; Herodian, *De prosod. cath.* 303.7, 382.20–22 Lentz; sch. H *Od.* 11.122; sch. vet. Lycoph. *Alex.* 799 and 800; Steph. Byz. s.v. Βούν(ε)ιμα (see also Τραμπύα); Eust. *Od.* 11.120 (402.26–28 Stallbaum). See also the summary of Sophocles' lost *Euryalus*. Eugammon's *Telegony* could also have covered the same aetiology.

Latinus, living in the 'holy islands' while at the same time ruling over the Etruscans. The *Theogony* passage is a mess. Mythographic accounts support different parts of it: in pseudo-Apollodorus epit. 7.37 Circe sends Telegonus and Penelope to live in the Isles of the Blessed; in pseudo-Hyginus *Fabulae* 127 Latinus is the son of Circe and Telemachus, and they all live in Italy near Etruscan lands. It seems that the fates of all these characters have become muddled in *Theogony* 1011–16, perhaps as a result of a scrambled quotation from the *Telegony*.

# APPENDIX: EDITIONS

## Intact poems

Editions of intact and near-intact poems (apart from the *Iliad* and *Odyssey*) are listed in the Loeb editions of M. L. West 2003a: 36–7; M. L. West 2003b: 23–5; and Most 2006: lxxvii–lxxxii. To these add the following:

Hesiodic corpus:
*Works and Days*: Ercolani 2010.
*Theogony* 1–115: Pucci 2007.
Entire corpus plus scholia: Cassanmagnago 2009.
Homeric hymns:
*Hymn to Apollo*: N. Richardson 2010.
*Hymn to Hermes*: N. Richardson 2010; Vergados 2012.
*Hymn to Aphrodite*: Faulkner 2008; N. Richardson 2010; Olson 2012.
*Hymns* 6, 9–12, 24, 27–29: Olson 2012.
Inscriptions: see pp. 31–2.
Verses attributed to Delphic Oracle: Parke and Wormell 1956; Andersen 1987.

## Fragmentary poems

Abbreviations:

| | |
|---|---|
| Bernabé i, ii¹, ii², ii³ | Bernabé 1996, 2004–7 (identified by volume) |
| Bethe | Bethe 1929 |
| Davies | Davies 1988 |
| D–K | Diels and Kranz 1952, vol. 1 |
| *FGrH* | F. Jacoby, *Fragmente der griechischen Historiker* |
| Kinkel | Kinkel 1877 |
| M–W | Merkelbach and West 1967, 1990 (cited with date) |

*SH*                          H. Lloyd-Jones and P. Parsons, *Supplementum*
                             *Hellenisticum* (Berlin, 1983)

References are given by page number unless indicated otherwise by
'test.' or 'fr.'. I have allowed the main modern compilations to supersede Kinkel, and Bernabé and D–K to supersede Colli's *La sapienza*
*greca*.

English translations are available for those fragments that are
included in West's and Most's Loeb editions or in the *New Jacoby*,
and numerous translations exist of Xenophanes, Parmenides, and
Empedocles. Otherwise the original Greek must usually be consulted.

Poems of unknown authorship are listed under 'Anon.' For poems of
uncertain authorship, ancient attributions are admitted even where it is
doubtful that the author actually existed (Epimenides, Hesiod, Homer,
Linus, Musaeus, the Orphica). Some poems that are often considered
anonymous are listed here with an attribution given in only one source.
Neither of these practices is intended as an argument for authorship.
Full details should be checked in the editions cited.

Excluded below are various late poems (Antimachus, Anyte,
Choerilus of Iasus, the *Meropis*; and many Orphic fragments, including
the *Rhapsodies*, the Hieronyman *Theogony*, the *Lyre*, the *Shorter Krater*,
and the *Sphere*); wholly spurious figures (Chersias, Demodocus,[1]
Hegesinous, Mnaseas, Perses, Phemius, Thamyris); and fragments
associated with hexameter poets but not themselves in hexameter
(Eumelus' *Prosodion*; the Homeric *Margites*; many Orphic fragments;
much of Xenophanes). Even among the works listed, many are of
uncertain date and may be late, especially the non-oracular works associated with Epimenides and Musaeus.

Abaris of Hyperborea, *Scythian Oracles; Marriage of the River Hebrus;*
    *Purifications*; and *Apollo's Arrival among the Hyperboreans*: Kinkel
    242–3; *New Jacoby* 34. See also Burkert 1972: 141–50; M. L. West
    1983: 54–5.
Agias (or Homer), *Returns* (or *Return of the Atreidae?*): Bethe 184–7; Davies
    66–71; Bernabé i: 93–9; M. L. West 2003a: 152–63; M. L. West 2013:
    244–87, with commentary. (See also Eumelus, *Returns*.)
Anon., *Alcmeonis*: Davies 139–40; Bernabé i: 32–6; M. L. West 2003a: 58–63.

---

[1] The mythical Demodocus of *Odyssey* 8 is here separated from the Demodocus who reportedly
authored a *Heraclea*; the latter is probably Demodocus of Leros, better known for his elegiac
aphorisms.

Anon., *Danais* or *Danaides*: Davies 141; Bernabé i: 121–2; M. L. West 2003a: 266–9.

Anon., *Minyas*: see Prodicus of Phocis.

Anon., *Naupactia*: see Carcinus.

Anon., *Phocais*: see Homer.

Anon., *Phoronis*: Davies 153–5; Bernabé i:118–21 l; M. L. West 2003a: 282–5.

Anon., *Return of the Atreidae*: see Agias.

Anon., *Theogony* (Cyclic): Bernabé i: 8–10.

Anon., *Theogony* (Orphic, Derveni, Eudemian): see Orphica.

Anon., *Theseis*: Davies 155–6; Bernabé i: 135–6; M. L. West 2003a: 216–19.

Antimachus of Teos, *Epigoni*: see Homer.

Antimachus, other poems: Kinkel 247; Davies 79.

Antiphon of Athens, poetry about divination by beasts: Kinkel 272–3; Davies 80.

Arctinus of Miletus (or Homer), *Aethiopis*: Bethe 167–9; Davies 45–8, 80; Bernabé i: 65–71; M. L. West 2003a: 108–17; M. L. West 2013: 129–62, with commentary.

Arctinus, *Sack of Ilion*: Bethe 179–83; Davies 61–6, 80, 143; Bernabé i: 86–92; M. L. West 2003a: 142–53; M. L. West 2013: 22–343, with commentary.

Arctinus, *Titanomachy*: see Eumelus.

Aristeas of Proconnesus, *Arimaspeia*: Davies 81–8; Bernabé i: 144–53; *New Jacoby* 35.

Asius of Samos, genealogical poetry: Davies 88–91; Bernabé i: 127–30; M. L. West 2003a: 254–61 (frs. 1–12).

Asius, *On the Customs of the Samians*: Davies 88–91 (test. and fr. 13); Bernabé i: 130–1; M. L. West 2003a: 260–3 (fr. 13).

Bacis of Eleon, oracles: see *New Pauly* s.v. 'Bacis', and add Paus. 9.17.5.

Boio of Delphi, *Hymns*: see *New Pauly* s.v. 'Boio'.

Carcinus, *Naupactia*: Davies 145–9; Bernabé i: 123–6; M. L. West 2003a: 274–83.

Cercops of Miletus, *Aegimius*: see Hesiod.

Cercops, *Descent to Hades*: see Orphica.

Choerilus of Samos, *Persica*: Radici Colace 1979; *SH* frs. 314–32; Bernabé i: 187–208.

*Chresmologoi*: see Abaris, Bacis, Boio, Epimenides, Musaeus, Olen, Onomacritus. See also Delphic Oracle ('intact poems', above).

Cinaethon of Lacedaemon, genealogical poetry: Davies 92–3; Bernabé i: 116; M. L. West 2003a: 250–3.

Cinaethon, *Heraclea*: Davies 142; Bernabé i: 117.

Cinaethon, *Oedipodea*: Davies 20–1; Bernabé i: 17–20; M. L. West 2003a: 38–43.

Cinaethon, *Telegony*: see Eugammon.

Cleostratus of Tenedos, *Astrology*: D–K 6; Bernabé i: 155–7.

Clonas (no titles known): Davies 93.

Conon, *Heraclea*: Kinkel 212; Davies 142.

Creophylus (or Homer), *Capture of Oichalia*: Davies 149–53; Bernabé i: 157–64; M. L. West 2003a: 172–5.

Cyclic *Theogony*: see Anon., *Theogony* (Cyclic).

Cynaethus of Chios, *Hymn to Apollo*: see 'intact poems' above. See also Davies 94.

Cyprias of Halicarnassus, *Cypria*: see Stasinus.

Demodocus of Leros, *Heraclea*: Kinkel 212–13; Davies 142.

Derveni *Theogony*: see Orphica.

Diotimus, *Cercopes*: see Homer.

Diotimus, *Heraclea*: Kinkel 213–14; *SH* frs. 393–4.

Empedocles of Agrigentum, *Physics*: D–K 31 frs. B 1–111; Inwood 1992 (equated with the *Purifications*).

Empedocles, *Purifications*: D–K 31 frs. B 112–53a; Inwood 1992 (equated with the *Physics*).

Epilycus of Athens (no titles known): Kinkel 272; Davies 95.

Epimenides, *Birth of the Kouretes and Korybantes*: Bernabé ii³: 159 (fr. 1).

Epimenides, *Building of the Argo* or *Argonautica*: Kinkel 233 (reassigned to *Oracles*/*Theogony* by D–K 3 frs. B 12–13); Bernabé ii³: 161–3 (frs. 57a–9).

Epimenides, *Cretica*: D–K 3 frs. B 20–5; Bernabé ii³: 136–42 (frs. 34–8).

Epimenides, *Genealogies*: Bernabé ii³: 160–1 (frs. 55–7).

Epimenides, *History of the Telchines*: Kinkel 233; Bernabé ii³: 142 (fr. 39).

Epimenides, *Oracles*: D–K 3 frs. B 1–19 (equated with the *Theogony*); Bernabé ii³: 143–52 (frs. 40–5).

Epimenides, *Purifications*: Bernabé ii³: 159–60 (fr. 54).

Epimenides, *Theogony*: D–K 3 frs. B 1–19 (equated with the *Oracles*); *FGrH* 456; Bernabé ii³: 152–9 (frs. 46–53).

'Eudemian' *Theogony*: see Orphica.

Eugammon of Cyrene (or Cinaethon), *Telegony*: Bethe 187–90; Davies 71–6; Bernabé i: 100–5; M. L. West 2003a: 164–71; M. L. West 2013: 288–315, with commentary. (Spelled 'Eugamon' by Eusebius and Syncellus, =test. 2 Davies.)

Eumelus of Corinth, *Bougonia*: Davies 96 (test. 2); Bernabé i: 106–7 (test. 4, 14).

Eumelus, *Corinthiaca*: Davies 96–101; Bernabé i: 108–12; M. L. West 2003a: 232–45.

Eumelus, *Europia*: Davies 102; Bernabé i: 112–13; M. L. West 2003a: 244–7.

Eumelus, *Returns*: Bernabé i: 93 (test. 3). (Usually understood as an alternate attribution of Agias' *Returns*; but *Returns* test. 2 Bernabé may indicate multiple poems with the same title.)

Eumelus (or Arctinus, or Telesis), *Titanomachy*: Davies 16–20; Bernabé i: 11–16; M. L. West 2003a: 222–33.

Herodicus of Perinthus, *Descent to Hades*: see Orphica.

Hesiod (or Cercops), *Aegimius*: M–W frs. 294–301 (1967: 151–4, 1990: 210–12); Most 2006: 212–13 (test. 79), 2007: 302–9 (frs. 230–8).

Hesiod, *Astronomy* or *Astrology*: D–K 4 frs. B 1–8; M–W frs. 288–93 (1967: 148–50, 1990: 208–9); Most 2006: 208–11 (test. 72–8), 2007: 298–303 (frs. 223–9).

Hesiod, *Bird Omens* or *Ornithomancy*: M–W 1967: 157; Most 2006: 212–13 (test. 80).

Hesiod, *Catalogue of Women*: M–W frs. 1–245 (1967: 1–120, 1990: 113–90a); Hirschberger 2004, with commentary; Most 2006: 200–5 (test. 56–65), 2007: 40–261 (frs. 1–184).

Hesiod, *Descent of Peirithous*: M–W frs. 280–1 (1967: 139–41, 1990: 203–4); Most 2006: 188–9 (test. 42), 2007: 292–5 (fr. 216).

Hesiod, *Dirge for Batrachus*: Most 2006: 154–7 (test. 1).

Hesiod, *Great Ehoiae*: M–W frs. 246–62 (1967: 121–8, 1990: 191–5); Hirschberger 2004, with commentary; d'Alessio 2005; Most 2006: 204–5 (test. 66), 2007: 262–77 (frs. 185–201).

Hesiod, *Great Works*: M–W frs. 286–7 (1967: 146–7, 1990: 207); Most 2006: 204–5 (test. 66), 2007: 298–9 (frs. 221–2).

Hesiod, *Idaean Dactyls*: M–W fr. 282 (1967: 142, 1990: 205); Most 2006: 154–7 (test. 1), 2007: 294–7 (frs. 217a, b).

Hesiod, *Melampodia*: M–W frs. 270–9 (1967: 133–8, 1990: 199–202); Most 2006: 188–9 (test. 42), 2007: 284–91 (frs. 206–15).

Hesiod, *Potters* (or *Caminus* or *Cerameis*): M–W 1967: 155–6 (fr. 302); Most 2006: 214–15 (test. 82).

Hesiod, *On Preserved Foods*: Most 2006: 212–13 (test. 81).

Hesiod, *Precepts of Chiron*: M–W frs. 283–5 (1967: 143–5, 1990: 206); Most 2006: 206–7 (test. 69–71), 2007: 296–9 (frs. 218–20).

Hesiod, *Wedding of Ceyx*: M–W frs. 263–9 (1967: 129–32, 1990: 196–8); Most 2006: 204–5 (test. 67–8), 2007: 287–83 (frs. 202–5).

Homer, *Aethiopis*: see Arctinus.

Homer, *Amazonia*: Davies 104 (Homer test. 1).

Homer, *Amphiaraus' Expedition against Thebes*: Kinkel 59–60. See also Homer, *Thebaid* (other editors treat these as alternate titles for one poem).

Homer, *Capture of Oichalia*: see Creophylus.

Homer (or Diotimus), *Cercopes*: Kinkel 69–70; M. L. West 2003b: 252–5. (See also Diotimus fr. 2 Kinkel=fr. 394 *SH*.)

Homer, *Cypria*: see Stasinus.

Homer, *Doloneia*: see *Iliad* 10 with sch. T on *Iliad* 10.1.

Homer (or Antimachus of Teos), *Epigoni*: Davies 26–7; Bernabé i: 29–32; M. L. West 2003a: 54–9.

Homer, *Epikichlides*: M. L. West 2003b: 254–7.

Homer, *Hymn to Dionysus*: Allen 1912: 1–2; M. L. West 2003b: 26–31.

Homer, *Little Iliad*: see Lesches.

Homer, *Phocais*: Davies 153; Bernabé i: 117.

Homer, *Returns*: see Agias.

Homer (or Cinaethon), *Thebaid*: Davies 21–6; Bernabé i: 20–8; M. L. West 2003a: 42–55.

Lesches of Mytilene (or Homer, or other authors), *Little Iliad*: Bethe 169–78; Davies 49–61; Bernabé i: 71–86; M. L. West 2003a: 118–43; M. L. West 2013: 163–222, with commentary. (Bernabé treats this as multiple poems of the same title; cf. *contra* Scafoglio 2006.)

Linus, *Laments*: Bernabé ii³: 104 (fr. 92).

Linus, *On the Nature of the Universe*: M. L. West 1983: 56– 67; Bernabé ii³: 94–104 (frs. 78–91).

Magnes of Smyrna, *Amazonia*: Davies 112.

Melanippides of Melos (no titles known): Kinkel 272; Davies 112.

Musaeus, *Curing of Diseases*: Kinkel 224; Bernabé ii³: 48–9 (frs. 92–3).

Musaeus, *Eumolpia*: Kinkel 223; Bernabé ii³: 35–6 (frs. 72–5).

Musaeus, *Hymns*: D–K 2 frs. B 19a–20; Bernabé ii³: 30–1 (frs. 57–61).

Musaeus, *Oracles*: D–K 2 frs. B 20a–2; Bernabé ii³: 32–4 (frs. 62–71). See also Onomacritus.

Musaeus, *Sphere*: Bernabé ii³: 38–9 (frs. 77–8).

Musaeus, *Theogony*: D–K 2 frs. B 1–19; Bernabé ii³: 39–48 (frs. 79–91).

Musaeus, *Thesprotis*: Bethe 187, 189 (frs. A 3, B 1); Davies 71, 73 (test. 3, fr. 1); Bernabé ii³: 27 (test. 50; =i: 100, test. 3); M. L. West 2003a: 164–5, 168–71 (test., fr. 3). See also Eugammon, *Telegony*.

Musaeus, *Titanography* (*Titanomachy*?): Bernabé ii³: 52 (fr. 100).

Niceratus of Heraclea (no titles known): Kinkel 272; *SH* frs. 564–5.

Olen of Lycia, *Hymns*: see M. L. West 1983: 53; *New Pauly* s.v. 'Olen'.

Onomacritus of Athens, *Oracles*: Bernabé ii²: 527–32 (frs. 1109–19). See also Musaeus, *Oracles*.

Oracles: see *chresmologoi*.

Orphica, Derveni *Theogony*: Bernabé ii¹: 2–33 (frs. 2–18); Kouremenos et al. 2006: 20–8; Bernabé 2007 (with translation and commentary).

Orphica, *Descent to Hades*: Bernabé ii²: 262–87 (frs. 707–17; multiple poems).

Orphica, 'Eudemian' *Theogony*: Bernabé ii¹: 33–42 (frs. 19–27).

Orphica, *Hieros logos* (or 'Egyptian *logos*'): Bernabé ii¹: 55–72 (frs. 40–63).

Orphica, *Hymns* (scil. *Hymni veteres*): Bernabé ii¹: 330–1 and ii²: 244–49 (frs. 398 and 680–90).

Orphica, *Mixing-bowl* or *Krater*: Bernabé ii¹: 340–1 (frs. 409–12).

Orphica, *Net* or *Diktyon*: Bernabé ii¹: 336–7 (frs. 403–5).

Orphica, *Physica*: Bernabé ii²: 337–8 (frs. 800–3).

Orphica, *Robe* or *Peplos*: Bernabé ii¹: 337–9 (frs. 406–7).

Orphica, *Theogony*: Bernabé ii¹: 42–55 and 72–80 (frs. 28–39 and 64–8). See also Orphica, Derveni and 'Eudemian' *Theogonies*.

Orphica, early fragments on the nature of the soul: Bernabé ii¹: 349–94 (frs. 421, 423–4, 428–34, 439–58, 463–5).

Palaephatus of Athens, *Creation of the World; Birth of Apollo and Artemis; Language of Aphrodite and Eros; Dispute of Athene and Poseidon*; and *Lock of Leto's Hair*: see M. L. West 1983: 55–6 (existence of poems doubtful).

Pamphos, *Hymns*: see M. L. West 1983: 53 (date uncertain).

Panyassis of Halicarnassus, *Heraclea*: Davies 113–29; Bernabé i: 171–87; M. L. West 2003a: 188–217.

Parmenides of Elea, poem (title not known): D–K 28; Gallop 1984; Coxon 2009.

Phaedimus of Bisanthe, *Heraclea*: Kinkel 214; *SH* fr. 669.

Phocus of Samos, *Astrology at Sea*: Bernabé i: 154–5.

Phocylides of Miletus (no titles known): see *New Pauly* s.v. Phocylides. (NB: not to be confused with the *Sentences*, a pseudo-Phocylidean poem of Roman date.)

Pisander of Cameirus, *Heraclea*: Davies 129–35; Bernabé i: 164–71; M. L. West 2003a: 176–87.

Pisinus of Lindos, *Heraclea*: Davies 143; Bernabé i: 164.

Polymnestus of Colophon, poem about Thales: Davies 135.

Prodicus of Phocis, *Minyas*: Davies 144–5; Bernabé i: 137–42; M. L. West 2003a: 268–75.[2]

Stasinus of Cyprus (or Cyprias, or Homer), *Cypria*: Bethe 152–67; Davies 27–45; Bernabé i: 36–64; M. L. West 2003a: 64–107; M. L. West 2013: 55–128, with commentary.

Telesis of Methymna, *Titanomachy*: see Eumelus.

Terpander of Lesbos, *Hymns*: Campbell 1988: 314–19.

Xenophanes of Colophon, *On Nature*: D–K 21 frs. B 23–41; Lesher 1992.

Xenophanes, *Parodies* or *Silloi*: D–K 21 fr. B 22; Lesher 1992.

---

[2] See also Clem. Al. *Strom.* 1.131.1.3 (=Orphica fr. 707 Bernabé), ascribing a *Descent to Hades* to Prodicus of Samos, the famous sophist; this is likely to be a corruption of 'Prodicus of Phocis'. M. L. West 1983: 10 n. 17 argues instead that it is a corruption of Herodicus (of Perinthus).

# BIBLIOGRAPHY

Journal titles are abbreviated as in *L'Année philologique*.

Alden, M. J. 2000. *Homer beside Himself. Para-narratives in the Iliad.* Oxford, Oxford University Press.

Allen, T. W. 1912. *Homeri Opera*, vol. 5. Oxford, Clarendon Press.

———— 1917–19. *Homeri Opera*. Second edition, vols. 3–4, Oxford, Clarendon Press; first published 1908.

Aloni, A. 1980. 'Prooimia, Hymnoi, Elio Aristide e i cugini bastardi', *QUCC* 4: 23–40.

Andersen, L. 1987. *Studies in Oracular Verses. Concordance to Delphic Responses in Hexameter.* Copenhagen, Scientiarum Danica Regia Academia.

Andersen, Ø. and Haug, D. (eds.) 2011. *Relative Chronology in Early Greek Poetry.* Cambridge, Cambridge University Press.

Andrews, A. D. 2005. 'Homeric Recitation, with Input from Phonology and Philology', *Antichthon* 39: 1–28.

Arend, W. 1933. *Die typischen Scenen bei Homer.* Berlin, Weidmann.

Auerbach, E. 2003. *Mimesis. The Representation of Reality in Western Literature.* Translated by W. R. Trask. Princeton, NJ, Princeton University Press. First published in German, Bern 1946.

Austin, N. 1991. 'The Wedding Text in Homer's *Odyssey*', *Arion* 1: 227–43.

Barker, A. 2007. *The Science of Harmonics in Classical Greece.* Cambridge, Cambridge University Press.

Barnes, H. R. 1986. 'The Colometric Structure of Homeric Hexameter', *GRBS* 27: 125–50.

Bassett, S. E. 1934. 'The Inductions of the *Iliad*, the *Odyssey*, and the *Aeneid*', *CW* 27: 105–10, 113–18.

Beall, E. F. 2004. 'The Plow that Broke the Plain Epic Tradition: Hesiod *Works and Days*, vv. 414–503', *ClAnt* 23: 1–32.

Becker, A. S. 1992. 'Reading Greek Poetry through a Distant Lens: Ecphrasis, Ancient Greek Rhetoricians, and the Pseudo-Hesiodic *Shield of Herakles*', *AJPh* 113: 5–24.

Beecroft, A. 2010. *Authorship and Cultural Identity in Early Greece and China. Patterns of Literary Circulation.* Cambridge, Cambridge University Press.

Bernabé, A. 1996. *Poetarum Epicorum Graecorum Testimonia et Fragmenta. Pars 1.* Second edition, Stuttgart, Teubner; first published 1987.

———— 2004–7. *Poetae Epici Graeci. Testimonia et Fragmenta. Pars 2.* 3 vols. Munich, Saur, and Berlin, De Gruyter.

———— 2007. 'The Derveni Theogony: Many Questions and Some Answers', *HSPh* 103: 99–133.

Bethe, E. 1887. *Quaestiones Diodoreae mythographae.* Göttingen (dissertation).

———— 1929. *Homer. Dichtung und Sage. Band 2.* Second edition, Leipzig, Teubner; first published 1922.

Boedeker, D. and Sider, D. (eds.) 2001. *The New Simonides. Contexts of Praise and Desire.* Oxford, Oxford University Press.

Bowden, H. 2005. *Classical Athens and the Delphic Oracle. Divination and Democracy.* Cambridge, Cambridge University Press.

Bundrick, S. D. 2005. *Music and Image in Classical Athens.* Cambridge, Cambridge University Press.

Burgess, J. 1996. 'The Non-Homeric *Cypria*', *TAPhA* 126: 77–99.

———— 2001. *The Tradition of the Trojan War in Homer and the Epic Cycle.* Baltimore, MD, Johns Hopkins University Press.

———— 2002. 'Kyprias, the *Kypria*, and Multiformity', *Phoenix* 56: 234–45.

———— 2004. 'Performance and the Epic Cycle', *CJ* 100: 1–23.

———— 2006. 'Neoanalysis, Orality, and Intertextuality: An Examination of Homeric Motif Transference', *Oral Tradition* 21: 148–89.

———— 2009. *The Death and Afterlife of Achilles.* Baltimore, MD, Johns Hopkins University Press.

Burkert, W. 1972. *Lore and Science in Ancient Pythagoreanism.* Cambridge, MA, Harvard University Press.

———— 1979. 'Kynaithos, Polycrates, and the Homeric Hymn to Apollo', in G. W. Bowersock, W. Burkert, and M. Putnam (eds.), *Arktouros. Hellenic Studies Presented to Bernard M. W. Knox.* Berlin, De Gruyter: 53–62.

Cameron, A. 2004. *Greek Mythography in the Roman World.* Oxford, Oxford University Press.

Campbell, D. A. 1988. *Greek Lyric 2. Anacreon, Anacreontea, Choral Lyric from Olympus to Alcman.* Loeb Classical Library. Cambridge, MA, Harvard University Press.

Canevaro, L. G. 2013. 'The Clash of the Sexes in Hesiod's *Works & Days*', *G&R* 60: 185–202.

———— 2015. *Hesiod's Works and Days. How to Teach Self-sufficiency.* Oxford, Oxford University Press.

Cassanmagnago, C. 2009. *Esiodo. Tutte le opere e i frammenti con la prima traduzione degli scolii.* Milan, Bompiani.

Càssola, F. 1986. *Inni omerici.* Milan, Mondadori.

Chappell 2011. 'The *Homeric Hymn to Apollo*: The Question of Unity', in Faulkner 2011a: 59–81.

Cingano, E. 2005. 'A Catalogue within a Catalogue: Helen's Suitors in the Hesiodic *Catalogue of Women* (frr. 196–204)', in Hunter 2005: 118–52.

———— 2009. 'The Hesiodic Corpus', in Montanari, Rengakos, and Tsagalis 2009: 91–130.

Clark, M. E. 1986. 'Neoanalysis: A Bibliographical Review', *CW* 79: 379–94.

Clay, J. S. 1989. *The Politics of Olympus. Form and Meaning in the Major Homeric Hymns.* Princeton, NJ, Princeton University Press.

—— 1997. 'The Homeric Hymns', in Morris and Powell 1997: 489–507.

—— 2003. *Hesiod's Cosmos*. Cambridge, Cambridge University Press.

—— 2009. '*Works and Days*: Tracing the Path to *Arete*', in Montanari, Rengakos, and Tsagalis 2009: 71–90.

—— 2011. 'The *Homeric Hymns* as Genre', in Faulkner 2011a: 232–53.

Coxon, A. H. 2009. *The Fragments of Parmenides*. Second edition, Las Vegas, NV, Parmenides Publishing; first published Assen, 1986.

Currie, B. 2006. 'Homer and the Early Epic Tradition', in M. J. Clarke, B. G. F. Currie, and R. O. A. M. Lyne (eds.), *Epic Interactions. Perspectives on Homer, Virgil, and the Epic Tradition Presented to Jasper Griffin*. Oxford, Oxford University Press: 1–45.

Daitz, S. G. 1991. 'On Reading Homer Aloud: To Pause or Not to Pause', *AJPh* 112: 149–60.

D'Alessio, G. B. 2005. 'The *Megalai Ehoiai*: A Survey of the Fragments', in Hunter 2005: 176–216.

Danek, G. 1998. *Epos und Zitat. Studien zu den Quellen der Odyssee*. Vienna, Österreichische Akademie der Wissenschaften.

—— and Hagel, S. 1995. 'Homer-Singen', *WHB* 37: 5–20.

Davies, M. 1986. 'Prolegomena and Paralegomena to a New Edition (with Commentary) of the Fragments of Early Greek Epic', *Nachrichten der Akademie des Wissenschaften in Göttingen. I Philologisch-historische Klasse* 1986.2: 91–111.

—— 1988. *Epicorum graecorum fragmenta*. Göttingen, Vandenhoeck & Ruprecht.

—— 2001. *The Epic Cycle*. Second edition, Bristol, Bristol Classical Press; first published 1989.

—— 2014. *The Theban Epics*. Cambridge, MA, Harvard University Press.

—— and Finglass, P. 2015. *Stesichorus. The Poems*. Cambridge, Cambridge University Press.

Debiasi, A. 2012. 'Homer ἀγωνιστής in Chalcis', in Montanari, Rengakos, and Tsagalis 2012: 471–500.

De Jong, I. J. F. 1987. *Narrators and Focalizers. The Presentation of the Story in the Iliad*. Amsterdam, B. R. Grüner Pub. Co.

—— 2001. *A Narratological Commentary on the Odyssey*. Cambridge, Cambridge University Press.

—— 2006. 'The Homeric Narrator and His Own *Kleos*', *Mnemosyne* 59: 188–207.

—— 2012. *Homer. Iliad Book XXII*. Cambridge, Cambridge University Press.

Diels, H. and Kranz, W. (eds.) 1952. *Die Fragmente der Vorsokratiker. Band 1*. Sixth edition, Berlin, Weidmann; first published 1903.

Dindorf, W. 1855. *Scholia graeca in Homeri Odysseam*. Vol. 1, Oxford, E Typographeo Academico.

Dowden, K. 1996. 'Homer's Sense of Text', *JHS* 116: 47–61.

Dräger, P. 1997. *Untersuchungen zu den Frauenkatalogen Hesiods*. Stuttgart, F. Steiner.

Eder, M. 2007. 'How Rhythmical is Hexameter: A Statistical Approach to Ancient Greek Poetry', in Digital Humanities 2007 conference abstracts, <http://www.digitalhumanities.org/dh2007/dh2007.abstracts.pdf>, retrieved 23 April 2015: 50–2.

Edmonds, R. G. 2011. 'Orphic Mythology', in K. Dowden and N. Livingstone (eds.), *A Companion to Greek Mythology*. Oxford, Wiley-Blackwell: 73–106.

Edwards, M. W. 1980. 'The Structure of Homeric Catalogues', *TAPhA* 110: 81–105.

—— 1986. 'Homer and Oral Tradition: The Formula, Part I', *Oral Tradition* 1/2: 171–230.

—— 1992. 'Homer and Oral Tradition: The Type-scene', *Oral Tradition* 7: 284–330.

Effe, B. 1988. 'Die Aristie des Herakles. Zur Homerrezeption der "Aspis"', *Hermes* 116: 156–68.

Eisenhut, W. 1973. *Dictys Cretensis*. Second edition, Leipzig, Teubner; first published 1958.

Erbse, H. 1997. 'The Ending of the *Odyssey*: Linguistic Problems', in G. M. Wright and P. V. Jones (eds.), *Homer. German Scholarship in Translation*. Oxford, Clarendon Press: 263–320. First published in German, 1972.

Ercolani, A. 2010. *Esiodo. Opere e giorni*. Rome, Carocci.

Evelyn-White, H. G. 1914. *Hesiod, the Homeric Hymns, and Homerica*. Loeb Classical Library. London, Heinemann.

Fantuzzi, M. and Papanghelis, T. (eds.) 2006. *Brill's Companion to Greek and Latin Pastoral*. Leiden, Brill.

Fantuzzi, M. and Tsagalis, C. (eds.) 2015a. *The Greek Epic Cycle and Its Ancient Reception. A Companion*. Cambridge, Cambridge University Press.

—— and —— 2015b. 'Introduction: *Kyklos*, the Epic Cycle and Cyclic Poetry', in Fantuzzi and Tsagalis 2015a: 1–40.

Faulkner, A. 2008. *The Homeric Hymn to Aphrodite*. Oxford, Oxford University Press.

—— (ed.) 2011a. *The Homeric Hymns. Interpretative Essays*. Oxford, Oxford University Press.

—— 2011b. 'Introduction', in Faulkner 2011a: 2–25.

Finkelberg, M. 2000. 'The *Cypria*, the *Iliad*, and the Problem of Multiformity in Oral and Written Tradition', *CPh* 95: 1–11.

—— 2004. 'The End of the Heroic Age in Homer, Hesiod and the Cycle', *Ordia Prima* 3: 11–24.

—— 2007. 'More on κλέος ἄφθιτον', *CQ* 57: 341–50.

—— 2011a. 'Homer and His Peers: Neoanalysis, Oral Theory, and the Status of Homer', *Trends in Classics* 3: 197–208.

Finkelberg, M. (ed.) 2011b. *The Homer Encyclopedia*. 3 vols. Oxford, Wiley-Blackwell.

Fontenrose, J. 1978. *The Delphic Oracle. Its Responses and Operations with a Catalogue of Responses*. Berkeley, CA, University of California Press.

Ford, A. 1992. *Homer. The Poetry of the Past*. Ithaca, NY, Cornell University Press.

———— 1997. 'Epic as Genre', in Morris and Powell 1997: 396–414.

Fränkel, H. 1975. *Early Greek Poetry and Philosophy. A History of Greek Epic, Lyric, and Prose to the Middle of the Fifth Century*. Translated by M. Hadas and J. Willis. New York, Harcourt Brace Jovanovich. First published in German, New York, 1951.

Francis, J. A. 2009. 'Metal Maidens, Achilles' Shield, and Pandora: The Beginnings of "Ekphrasis"', *AJPh* 130: 1–23.

Fraser, L.-G. 2011. 'A Woman of Consequence: Pandora in Hesiod's *Works and Days*', *Cambridge Classical Journal* 57: 9–28.

Friedländer, P. 1948. *Epigrammata. Greek Inscriptions in Verse from the Beginnings to the Persian Wars*. Berkeley, CA, University of California Press.

Friedrich, R. 2007. *Formular Economy in Homer. The Poetics of the Breaches. Hermes Einzelschriften* 100. Stuttgart, Franz Steiner Verlag.

Friis Johansen, K. 1967. *The Iliad in Early Greek Art*. Copenhagen, Munksgaard.

Gainsford, P. 2012a. 'The Deaths of Beowulf and Odysseus: Narrative Time and Mythological Tale-types', *C&M* 63: 247–78.

———— 2012b. 'Diktys of Crete', *Cambridge Classical Journal* 58: 58–87.

Gallop, D. 1984. *Parmenides of Elea. Fragments*. Toronto, University of Toronto Press.

Gantz, T. 1993. *Early Greek Myth. A Guide to Literary and Artistic Sources*. Baltimore, MD, Johns Hopkins University Press.

González, J. M. 2010. 'The *Catalogue of Women* and the End of the Heroic Age (Hesiod fr. 204.94–103 M–W)', *TAPhA* 140: 375–422.

Graziosi, B. 2002. *Inventing Homer. The Early Reception of Epic*. Cambridge, Cambridge University Press.

———— 2013. 'The Poet in the *Iliad*', in A. Marmodoro and J. Hill (eds.), *The Author's Voice in Classical and Late Antiquity*. Oxford, Oxford University Press: 9–38.

———— and Haubold, J. 2005. *Homer. The Resonance of Epic*. London, Duckworth.

Grieve, J. 2007. 'Quantitative Authorship Attribution: An Evaluation of Techniques', *Literary and Linguistic Computing* 22: 251–70.

Griffin, J. 1977. 'The Epic Cycle and the Uniqueness of Homer', *JHS* 97: 39–53.

———— 1980. *Homer on Life and Death*. Oxford, Oxford University Press.

Guillon, P. 1963. *Le Bouclier d'Héraclès et l'histoire de la Grèce centrale dans la période de la première guerre sacrée*. Aix-en-Provence, Éditions Ophrys.

Gutzwiller, K. 2006. 'The Herdsman in Greek Thought', in Fantuzzi and Papanghelis 2006: 1–23.

Hagel, S. 2009. *Ancient Greek Music. A New Technical History*. Cambridge, Cambridge University Press.

Hainsworth, J. B. 1968. *The Flexibility of the Homeric Formula*. Oxford, Clarendon Press.

———— 1990. 'Books V–VIII', in A. Heubeck, S. West, and J. B. Hainsworth, *A Commentary on Homer's Odyssey. Volume I. Introduction and Books I–VIII*. Oxford, Clarendon Press: 247–385.

———— 1991. *The Idea of Epic*. Berkeley, CA, University of California Press.

Hall, J. M. 2014. *A History of the Archaic Greek World ca. 1200–479 BCE*. Second edition, Malden, MA, Blackwell; first published 2007.

Hansen, P. A. 1983. *Carmina Epigraphica Graeca, saec. VIII–V a.Chr.n.* Berlin, De Gruyter.

Harden, S. and Kelly, A. 2013. 'Proemic Convention and Character Construction in Early Greek Epic', *HSPh* 107: 1–34.

Hartmann, A. 1917. *Untersuchungen über die Sagen vom Tod des Odysseus*. Munich, C. H. Beck.

Haug, D. 2002. *Les Phases de l'évolution de la langue épique*. Göttingen, Vandenhoeck & Ruprecht.

Hirschberger, M. 2004. *Gynaikōn Katalogos und Megalai Ēhoiai. Ein Kommentar zu den Fragmenten zweier hesiodeischer Epen*. Munich, K. G. Saur.

Hoekstra, A. 1957. 'Hésiode et la tradition orale', *Mnemosyne* 10: 193–225.

———— 1981. *Epic Verse before Homer. Three Studies*. Amsterdam, North-Holland Pub. Co.

Horrocks, G. 1997. 'Homer's Dialect', in Morris and Powell 1997: 193–217.

———— 2010. *Greek: A History of the Language and Its Speakers*. Second edition, Chichester, Wiley-Blackwell; first published 1997.

Horsfall, N. 1979. 'Stesichorus at Bovillae?', *JHS* 99: 26–48.

Hunter, R. (ed.) 2005. *The Hesiodic Catalogue of Women. Constructions and Reconstructions*. Cambridge, Cambridge University Press.

———— 2014. *Hesiodic Voices. Studies in the Reception of Hesiod's Works and Days*. Cambridge, Cambridge University Press.

Hutchinson, G. 2013. 'Genre and Super-genre', in T. Papanghelis, S. J. Harrison, and S. Frangoulidis (eds.), *Generic Interfaces in Latin Literature. Encounters, Interactions and Transformations*. Berlin, De Gruyter, 19–34.

Huxley, G. L. 1960. 'Homerica II: Eugamon', *GRBS* 3: 23–8.

———— 1969. *Greek Epic Poetry from Eumelos to Panyassis*. London, Faber and Faber.

Immerwahr, H. R. 2009. *Corpus of Attic Vase Inscriptions*. <http://avi.unibas.ch/home.html>, retrieved 3 May 2015.

Inwood, B. 1992. *The Poem of Empedocles*. Toronto, Toronto University Press.

Irwin, E. 1998. 'Biography, Fictions and the Archilochean *Ainos*', *JHS* 118: 177–83.

———— 2005a. 'Gods among Men? The Social and Political Dynamics of the Hesiodic *Catalogue of Women*', in Hunter 2005: 35–84.

———— 2005b. *Solon and Early Greek Poetry. The Politics of Exhortation*. Cambridge, Cambridge University Press.

Janko, R. 1981. 'The Structure of the Homeric Hymns: A Study in Genre', *Hermes* 109: 9–24.

—— 1982. *Homer, Hesiod and the Hymns. Diachronic Development in Epic Diction.* Cambridge, Cambridge University Press.

—— 1986. 'The *Shield of Heracles* and the Legend of Cycnus', *CQ* 36: 38–59.

—— 1994. *The Iliad. A Commentary. Vol. 4. Books 13–16.* Cambridge, Cambridge University Press.

—— 2011. 'πρῶτόν τε καὶ ὕστατον αἰὲν ἀείδειν: Relative Chronology and the Literary History of the Early Greek Epos', in Andersen and Haug 2011: 20–43.

Johnston, S. I. 2002. 'Myth, Festival, and Poet: The *Homeric Hymn to Hermes* and Its Performative Context', *CPh* 97: 109–32.

—— 2003. '"Initiation" in Myth, "Initiation" in Practice', in D. B. Dodd and C. A. Faraone (eds.), *Initiation in Ancient Greek Rituals and Narratives.* London, Routledge: 155–80.

Jones 2011. 'Relative Chronology and an "Aeolic Phase" of Epic', in Andersen and Haug 2011: 44–64.

Junker, K. 2012 [2005]. *Interpreting the Images of Greek Myths.* Translated by A. Kunzi-Snodgrass and A. Snodgrass. Cambridge, Cambridge University Press. First published in German, Stuttgart, 2005.

Juola, P. 2006. 'Authorship Attribution', *Foundations and Trends in Information Retrieval* 1: 233–334.

Kakridis, J. T. 1949. *Homeric Researches.* Lund, C. W. K. Gleerup.

Kannicht, R. 1982. 'Poetry and Art: Homer and the Monuments Afresh', *ClAnt* 1: 70–86.

Kazantzakis, N. 1938. *Οδύσεια.* Athens, Πυρσός.

Kelly, A. 2006. 'Neoanalysis and the *Nestorbedrängnis*: A Test Case', *Hermes* 134: 1–25.

—— 2007. 'How to End an Orally-derived Epic Poem', *TAPhA* 137: 371–402.

—— 2012. 'The Audience Expects: Odysseus and Penelope', in E. Minchin (ed.), *Orality, Literacy and Performance in the Ancient World.* Leiden, Brill: 3–24.

Kinkel, G. 1877. *Epicorum graecorum fragmenta.* Leipzig, Teubner.

Kirk, G. S. 1962. *The Songs of Homer.* Cambridge, Cambridge University Press.

—— 1985. *The Iliad. A Commentary. Vol. 1. Books 1–4.* Cambridge, Cambridge University Press.

Koenen, L. 1994. 'Greece, the Near East, and Egypt: Cyclic Destruction in Hesiod and the *Catalogue of Women*', *TAPhA* 124: 1–34.

Kõiv, M. 2011. 'A Note on the Dating of Hesiod', *CQ* 61: 355–77.

Koning, H. H. 2010. *Hesiod. The Other Poet. Ancient Reception of a Cultural Icon.* Leiden, Brill.

Kopff, E. C. 1983. 'The Structure of the Amazonia (*Aethiopis*)', in R. Hägg (ed.), *The Greek Renaissance of the Eighth Century.* Stockholm, Svenska Institutet i Athen: 57–62.

Kouremenos T., Parássoglou G. M., and Tsantsanoglou K. (eds.) 2006. *The Derveni Papyrus. Edited with Introduction and Commentary.* Florence, L. S. Olschki.

Kullmann, W. 1960. *Die Quellen der Ilias.* Wiesbaden, F. Steiner.

——— 1984. 'Oral Poetry Theory and Neoanalysis in Homeric Research', *GRBS* 25: 307–23.

——— 1992. *Homerische Motive. Beiträge zur Entstehung, Eigenart und Wirkung von Ilias und Odyssee.* Stuttgart, Franz Steiner.

Landels, J. G. 1999. *Music in Ancient Greece and Rome.* London, Routledge.

Lane Fox, R. 2008. *Travelling Heroes. Greeks and Their Myths in the Epic Age of Homer.* London, Allen Lane.

Lardinois, A. P. M. H. 1994. 'Subject and Circumstance in Sappho's Poetry', *TAPhA* 124: 57–84.

——— 2003. 'The Wrath of Hesiod: Angry Homeric Speeches and the Structure of Hesiod's *Works and Days*', *Arethusa* 36: 1–20.

Larson, J. 2005. 'Lugalbanda and Hermes', *CPh* 100: 1–16.

Latacz, J. 2004. *Troy and Homer. Towards a Solution of an Old Mystery.* Translated by K. Windle and R. Ireland. Oxford, Oxford University Press. First published in German, Stuttgart, 2001.

Leaf, W. 1902. *The Iliad. Vol. 2. Books XIII–XXIV.* Second edition, London, Macmillan and Co.; first published 1888.

Ledbetter, G. M. 2003. *Poetics before Plato. Interpretation and Authority in Early Greek Theories of Poetry.* Princeton, NJ, Princeton University Press.

Lesher, J. H. 1992. *Xenophanes of Colophon. Fragments.* Toronto, University of Toronto Press.

Lewis, C. S. 1942. *A Preface to Paradise Lost.* London, Oxford University Press.

Lord, A. B. 1960. *The Singer of Tales.* Cambridge, MA, Harvard University Press.

Lowenstam, S. 1992. 'The Uses of Vase-depictions in Homeric Studies', *TAPhA* 122: 165–98.

——— 2008. *As Witnessed by Images. The Trojan War Tradition in Greek and Etruscan Art.* Baltimore, MD, Johns Hopkins University Press.

Lynn-George, J. M. 1978. 'The Relationship of Σ 535–540 and Scutum 156–160 Re-examined', *Hermes* 106: 396–405.

MacFarlane, K. A. 2009. 'Choerilus of Samos' Lament (*SH* 317) and the Revitalization of Epic', *AJPh* 130: 219–34.

Mansilla, R. and Bush, E. 2002. 'Increase of Complexity from Classical Greek to Latin Poetry', arXiv preprint, <http://arxiv.org/abs/cond-mat/0203135>, edition of 18 March 2002, retrieved 23 April 2015.

Marks, J. 2010. 'Inset Narratives in the Epic Cycle', *Classics@* 6. Center for Hellenic Studies, Harvard University, <http://chs.harvard.edu/CHS/article/display/3230>, edition of 21 December 2010, retrieved 16 December 2011.

Mathiesen, T. J. 1999. *Apollo's Lyre. Greek Music and Music Theory in Antiquity and the Middle Ages.* Lincoln, NE, University of Nebraska Press.

Matthews, V. J. 1996. *Antimachus of Colophon. Text and Commentary.* Leiden, Brill.

Martin, R. P. 2005. 'Pulp Epic: The *Catalogue* and the *Shield*', in Hunter 2005: 153–75.

Merkelbach, R. 1969. *Untersuchungen zur Odyssee*. Second edition, Munich, Beck; first published 1951.

—— and West, M. L. 1967. *Fragmenta Hesiodea*. Oxford, Clarendon Press.

—— and —— 1990. 'Fragmenta Selecta', in F. Solmsen (ed.), *Hesiodi Theogonia, Opera et dies, Scutum*. Oxford, Clarendon Press, 109–230; first published 1970.

Minchin, E. 2001. *Homer and the Resources of Memory*. Oxford, Oxford University Press.

—— 2007. *Homeric Voices. Discourse, Memory, Gender*. Oxford, Oxford University Press.

Monro, D. B. 1883. 'On the Fragment of Proclus' Abstract of the Epic Cycle Contained in the Codex Venetus of the *Iliad*', *JHS* 4: 305–34.

—— 1901. *Homer's Odyssey. Books XIII–XXIV*. Oxford, Clarendon Press.

—— and T. W. Allen. 1920. *Homeri Opera. Ilias*. 2 vols. Third edition, Oxford, Clarendon Press; first published 1908.

Montanari F., Rengakos A., and Tsagalis C. (eds.) 2009. *Brill's Companion to Hesiod*. Leiden, Brill.

——, ——, and —— (eds.) 2012. *Homeric Contexts. Neoanalysis and the Interpretation of Oral Poetry*. Berlin, De Gruyter.

Moreno, P. and Stefani, C. 2000. *The Borghese Gallery*. Milan, Touring Club Italiano.

Morris, I. and Powell, B. B. (eds.) 1997. *A New Companion to Homer*. Leiden, E. J. Brill.

Most, G. W. 2006. *Hesiod. Theogony, Works and Days, Testimonia*. Loeb Classical Library. Cambridge, MA, Harvard University Press.

—— 2007. *Hesiod. The Shield, Catalogue of Women, Other Fragments*. Loeb Classical Library. Cambridge, MA, Harvard University Press.

Moulton, C. 1974. 'The End of the *Odyssey*', *GRBS* 15: 153–69.

Muellner, L. 1996. *The Anger of Achilles. Mênis in Greek Epic*. Ithaca, NY, Cornell University Press.

Murray, O. 2008. 'The *Odyssey* as Performance Poetry', in M. Revermann and P. Wilson (eds.), *Performance, Iconography, Reception. Studies in Honour of Oliver Taplin*. Oxford, Oxford University Press: 161–76.

Myres, J. L. 1941. 'Hesiod's "Shield of Herakles": Its Structure and Workmanship', *JHS* 61: 17–38.

Nagy, G. 1974. *Comparative Studies in Greek and Indic Meter*. Cambridge, MA, Harvard University Press.

—— 1979. *The Best of the Achaeans. Concepts of the Hero in Archaic Greek Poetry*. Baltimore, MD, Johns Hopkins University Press.

—— 1990. *Pindar's Homer. The Lyric Possession of an Epic Past*. Baltimore, MD, Johns Hopkins University Press.

—— 1994. 'Genre and Occasion', *Mètis* 9–10: 11–25.

——— 1996. *Homeric Questions*. Austin, TX, University of Texas Press.

——— 2009. *Homer the Classic*. Cambridge, MA, Harvard University Press.

Nelson, S. A. 1998. *God and the Land. The Metaphysics of Farming in Hesiod and Vergil*. New York, Oxford University Press.

Nikolaev, A. 2013. 'The Aorist Infinitives in -έειν in Early Greek Hexameter Poetry', *JHS* 133: 81–92.

Northrup, M. D. 1980. 'Homer's Catalogue of Women', *Ramus* 9: 150–9.

Obbink, D. 2014. 'Two New Poems by Sappho', *ZPE* 189: 32–49.

Olson, S. D. 1995. *Blood and Iron. Stories and Storytelling in Homer's Odyssey*. Leiden, Brill.

——— 2012. *The Homeric Hymn to Aphrodite and Related Texts*. Berlin, De Gruyter.

Ormand, K. 2014. *The Hesiodic Catalogue of Women and Archaic Greece*. Cambridge, Cambridge University Press.

Oxford University Press 2015. *Oxford English Dictionary*. Online edition, <http://www.oed.com>, retrieved 8 May 2015.

Pache, C. 2008. 'Mortels et immortelles dans la *Théogonie*', *Mètis* n.s. 6: 21–38.

Page, D. 1955. *The Homeric Odyssey*. Oxford, Clarendon Press.

Papakitsos, E. C. 2013. 'Computerized Scansion of Ancient Greek Hexameter', *Literary and Linguistic Computing* 26: 57–69.

Parke, H. W. 1985. 'What Kind of Oracle is IG II$^2$, 4968?', *ZPE* 60: 93–6.

——— and Wormell, D. E. W. 1956. *The Delphic Oracle. Vol. II. The Oracular Responses*. Oxford, Basil Blackwell.

Pedrick, V. 1992. 'The Muse Corrects: The Opening of the *Odyssey*', *YClS* 29: 39–62.

Peradotto, J. 1990. *Man in the Middle Voice. Name and Narration in the Odyssey*. Princeton, NJ, Princeton University Press.

Pestalozzi, H. 1945. *Die Achilleis als Quelle der Ilias*. Zürich.

Pretagostini, R. 2006. 'How Bucolic Are Theocritus' Bucolic Singers?', in Fantuzzi and Papanghelis 2006: 53–73.

Pucci, P. 2007. *Inno alle Muse (Esiodo, Teogonia, 1–115)*. Pisa, Fabrizio Serra.

——— 2009. 'The Poetry of the *Theogony*', in Montanari, Rengakos, and Tsagalis 2009: 37–70.

Radici Colace, P. 1979. *Choerili Samii reliquiae*. Rome, L'Erma di Bretschneider.

Redfield, J. M. 1975. *Nature and Culture in the Iliad. The Tragedy of Hector*. Chicago, IL, University of Chicago Press.

Reece, S. 1993. *The Stranger's Welcome. Oral Theory and the Aesthetics of the Homeric Hospitality Scene*. Ann Arbor, MI, University of Michigan Press.

Richardson, N. J. 1974. *The Homeric Hymn to Demeter*. Oxford, Clarendon Press.

——— 1981. 'The Contest of Homer and Hesiod and Alcidamas' *Mouseion*', *CQ* 31: 1–10.

——— 2010. *Three Homeric Hymns to Apollo, Hermes, and Aphrodite*. Cambridge, Cambridge University Press.

Richardson, S. D. 1990. *The Homeric Narrator*. Nashville, TN, Vanderbilt University Press.

Roscher W. H. (ed.) 1884–1937. *Ausführliches Lexikon der griechischen und römischen Mythologie*. 7 vols. Leipzig, Teubner.

Rosen, R. M. 2004. 'Aristophanes' *Frogs* and the *Contest of Homer and Hesiod*', *TAPhA* 134: 295–322.

Ruijgh, C. J. 2011. 'Mycenaean and Homeric Language', in Y. Duhoux and A. Morpurgo Davies (eds.), *A Companion to Linear B. Vol. 2*. Louvain, Peeters: 253–98.

Russo, C. F. 1965. *Hesiodi Scutum. Introduzione, testo critico e commento con traduzione*. Second edition, Florence, La Nuova Italia; first published 1950.

Rutherford, I. 2000. 'Formulas, Voice, and Death in *Ehoie*-poetry, the Hesiodic *Gunaikon Katalogos*, and the Odyssean *Nekuia*', in M. Depew and M. Obbink (eds.), *Matrices of Genre. Authors, Canons, and Society*. Cambridge, MA, Harvard University Press: 81–96.

——— 2001. 'The New Simonides: Toward a Commentary', in Boedeker and Sider 2001: 33–54.

——— 2009. 'Hesiod and the Literary Traditions of the Near East', in Montanari, Rengakos, and Tsagalis 2009: 9–35.

Rutherford, R. 1982. 'Tragic Form and Feeling in the *Iliad*', *JHS* 102: 145–60.

——— 2013. *Homer*. Second edition, Cambridge, Cambridge University Press; first published 1996.

Sadurska, A. 1964. *Les Tables Iliaques*. Warsaw, Państwowe Wydawnictwo Naukowe.

Sammons, B. 2010. *The Art and Rhetoric of the Homeric Catalogue*. Oxford, Oxford University Press.

——— 2013. 'Narrative Doublets in the Epic Cycle', *AJPh* 134: 529–56.

Scafoglio, G. 2004. 'La questione ciclica', *RPh* 78: 289–310.

——— 2006. 'Two Fragments of the Epic Cycle', *GRBS* 46: 5–11.

Schadewaldt, W. 1965. *Von Homers Welt und Werk. Aufsätze und Auslegungen zur homerischen Frage*. Fourth edition, Stuttgart, Koehler; first published 1952.

Schmidt, J.-U. 1986. *Adressat und Paraineseform. Zur Intention von Hesiods Werken und Tagen*. Göttingen, Vandenhoeck & Ruprecht.

Schwarz, G. 2006. 'Schwester, Gattin, Mutter? Die Rolle der Frauen in der Ikonographie von "Hektors Lösung"', in C. C. Mattusch, A. A. Donohue, and A. Brauer (eds.), *Common Ground. Archaeology, Art, Science, and Humanities*. Oxford, Oxbow Books: 575–9.

Severyns, A. 1928. *Le Cycle épique dans l'école d'Aristarque*. Liége, H. Vaillant-Carmanne.

——— 1938–63. *Recherches sur la Chrestomathie de Proclos*. 4 vols. Paris, Société d'Édition 'Les Belles Lettres'.

Sider, D. 2001. '"As is the Generation of Leaves" in Homer, Simonides, Horace, and Stobaeus', in Boedeker and Sider 2001: 272–88.

Sinn, U. 1979. *Die homerischen Becher*. Berlin, Gebr. Mann.

Slatkin, L. 1991. *The Power of Thetis. Allusion and Interpretation in the Iliad*. Berkeley, CA, University of California Press.

Smith, R. S. and Trzaskoma, S. 2007. *Apollodorus' Library and Hyginus' Fabulae*. Indianapolis, IN, Hackett Pub.

Snell, B. 1953. *The Discovery of the Mind. The Greek Origins of European Thought*. Oxford, Blackwell; first published in German, Hamburg, 1948.

Snodgrass, A. 1998. *Homer and the Artists. Text and Picture in Early Greek Art*. Cambridge, Cambridge University Press.

Stamatopoulou, Z. 2013. 'Reading the *Aspis* as a Hesiodic Poem', *CPh* 108: 273–85.

Steiner, D. 2012. 'Fables and Frames: The Poetics and Politics of Animal Fables in Hesiod, Archilochus, and the *Aesopica*', *Arethusa* 45: 1–41.

Stoddard, K. 2004. *The Narrative Voice in the Theogony of Hesiod*. Leiden, Brill.

Swift, L. 2012. 'Archilochus the "Anti-hero"? Heroism, Flight and Values in Homer and the New Archilochus Fragments (P.Oxy LXIX 4708)', *JHS* 132: 139–55.

Thalmann, W. G. 1984. *Conventions of Form and Thought in Early Greek Epic Poetry*. Baltimore, MD, Johns Hopkins University Press.

Toohey, P. 1988. 'An [Hesiodic] *danse macabre*: The Shield of Heracles', *ICS* 13: 19–35.

Tsagalis, C. 2010. 'The Dynamic Hypertext: Lists and Catalogues in the Homeric Epics', *Trends in Classics* 2: 323–47.

———— 2011. 'Towards an Oral, Intertextual Neoanalysis', *Trends in Classics* 3: 209–44.

———— 2014. 'Epic Diction', in G. K. Giannakis (ed.), *Encyclopedia of Ancient Greek Language and Linguistics*. 3 vols. Leiden, Brill: i.548–57.

Van der Valk, M. H. A. L. H. 1953. 'A Defence of Some Suspected Passages in the *Scutum Hesiodi*', *Mnemosyne* 6: 265–82.

Van Wees, H. 1994. 'The Homeric Way of War: The *Iliad* and the Hoplite Phalanx', *G&R* 41: 1–18, 131–55.

Vergados, A. 2011. 'The *Homeric Hymn to Hermes*: Humour and Epiphany', in Faulkner 2011a: 82–104.

———— 2012. *A Commentary on the Homeric Hymn to Hermes*. Berlin, De Gruyter.

Visser, E. 1997. *Homers Katalog der Schiffe*. Stuttgart, Teubner.

Wachter, R. 2001. *Non-Attic Greek Vase Inscriptions*. Oxford, Oxford University Press.

Wagner, R. 1892. 'Proklos und Apollodoros', *Neue Jahrbücher für Philologie und Paedagogik* 145, 62. Jahrgang (=*Jahrbücher für classische Philologie*, 38. Jahrgang): 241–56.

Watkins, C. 1995. *How to Kill a Dragon. Aspects of Indo-European Poetics*. Oxford, Oxford University Press.

Weitzmann, K. 1959. *Ancient Book Illumination*. Cambridge, MA, Harvard University Press.

West, M. L. 1966. *Hesiod. Theogony*. Oxford, Clarendon Press.

—— 1973a. 'Greek Poetry 2000–700 B.C.' *CQ* 23: 179–92.

—— 1973b. *Textual Criticism and Editorial Technique Applicable to Greek and Latin Texts*. Stuttgart, Teubner.

—— 1978. *Hesiod. Works and Days*. Oxford, Clarendon Press.

—— 1983. *The Orphic Poems*. Oxford, Clarendon Press.

—— 1985. *The Hesiodic Catalogue of Women. Its Nature, Structure, and Origins*. Oxford, Clarendon Press.

—— 1988. 'The Rise of the Greek Epic', *JHS* 108: 151–72.

—— 1992. *Ancient Greek Music*. Oxford, Clarendon Press.

—— 1997. *The East Face of Helicon. West Asiatic Elements in Greek Poetry and Myth*. Oxford, Clarendon Press.

—— 1998–2000. *Homeri Ilias*. 2 vols. Stuttgart, Teubner and Munich, K. G. Saur.

—— 1999. 'The Invention of Homer', *CQ* 49: 364–82.

—— 2001. *Studies in the Text and Transmission of the Iliad*. Munich, Saur.

—— 2003a. *Greek Epic Fragments from the Seventh to the Fifth Centuries BC*. Loeb Classical Library. Cambridge, MA, Harvard University Press.

—— 2003b. *Homeric Hymns, Homeric Apocrypha, Lives of Homer*. Loeb Classical Library. Cambridge, MA, Harvard University Press.

—— 2005. '*Odyssey* and *Argonautica*'. *CQ* 55: 39–64.

—— 2007. *Indo-European Poetry and Myth*. Oxford, Oxford University Press.

—— 2011a. *The Making of the Iliad*. Oxford, Oxford University Press.

—— 2011b. 'Towards a Chronology of Early Greek Epic', in Andersen and Haug 2011: 224–41.

—— 2013. *The Epic Cycle. A Commentary on the Lost Troy Epics*. Oxford, Oxford University Press.

West, S. 1989. 'Laertes Revisited', *PCPhS* 35: 113–43.

Wheeler, E. L. 1987. 'Ephorus and the Prohibition of Missiles', *TAPhA* 117: 157–82.

Wheeler, G. 2002. 'Sing, Muse…: The Introit from Homer to Apollonius', *CQ* 52: 33–49.

Wilamowitz-Moellendorff, U. von 1905. 'Lesefrüchte', *Hermes* 40: 116–53.

Willcock, M. M. 1997. 'Neoanalysis', in Morris and Powell 1997: 174–89.

Zardini, F. 2009. *The Myth of Herakles and Kyknos. A Study in Greek Vase-painting and Literature*. Verona, Edizioni Fiorini.

Zarecki, J. P. 2007. 'Pandora and the Good Eris in Hesiod', *GRBS* 47: 5–29.

# INDEX

## Ancient sources cited

Ancient sources are in bold, page numbers in italics, with editions indicated in parentheses. Authorship attributions are given as in the Appendix.

# General index

Index entries for poems list only places where the poem is discussed as a whole, or without reference to a specific passage. Cyclic epics are listed under 'Epic Cycle'.